I0787583

Robert Reich
@RBReich

The GOP including $0 for the USPS,
$0 for our elections, and
$21,300,000,000 for the Pentagon in
a COVID relief bill is the real looting in
America.

3:38 PM · 8/12/20 · Twitter Web App

Strategic Book Publishing & Rights Co., LLC
USA | Singapore
www.sbpra.net

For information about special discounts for bulk purchases, please contact Strategic Book Publishing and Rights Co. Special Sales, at bookorder@sbpra.net.

ISBN: 978-1-951530-45-7

FOREWORD

IF you have a toothache, then you should see the dentist. However, people usually procrastinate doing this because of the pain that would have to be endured by seeing the dentist—but by putting it off the toothache only gets worse. The longer one waits to deal with the inevitable, then the worse the inevitable will become.

Essentially, this work is like a visit to the dentist for society; and the dentist surely has her work cut out for her. As such, it is sometimes a disturbing read because it embraces a "bite the bullet" attitude.

It also is analogous to the time in high school when several buddies and I were horsing around on the school bus and a pile-on ensued. At one point I was on the bottom, face up, and I was laughing like everyone else. But then another 200-pound guy jumped on top, which prompted me to plead for everyone to get off because I couldn't breathe; but, to no avail, since I wasn't loud enough. Luckily, the guy on top of me was not diminutive, so when I yanked the hell out of his hair he instantly got the message and shoved everyone off. Well, this work is an attempt to yank the hell out of the hair of a lot of people at the top who are suffocating everybody else.

That may seem histrionic, but that is the nature of the tone one must adopt when utilizing the philosophy of William James' essay, **"The Will to Believe**," which states that "If we believe in the possibility of some future event taking place, then this belief increases our power to help make the event happen when the time comes for action."

"Genius…means little more than the faculty of perceiving in an unhabitual manner."

~ William James

Reality Check

PREFACE

"PERHAPS the sentiments contained in the following pages, are not yet sufficiently fashionable to procure them general favor; a long habit of not thinking a thing <u>wrong</u>, gives it a superficial appearance of being <u>right</u>, and raises at first a formidable outcry in defense of custom. But the tumult soon subsides. Time makes more converts than reason.

"As a long and violent abuse of power is generally the Means of calling the right of it in question and as the good people of this country are grievously oppressed by the combination, they have an undoubted privilege to inquire into the pretensions of both, and equally to reject the usurpation of either.

"The cause of America is in great measure the cause of all mankind. Many circumstances hath, and will arise, which are not local, but universal, and through which the principles of all Lovers of Mankind are affected, and in the Event of which, their Affections are interested. The laying a Country desolate with Fire and Sword, declaring War against the natural rights of all Mankind, and [obliterating] the Defenders thereof from the Face of the Earth, is the Concern of every Man to whom nature hath given the Power of feeling; of which Class, regardless of Party Censure, is the

~ AUTHOR

"P.S. Who the Author of this production is, is wholly unnecessary to the Public, as the Object for Attention is the <u>Doctrine</u> <u>itself</u>, not the <u>Man</u>. Yet it may not be unnecessary to say, That he is unconnected with any Party, and under no sort of Influence public or private, but the influence of reason and principle.

<u>Philadelphia</u>, February 14, 1776."

The preceding excerpt is from the introduction to Thomas Paine's *Common Sense*.

The following is the introduction to…

©REALITY CHECK

i.e., The Conclusion To Which I Have Come

Which is that, in order to work, this presentation needs to be

self-described as the necessary means to creating a practical

solution to reversing society's self-destructive course.

In other words: **A Piece of Cake**

Reality Check

♫ "Dear God, hope you got the letter and…
I pray you can make it better down here
I don't mean a big reduction in the price of beer
But all the people that you made in your image
See them starving on their feet
'Cause' they don't get enough to eat from
God, I can't believe in you

Dear God, sorry to disturb you but…
I feel that I should be heard loud and clear
We all need a big reduction in amount of tears
And all the people that you made in your image
See them fighting in the street
'Cause they can't make opinions meet about
God,
I can't believe in you…
Did you make disease and the diamond blue?
Did you make mankind after we made you?
And the devil too?

Dear God, don't know if you've noticed but…
Your name is on a lot of quotes in this book
And us crazy humans wrote it, you should take a look
And all the people that you made in your image
Still believing that junk is true
Well I know it ain't, and so do you, Dear God
I can't believe in
I don't believe in

I won't believe in heaven and hell
No saints, no sinners, no devil as well
No pearly gates, no thorny crown
You're always letting us humans down
The wars you bring, the babes you drown
Those lost at sea and never found
And it's the same the whole world 'round
The hurt I see helps to compound
That Father, son and Holy Ghost
Is just somebody's unholy hoax
And if you're up there you'd perceive
That my heart's here upon my sleeve
If there's one thing I don't believe in

It's You,
Dear God." [1]

Pivot

What a mess. Every time I look at Earth, it's gotten worse. Maybe I ought to stop looking.

Millions of planets and that one has always been a problem. Why that one?

I know why.

People.

Maybe I ought to go down there and look around.

I've gotta do something.

~ God, from the movie, *Oh, God! Book II*

Reality Check

"In Praise of Eloquence" [2]

Surely whoever speaks to me in the right voice, him or her I shall follow.

~ Walt Whitman

Eloquence may set fire to reason.

~ Oliver Wendell Holmes, Jr.

To disparage eloquence is to disparage mankind.

~ John Morley

Speeches are veritable transactions in the human commonwealth; in fact, very gravely influential transactions.

~ G.W.F. Hegel

Every investigation that can be made as regards those duties for which an orator should be held responsible, I bid you make. And what are those duties? To discern events in their beginnings, to foresee what is coming, and to forewarn others.

~ Demosthenes

The breastplate and the sword are not a stronger defense on the battlefield than eloquence is to man amid the perils of prosecution.

~ Tacitus

The power of eloquence—so very effective in convincing us of either right or wrong—lies open to all. Why, then, do not the good zealously procure it that it may serve the truth, if the wicked, in order to gain unjustifiable and groundless cases, apply it to the advantages of injustice and error?

~ St. Augustine

Rhetoric, or the art of conveying our thoughts to others by speech with advantages of clearness, force, and elegancy, so as to instruct, to persuade, to delight the auditors: of how great benefit is it, if it be well used! How much may it conduce to the service of God and edification of men!

~ Isaac Barrow

Oratory, phrases, the evocative power of verbal symbols must not be despised, for these are and have been one of the chief means of uniting the United States and keeping it united.

~ D.W. Brogan

Our statesmen have been compelled, by the very exigencies of their position, to be "masters of the word"; and, however much men may decry the word, in this the age of the brutal act, the fact remains that the word—the word which expresses creative thought—is the ultimate master of the act.

~ Earnest Baker

Philosophers have merely interpreted the world; …the point is to change it.

~ Karl Marx

Eventually poets will lead men's souls back to God.

~ Walt Whitman

Pivot

♫ "What if God was one of us? Just a stranger on the bus trying to make His way home." [3]

What if God was all of us? (but only some of us knew it…and we couldn't go home unless we brought everyone with us).

♫ "The millennium has come at last. My one-horse town is made of glass." [4]

♫ "My century is turnin', to me." [4]

We continue Our story with the assumption that everyone wants to be happy….

Reality Check

Along the course of events I couldn't help noticing that I was not the only one who was, generally, unhappy, lonely, and fraught with self-pity. It was evident from conversations that all of my friends, relatives and acquaintances were also, by and large, feeling disillusionment towards life. What really struck me, though, was that even my friend Jarrod—who was not only exceptionally sharp, honest, captivating, industrious and genuine, but also the son of a mega-millionaire—was more often than not very discontented with life.

It got me to (keep) thinking.

During the same period, fall of 1995, Jarrod and I had been playing three-wall racquetball almost every day for four months. We both considered our matches to usually be the best part of the day. Personally, I couldn't remember when I was so consistently being thrilled by life on a day-to-day basis since the time that I was fortunate enough to live within a courtyard that had a volleyball court and I was able to play every day with all of my neighbors. I concluded that as long as the rest of my life was in balance, then I could play racquetball every day until I died and it would always remain exciting because it would always remain a challenge. Additionally, it occurred to me that not only are these activities fun, but, over the long run, when shared with many, they cost virtually nothing to play. So, somewhere in the back of my mind, I wondered: *How come we don't just design a society that allows us to play as much as possible?*

I mean, that is possible, right?

♫ "I've got to be a boy again." [4]

Then one day in December, 1995, I happened to catch on The Learning Channel a program on how to properly raise babies, which included the seven reasons why they cry. This discovery of the reason for/solution to all of mankind's problems left me reeling. But I was confused, flustered and concerned, wondering: *How come this profound bit of knowledge isn't being broadly disseminated? Isn't the point of such constructive knowledge to apply it?*

Well, first it has to be shared.

Meanwhile, I continued asking myself why I had come to be so disappointed over my fruition into an "adult." A component of the answer was that I constantly felt anxiety from always being afraid that there wouldn't be enough money to do all the things I wanted to do during my life, let alone ever achieve financial freedom. I also realized that the other component of the answer was that my parents had failed to guide me away from developing the shortcomings that left me feeling so unprepared for life; so beneath my potential—because their efforts towards my eventual fruition were vague, and often misguided. What struck me even more, though, was that this problem was, of course, occurring not just with me, but with virtually everybody. The coalescence of these two thoughts is what really made my jaw drop, thinking: "*Now it all makes sense! The reason that society is so out of whack is because nobody is ever taught how to develop into a functioning and prosperous member of the society. What we are conditioned for is how to develop into a functioning member of the* economy."

Then one day in early January 1996, I was thinking, "*The world is* really *screwed up. It's hopeless in fact. Yet, everyone continues to act as if nothing is drastically wrong; as if we could continue well into my lifetime with our pattern of destruction and neglect that's built into the system and our attitudes without having a complete collapse. Did my parents go through this? Well, apparently they did, judging by what went on in the sixties. So, then, why did they and everyone else continue bringing children into such a hopeless world??*"

"[*EUREKA!!!*]"

Because thirty years ago, as today, everyone pretended that the system wasn't doomed to inevitably collapse in upon itself—because *sixty* years ago the attitude was the same. BECAUSE WHEN WE'RE FIVE YEARS OLD WE CANNOT PERCEIVE JUST HOW BAD IT IS, AND ONCE WE GROW UP AND LEARN THAT MOST OF OUR MEANS OF SURVIVAL ARE ACTUALLY PERPETUATING OUR DEMISE WE ARE VIRTUALLY HELPLESS TO DO ANYTHING ABOUT IT, OR RE-DIRECT THAT CURRENT, *BECAUSE WE ARE INSIDE THE CURRENT*; AND IT IS THE CURRENT THAT IS SUSTAINING US.

Two weeks prior to having the above revelation I was telling my friend Shimón some ideas I was excited about; ideas I had come up with for how a utopian society would probably function in the future. I insisted that I was on to something, and at first he tried to refute my logic, but, then, finally, he grudgingly conceded to the soundness of my reasoning. However, he insisted, "But the bottom line is that it's never going to happen, so there's no point even discussing it! Because it's just not possible! Because THAT'S JUST THE WAY IT IS." In an earlier discussion regarding a problem he retorted with the ever-popular cliché, "You have to take the good with the bad."

Why? Why is it never going to happen? Why is it just not possible? *Why* is it the way it is? Why do I *have* to take it? I'm sure he must be wrong. I mean, even if it doesn't happen for centuries, it has to happen eventually. Doesn't it?

Way in the back of my mind his message lingered. Then his echoing voice finally came streaming to the front of my mind not long after I had the aforementioned revelation—and I experienced an epiphany like no other: Shimón didn't put any thought into his statement—**BECAUSE IT'S THE SAME THING EVERYONE HAS BEEN TELLING EACH OTHER SINCE FOREVER!!!**

Can we say, "Self-fulfilling prophecy"?

Yet, that was only a minor part of the epiphany. The major part was the following train of thought: *"Then doesn't that mean that I have the power and responsibility to create the necessary catalyst for altering the system into one that will be self-perpetuating, instead of self-destructive, just by writing down what I understand* (and was soon to discover) *and then spreading it? But, by definition, that's crazy, even if the logic of my premise is sound. Besides, who am I to possess the answer to how to make such an adjustment?"* But, then I thought, *"Yeah, but that's what everyone would think if they had such an original thought, even someone such as Michael Stipe."* But that made me realize that everybody who has ever become somebody started out as nobody. Therefore, everybody is anybody; and anybody can become somebody.

I'm anybody.

So I began to write it all down. With frenzied glee I told friends, "I know you're going to say it's crazy talk, but I'm writing a work to solve all of Earth's major root problems! A month ago I would have told myself that it was crazy talk, but in a few weeks when I'm done, you'll see."

While trying to organize my thoughts into writing I continuously crosschecked the perspective of friends and strangers in order to make sure that I wasn't just being presumptuous. This work, in a sense, began to write itself, much the same way a crossword puzzle does.

And the funniest thing I learned along the way is that when you tell people that you have figured out exactly why the world is so disjointed, along with the philosophy to correct it, everyone will tell you that that's malarkey; that such a proposal is not possible. Yet, at the same time they would tell me *their* theories on society and human behavior with such conviction that one would think that *they* should write an opus. And after every such encounter I was prompted to clarify and modify my ideas as necessary.

The first draft of this work was like reading the menu at a very fancy restaurant. My friend Marah's response: "We've all been talking about it, and it's really made us all think. This needs to be widely read." With that bold confirmation I knew that I could serve up a meal to meet the highest expectations.

And I did.

♫ "Consider this the hint of the century." [5]

"God, grant me the serenity to accept the things I can't change, the courage to change the things I can … and the wisdom to know the difference."

~ St. Francis

I clearly remember the moment when that prayer first came to my attention while listening to the album *I Do Not Want What I Haven't Got.* I thought, *"Wow, I'm really impressed by Sinead O'Connor's insight."* To verbalize my reaction to it now, I'd say that it was the Totality of its wisdom that really struck me. I mean, it just made me think, "Yeah, *if one could know* that, *then it would be like, problem solved."* I never actually thought to invoke the prayer, (although I did make a similar proposition to God a few years earlier).

Now, looking back, it occurs to me that praying isn't going to provide anyone with this insight. After all, if it were, then wouldn't the world be a much saner place with so many invoking this prayer for so long? (Although I bet Voltaire would say that the prayers *have* been answered, and that this is as sane as it gets, at this point in time, *for each individual*—because this is the best of all possible worlds.)

So, for the record, God, thanks for creating me and all, but I don't need You to gain such insight. I can help myself; and I can help others. Thanks to my God-given ability to think.

♫ "I don't know what the worlds needs now, but I'm sure as hell that [change] starts with me. And that's wisdom that I have [previously] laughed at." [6]

[A few months before I started to write this… proof that the system needs major revamping, my money-driven mind was planning on marketing the bumper sticker "WELCOME TO PLANET LAME."]

A Brief History of History

Insecure men with low self-esteem got together to validate their weak egos by dominating others through force, oppression and the acquisition of property. It didn't work.

We studied this failure.

The insecure descendants and victims of those men get together to validate their weak egos by dominating others through force, oppression and the acquisition of property. It doesn't work.

We study this failure.

The insecure descendants and victims of those descendants will get together to validate their weak egos by dominating others through force, oppression and the acquisition of property. It won't work.

We'll have nothing left to study.

THE END?

My second favorite movie is *BACK to the FUTURE*.

My second favorite line from that movie is: "If you put your mind to it, you can accomplish anything."

My third favorite line from it is: "EIGHTY-EIGHT MILES PER HOUR!!!!!"

My fourth favorite line from it is: "No, Biff: You leave her alone."

My fifth favorite line from it is: "Yeah? Well, history is going to change."

"You can see a lot of things that are wrong. Small changes you can propose. But, to be realistic, substantial change (which will really alter the large-scale direction of things and overcome major problems) will require **profound democratization of the society and the economic system**."

~ from Noam Chomsky's *The Prosperous Few and the Restless Many*

Reality Check

[Well, we can kiss "Planet Lame" goodbye.]

Clichés are ironic in that they have much weight and truth, but because they are clichés their weight is often overlooked since they are "so cliché." Yet, it is the most repeated sentiments that need to be internalized the most. If people would just start taking their weight to heart the first time they heard them, then they wouldn't need to be repeated. So when I use clichés, and repeat points, don't get impatient and think, "*Yeah, yeah. You already made that point.*" By continuing to forever ignore the truest clichés we have all made it necessary for us to have to continually repeat them. So don't let your mind tune out so that all that registers is "words, words, words." If everyone would stop shrugging off the clichés, then we could move on, already.

"Two wrongs don't make a right." Don't contradict yourself by saying, "No kidding," but then continuing to do wrong in order to get even. Who started it is not the issue; the issue is that keeping it going is counterproductive.

Ironically, the cliché we do listen to is, "Don't talk to strangers." Let's put a bullet in that one. (So that we won't have guns, anymore.)

If you do "right," and explain "right," then the righteous will follow, then the meek will proceed, then the vengeful will be appeased, then the downtrodden will be motivated… and the mistaken will be awaken.

Part I
The Truth
(pages 1 – 54)

"The object of the Freethinker is to ascertain the truth—the conditions of well-being—to the end that his life will be made of value."

~ Robert G. Ingersoll

Reality Check

"Until philosophers are queens, or the queens and princesses of this world have the spirit and power of philosophy, and political greatness and wisdom meet in one…cities will never have rest from their evil—no, nor the human race, as I believe."

~ Plato

"An unexamined idea, to paraphrase Socrates, is not worth having; and a society whose ideas are never explored for possible error may eventually find its foundations insecure."

~ Mark Van Doren

"Artists and statesmen, merchants and saints, all busy themselves with their more or less partial tasks without necessarily concerning themselves with what it is that they are doing. According to **George Hegel**, it is the function of the philosopher to make men conscious of what art and politics, commerce and religion, are, so that mind can exert itself to its utmost, and, thus, become absolute."

~ The Encyclopedia of Philosophy

"There is a destiny that makes us brothers,
None goes his way alone—
All that we send into the lives of others,
Comes back into our own."

(AUTHOR UNKNOWN)

irony: 1/ use of words to express the opposite of the literal meaning; 2/ incongruity between the actual and expected result of events.

Irony is created inadvertently, therefore its creation often goes unnoticed—we cannot be aware of irony if we don't recognize how it was created. But, once realized, that same irony cannot be created again. Irony is ironic in that it ceases to further exist once its existence is discovered. How ultimately ironic.

Examples of the first definition of 'irony': It's as clear as fog. And, I hate how everyone generalizes, these days.

An example of definition two would be the case of two black fellows that I knew—neither of whom knew the other—who both told me that sometimes when they walk down the street they purposely do not compromise space for white fellows. Both admitted that it was wrong, but said it was their one harmless way of making a point to white people that they are bitter for still having to put up with slights due to racist attitudes that still persist. This was one little way to "get back some dignity." What they don't realize is the irony. The irony is that the white guy whom they so rudely hog the sidewalk from may then become the type to slight black people—thereby causing such people to hog the sidewalk from other white people…

…WHAT GOES AROUND,

COMES AROUND…

Life is ironic if and while we are living in an ironic world where we are not aware that the world is ironic. Our current world is ironic because we have fear, anger, pain and sorrow—and an awareness of that fear, anger, pain and sorrow—which leads us to *create more situations* that cause us to be fearful, etc.; which causes us to have a greater awareness of fear, anger, pain and sorrow, thereby causing us to create more situations…ad infinitum.

Life *would be* ironic if and while we were living in an ironic world where we were not aware of the above-mentioned cycle of inadvertently perpetuating negativity—because if it didn't exist, then we couldn't be aware of it and, thus, inadvertently enable it. This absence of negativity would allow us to live with a minimal awareness of negativity—and that minimal awareness would enable us to have unbridled potential. (!!!!)

This is the world that will exist.

In both worlds we can't have our cake and eat it, too. In the first world we have our cake, but regret not being able to eat it, (or at least not being able to fully enjoy it, let alone share it). In the second world we eat our cake, but cannot appreciate it since it is all there is to eat, so we take it for granted.

The bridge between the two worlds is eating what we have. That means giving up the cake so that we can't have it, anymore, but, instead, we can eat it.

paradox: statement that seems contrary to common sense, yet is perhaps true.

By giving up the cake so that future generations can eat it we will receive even more fulfillment than if we ate it ourselves.

Reality Check

A man sits comfortably with all of his material needs met. He has a family and friends; no regrets, no complaints. He's just happy. We'll quantify his happiness, arbitrarily, as 80 on the happiness scale. The man assumes that everyone is as comfortable and happy as he is. Ignorance is bliss.

Then a commercial for Save the Children comes on, so he is shocked and horrified to learn that such suffering and disparity exists. Now he is very unhappy with this new awareness. (Ignorance was bliss.) So, now he is only at 30 on the happiness scale. Perhaps, though, he can force himself to forget this knowledge through suppression and denial. He can create an untrue reality. However, such suppression will affect his whole psyche, so he'll only be at 60 on the happiness scale. Or, he can accept the real reality, and allow his empathy to compel him to make the effort necessary to save the children. Being as how he completely accepts the reality he understands that the level of effort needed will be extraordinary; in fact, more effort than he alone is capable of. So, he gets help, and the help gets help. Then they make whatever effort and personal sacrifice required to save the children. They save the children. Now he's at 220 on the happiness scale even though he may have lost many of his material possessions. Of course, though, not only will he still have his family and friends, but they'll be that much closer from the process.

Awareness is bliss.

Pivot

"We'll cross that bridge when we come around to it."

The bridge is upon us; and the reason we are going to cross it is because going over the bridge is the best of both worlds—while crossing the bridge we get to have our cake and eat it, too. So, not only is the bridge better than the side we are leaving behind, but it is even better than the side we are going towards.

I brought the first draft of this work to a priest in order to get his objective feedback. Before even reading it he told me a story to alleviate my excited sense of urgency.

"There's a rooster who crows every morning just as the sun is about to rise. The [cocky] rooster is arrogant enough to believe that the sun rises because he crows. One day, though, he oversleeps and is greatly embarrassed and humbled to discover that the sun came up, anyway.

"The rooster learns that he is still important because he announces the sun's rising,

hence enabling others to become aware of its presence." The pastor said that my opus is

good because it announces the sun to others, but I should relax since the sun will still rise.

(Yeah, tell that to all of the puppy mill dogs whose lives are constant torment.)

Pastor, I see your point, but there's a glaring contradiction to your analogy—THE EARTH REVOLVES AROUND THE SUN.

So, Everyone, this is the announcement that the sun/bridge is here—**but it's up to us to actually circle/cross it.**

Some of you may contend that you do go around the sun, and already live happily and properly. Maybe you do and maybe you do. Yet, you still must live in a world with others who don't, and others who can't. You live in a world threatened by war, economic instability, and mass destruction of the habitat. You/we are like the moon; we go around the sun, but, indirectly, by directly circling the Earth, instead, thereby thus wasting our momentum.

We're supposed to just be going around the sun directly in order to appreciate it completely. It's inherently impossible for some to live on the Earth, and some to live on the Moon. We'll just say that some tend to live more on the bright side of the Moon, and some tend to live more on the dark side—but it's still the same indirect path for all of us.

So, buckle up, Everyone: we're goin' **BACK to the EARTH**.

****

Reality Check

The Cake Analogy

You're born with a cake in the refrigerator; your favorite kind. You can have a piece or the whole cake whenever you want; you have free will. But there's a catch: this particular cake gets better and bigger the longer that it sits in the fridge.

You may be thinking: *"What if he's wrong, and the cake will only get worse, and diminish as I get older?"* But, if I'm right, then if most of it is eaten now during your younger years, then the cake will only be an ordinary delicious cake, whereas if most of the cake is saved for later in life then just imagine what an amazingly delicious and fulfilling cake it will be by then.

Some advice: expect guests, so save cake for them. But be careful of guests who come over just to mooch off of your cake because they already ate most of theirs.

Now, if everyone waits long enough to ration out the cake at a staggered pace then everyone will wind up with ample cake of the sweetest caliber and of all varieties.

Don't forget to save cake for children. Otherwise they won't have anything to look forward to and get excited about. They won't have motivation.

Here's a big secret: everyone started off with a different size cake, and some got practically none at all.

(But that's not *THE* BIG secret…)

Pivot

♫ "We'll Inherit the Earth" 7

"Shocking how nothing shocks anymore,"
The message read as it washed ashore.
Skies turn black as my eyes look down,
Written on the back are these words I found:

We'll inherit the Earth, but we don't want it.
It's been ours since birth, what ya doin' on it?
We'll inherit the Earth, but we don't want it.
Laying claim at birth, what ya doin' on it?

Waterfalls of grain fall through our hands,
We're too weak to stand, and too meek to stray.
Big trees sway, and the air is still,
Lovers climb to the top of a hill and say:

We'll inherit the Earth, but we don't want it.
It's been ours since birth, what ya doin' on it?
We'll inherit the Earth, but we don't want it.
Laid our claim at birth, what ya doin' on it?

…We watch the world from the padded cell
And our eyes scream what our lips must quell,
Oh, well…

Last bundle of twigs grew strong and young,
We can't hold our tongues …AT THE TOP OF OUR LUNGS!!!

We'll inherit the Earth, but don't tell anybody.
It's been ours since birth, and it's ours already.
We'll inherit the Earth, but don't tell anybody,
(Don't tell a soul.)

I've got my hands in my pockets, and I'm waiting for the day to come…

"We do not inherit the Earth from our ancestors.

We borrow it from our children."

~ Old Indian Proverb

♪ "Some say that's progress.

Gerd Ludwig/INSTITUTE

Moscow 1993

Arms without hands may point to pollution's gruesome price. Eight children were among 90 born since 1973 with missing terminal limbs in homes clustered around industrial sections of the city.

...I say that's cruel." [8]

Pivot

♫ "You may find yourself living in a shotgun shack. You many find yourself in another part of the world. And you may find yourself behind the wheel of a large automobile. And you may find yourself in a beautiful house, with a beautiful wife. And you may ask yourself: Well, how did I get here?

…letting the days go by, letting the water hold me down; into the blue again, after the money's gone. Once in a lifetime.

And you may ask yourself: How do I work this? And you may ask yourself: Where is that large automobile? And you may tell yourself: This is not my beautiful house, and this is not my beautiful wife.

…same as it ever was, same as it ever was, same as it ever was, same as it ever was…

You may ask yourself: What is this beautiful house? And where does that highway go to? And am I right, or am I wrong? And you may say to yourself: My, God! What have I done?!

…same as it ever was, same as it ever was, same as it ever was, same as it ever was…

Time isn't holding up, time isn't after us.

Here comes the twister…" [9]

How can one truly live properly and happily if one doesn't know why he is living, or what the purpose is? An actor will typically ask, "What's my motivation?" because without that knowledge, that foundation, the actor cannot know how to behave. That actor will have no conviction.

What are our motivations, intentions, and convictions? I assert that no one really knows the answer to this question. After all, if you ask any child why they go to school, 95% of the time they'll answer: "to get a job." But shouldn't that answer be the same even for children set to inherit billions of dollars?

Since when are children explained why human beings should want to learn, should want to be honest, should want to care, should want to share, should want to try, should want to live?

While learning how to tell time you might have told someone that the time was 2:05 when it was actually 5:02. You may have even claimed to be sure. You believed that you knew. But the proof that you didn't know was that you wouldn't have been able to teach it to others. Once you finally grasped it, though, you always knew how to tell time.

If any of us really knew how to tell time, so to speak, then we wouldn't still be conditioning children to believe that money is the ends, and not the means. (If anyone does know, then he or she needs a new **P**ublic **R**elations agent.)

A 6-year-old can believe that he knows how to tell time, and go about falsely living in a world where he "knows" the time. But if an adult were to assert that it is 4 o'clock when it is actually 10 o'clock, then the rest of us would have to consider that person insane, or not accepting reality.

Grasping time, however, is not black and white. Animals don't have "time." They merely have instinct to regulate their behavior according to the changing environment. But, we, by definition, have a higher level of perception than animals because of the very nature of our ability to conceive. Earliest man must have had a conception of time but did not have the tools to demarcate, or articulate, the progression

of time; so his perception of the conception of time was minimal. Of course, as time went on, man increased the level of his perception as he created devices such as the sundial and computer.

The ability to perceive time is not absolute, though, as the very nature of numbers is endless. Suffice it to say, we do not have infinite perception. We can, though, conceive of infinity.

There are countless levels of perception.

♪ "I've never been the kind to close an open mind." [10]

"Philosophers of The Age of Reason believed man can 'make himself do the right thing,' instead of doing what may seem easier or more appealing.

"To the philosophers of The Age of Reason, progress in human affairs seemed assured. It was only a question of time, they believed, until people learned to let reason—not ignorance, emotion or superstition—guide them. When people did so, they would have happy lives." [11]

Never be the kind to close an open mind.

What the philosophers of The Age of Reason seemed to be saying is: "Do you really want to have fun? …or are you just saying that you want to have fun?" [12]

Obviously everyone ever born was born into a society that they did not create. Moreover, most people did not have perfect parents; perfect parents who would lavish abundant love and affection and perfect parents who would properly teach right from wrong. And all of those imperfect parents also did not have perfect parents. And all of *those* imperfect parents' parents', etc. However, even those people who *were* reared by outstanding parents to become very self-secure individuals still had to grow up amidst others who were lacking in self-identity, self-esteem and a general sense of purpose that comes from recognizing that one belongs to a community. Furthermore, everyone who has ever lived has been socialized from childhood to accept their reality—the status quo, as it were—as right, normal, and inevitable. That is to say, children naturally assume that the way things are done is the way things are supposed to be done simply because that's the way it's always been done.

This pattern has continuously perpetuated itself in a downward spiral. Understand how and why this is so, then it will not continue to be so. The pattern will reverse, and perpetuate in an ascending, outwardly expanding spiral at an exponential rate directly proportional to how fast this idea is shared.

"As we learn through imitation, identification, and instruction, values are internalized. They provide security and contribute to a sense of personal and social identity. For this reason, individuals in every society cling tenaciously to the values they have acquired and feel threatened when confronted with others who live according to different conceptions of what is desirable." [13]

"Some scholars explain the dynamic of conflict between different cultures, or just differences, by linking cultural conflict to a competitive strategy of behavior. For example, if there is a high value placed on attaining power and status within a group, the stage is set for competition [to defeat]. A competitive spirit arising, for instance, from scarce resources, can pit individuals, micro-cultures, and whole cultures against each other. Therefore, rejecting others who do not look or behave like us is reinforced if one of our cultural values is to compete against, and attempt to, among other things, seek status higher than another individual or group. This competitive spirit that lays the ground work for conflict is in direct contradiction to the conforming and co-operative mode of behavior we need to survive." [14]

"The bottom line is, if we want to be accepted by others and be happy, conforming to the rules is essential. Ultimately, conforming members of society create group cohesion, which assures the group's ongoing existence." [14]

But, because we go about with a narrow vision and lack of intention, we contradict ourselves. Yes, following the rules will assure the group's cohesion and ongoing existence—but not if the rules are contradictory and stress elimination of "the other guy." THE OTHER GUY IS PART OF YOUR/OUR GROUP. The group will not be assured if the individuals within it are not assured.

So, if we are selfishly concerned about our own individual welfare, instead of altruistically concerned about the welfare of others, that is, the group we belong to, then our individual welfare will be left wanting. If you/we are concerned with others ahead of ourselves, then we will be rewarded ourselves. That's the circle of irony we should be traversing.

Reality Check

YOU ARE SOCIETY IS YOU ARE SOCIETY IS YOU ARE SOCIETY IS YOU ARE SOCIETY IS…

It is not a "competition to obtain material goods, power and/or status." It is about aspiring for self-improvement, enhancement of relationships, and general evolution of human potential.

Irony creates contradiction, confusion and chaos. It creates destruction. Destruction creates nothing. I will be repeatedly referring to this creative cycle of destruction as "bullshit." Yes, this is a crude, vulgar and offensive term, but that's the point of using it. The term "bullshit" also is the only word in the English lexicon that so accurately defines the nonsense that I'm talking about since we all constantly use it since it is constantly being created.

WARNING: AVOID BULLSHIT. Because once it gets you, you won't be able to recognize it, anymore.

Obviously it is too late to avoid, and perhaps it was inevitable for man to avoid from the get-go since, at the time, man didn't know that he was supposed to avoid it. Now, though, we have the weapon to defeat bullshit. We have the understanding of what it is, and how it manifests. We have the ability to recognize it: and the way to defeat bullshit is to simply point it out. What's more, now that we know to be vigilant of bullshit it should become next to impossible to perpetuate it. Once all of the bullshit is gone, potential potentially becomes infinite.

BULLSHIT IS BULLSHIT

"Hey, we're only human." That cliché is bullshit. That attitude falsely implies that our potential is not reachable, thereby becoming a self-fulfilling prophecy. It gives us an excuse to not do our best. It makes failure acceptable, and even expected. It is a negative, pessimistic attitude that is self-defeating and pointless.

Pivot

Man is here to feel emotion. This occurs by satiating our innate curiosity and desire for awareness by using our innate creative imagination; by integrating our bodies with our environment, and by satisfying our innate social instincts to relate to others, to share.

Unfortunately, when there has been inadequate parenting, particularly in infancy, a person will have a lower threshold for becoming afraid. This can manifest as anger and unhappiness and denial. This insecurity is a result of parenting that is lacking in attention, particularly affection. Such neglect of a child's mental and physical needs will decrease their curious and creative natures, preventing them from achieving their full potential. Hence, bullshitting becomes the modus operandi.

Ideally, when absolutely everyone is nurtured properly from birth, our social instincts will completely be fulfilled. This is because we will all be so secure and happy that we will all strive to our full creative potential, instead of venting our anger by quashing others' potential. Therefore, we will always have an abundance to share with each other. We will play and challenge as a group, advancing and achieving faster and greater as a group than we would as mere scattered individuals. Yet, since the real world isn't ideal, even those lucky enough to be born to qualified parents who know how to fully nurture human potential, bullshit will still become a hazard. Because even though such a person will have a gung-ho attitude towards life, if he's the only one in the community who takes life by the horns, then he'll end up even more unhappy than everyone else because he won't have anyone else around to grab the horns with. So, in order to avoid being lonely, he'll start hanging around with those who are not yet on his level. Yet, in order to assimilate he'll have to be dishonest by bullshitting them and himself. Though, by doing so he facilitates negative emotions and suppresses the life-affirming ones. Dishonesty isn't real, and unreal living will leave a person wanting.

For instance, give a child a strange-looking rock, say it is from the moon and watch him admire and appreciate it. Then confess that it is actually just a regular Earth rock and watch as he feels contempt and disappointment even though it's still the same rock. Now he will understand how and why dishonesty is undesirable. Think of a movie that was very good except it had some major plot holes that lead to disbelief. The movie becomes difficult, if not impossible, to accept and enjoy. Instead of feeling the fulfillment that a good drama should invoke, you feel gypped. Conversely, think of how much more riveting a good story is when it's true. This same notion of Realism applies to our everyday lives: the level of isolationism in a society is directly proportional to its level of dishonesty.

Phoniness is next to loneliness.

Honesty is the best policy.

"One can only be honest with others when one is being honest with oneself."

There are two kinds of people. Those who would choose the bumper sticker: "I WANT THE TRUTH!"; and those who would choose: "I CAN'T HANDLE THE TRUTH!"

♪ "Do you want to hear that ignorance is bliss?" [10]

THE TRUTH SHALL SET YOU FREE.

Reality Check

Fear, anger, loneliness and apathy are negative. In and of themselves they have no redeeming value. Their purpose is to direct one back towards the positive, life-affirming emotions. Apathy will create boredom; its purpose is to create desire to overcome the apathy, because it ultimately results in death. Loneliness' purpose is to create the desire to return towards group-oriented, altruistic behavior; towards man's innately self-perpetuating motivations. Anger's purpose is to correct behavior that is counterproductive.

There are only two logical reasons for having fear: to avoid physical harm, and to avoid isolation. These are very real fears in the current real world, but in an ideal world such fears would virtually never exist because there would be no genesis for threatening circumstances stemming from non-altruists.

In the real world of course the average child is brimming with insecurity and self-doubt. Amongst those children whose self-worth is particularly pronounced their sense of exclusion will manifest as violence and/or as petty attempts to create a hierarchical social order. For those children whose self-esteem is above average but still lacking they'll usually pretend to share the same opinions as their domineering counterparts merely for the sake of not being excluded from the group.

If adults would explain to these children that if they stopped worrying about not being accepted, and just trusted that if they listen to their subconscious inclinations, then they'll develop into self-secure and self-fulfilled individuals. Then others with similar dispositions will naturally gravitate towards them due to their substance. Whereas simply following for the sake of avoiding being excluded from the group is disingenuous. And, without exception, being disingenuous will result in regret.

"Don't go for the glitter, go for the substance."

~ Lisa Simpson

Just as we can experience positive emotion merely through the imagination, we can also deny and be dishonest, which is simply creating unrealness. Denial and negative emotions perpetuate each other. The longer the cycle is allowed to continue, then the more difficult it is to break the cycle since denial and unconscious negative emotions quash the real potential of curiosity and creativity. If they haven't been developed, then there would be hardly any foundation from which to start over again.

When an individual has to make such a fresh start the challenge can seem daunting, and may very well be impossible if doing it alone. If, however, society provided adequate crutches for those seeking to escape their cycle of bullshit, then everyone would be capable of a fresh start. Since it is society as a whole that is ensconced in bullshit we can only climb out of it if we build one collective ladder, instead of just many ladders for each individual. Because the only way for everyone to overcome their micro-cosmic problems is for everyone to address them at a macro-cosmic level.

This new awareness of the bullshit that we have to climb out of can be overwhelming; and perhaps seem like a futile prospect. But it can also be cause for hope that we can now accomplish an intentional society that's devoid of bullshit and rife with congruity. Of course, it goes without saying that it's simple enough to state grandiose goals, but it's unrealistic to believe that achieving them is possible. It's even, perhaps, an imposition to declare that everyone should now be expected to confront the inconvenient truth of reality. Hopefully, though, by simply stating what will happen if we don't act collectively, and what could happen if we do, most everyone will believe that attempting to achieve the ideal is not merely possible, but desirable. …And that it's actually the opposite point of view that is futile and pointless.

"I didn't create this situation; I'm just dealin' with it!" 15 Deal with what's real, otherwise real accomplishment will be impossible.

I didn't create this reality, I just accepted it. (But, man, I just can't accept this.)

Reality Check

Basically, everyone lives with some degree of fear since we have yet to create an ideal world. Also, fear is an inherent vestigial quality left in us from our ascendance from the animals. We have risen above the animals by gaining awareness, by achieving a higher consciousness; it is what separates us from them. Yet, our inherent fears which we've not yet escaped from confines us closer to their level and prevents us from achieving an even greater consciousness. Awareness of fear can be on a conscious or subconscious level. If it is on a conscious level, above the surface, it can be the impetus for us to avoid it and run away, which is how it gains strength and causes one's consciousness to diminish even further. Yet, as fear decreases, consciousness goes up. Life gets better. You become more passionate and less apathetic. As stated earlier, the most extreme apathy results in death. Extreme passion results in extremely complete fulfillment. And understanding this should inspire us to strive for the ideal.

TRY UNTIL YOU DIE: **"Failure is not an option!"**

♫ "It may have been Camelot for Jack and Jacqueline
But on the Ché Guevara highway filling up with gasoline
Fidel Castro's brother spies a rich lady who's crying
Over luxury's disappointment, so he thinks that he should warn her
That the Third World is just around the corner/
Mixing Pop and Politics…he asks me what the use is
I offer him embarrassment and my usual excuses while looking down the corridor
Out to where the van is waiting: I'm looking for the Great Leap Forwards
You can be active with the activists or sleep in with the sleepers
While you're waiting for the Great Leap Forwards/
One leap forwards, two leaps back

Here comes the future and you can't run from it
If you've got a black list I want to be on it
If no one seems to understand, start your own revolution, cut out the middleman.
In a perfect world we'd all *sing in tune*
But this is reality, so give me some room!

So join the struggle while you may
The Revolution is just a T-shirt away!
…Waiting for the Great Leap Forwards" [16]

"The mode by which the inevitable comes to pass is effort."

~ Oliver Wendell Holmes

Boredom causes laziness, and vice versa. Don't give in to it by letting it sap your motivation. If you don't fight it, then it will overtake you. The longer you don't fight it, the more there will be to overcome and resist.

"Abhor laziness in yourself and in others." [20]

Pivot

The only way to live life fully is to do everything you feel the impulse for, instead of not bothering to do the littlest and biggest things because we just don't feel like bothering. Otherwise, don't talk about what you want if you don't want it enough to do it.

"Tomorrow has been canceled due to a lack of interest." That would be the ultimate shame.

My cousin Judy told me that my perspective is one that focuses on the negative, when we're supposed to focus on the positive. But what I'm actually doing *is* positive—a positive attempt to eradicate the negative by focusing on it. It is hypocritical to say that my attitude is negative since one wouldn't say it to the hungry and homeless while living lavishly. It also implies misery and suffering are acceptable…as long as it's not you. "There are problems in these times, but none of them are mine."

A negative attitude is accepting the bad because it is "inevitable." If a commercial for Save the Children comes on and you turn it off to avoid viewing very sad situations, then all you are doing is playing the denial game: If I don't see it, then it doesn't exist. But obviously it does exist. And if we don't accept it, then it will only get worse. If you had such a miserable life wouldn't you hope that the lucky ones would be considerate enough to rescue you?

Of course the bad is complicated, and permeated throughout practically all elements of society to a point that it seems impossible to fix. We can, however, get everyone to realize that it's not impossible if we get everyone to realize that it's not impossible. Let's not accept less than (trying for) perfection. We don't necessarily have to take the bad with the good.

The higher one's standards are, then the greater the rewards. Therefore, be idealistic.

According to my friend Jarrod, there are 2 kinds of people: those who would pick up the spoon, and those who would kick it under the table. He said that he happened to notice a fellow waiter cleaning up her station when she spotted a spoon on the floor. She looked around to see if anyone was watching, saw no one, then kicked it further underneath. Either someone else will eventually have to pick it up, or they'll have to needlessly replace it.

Incidentally, Jarrod's most memorable retort, upon being asked, "What's the big deal about being honest?": "It just feels good to be honest."

Reality Check

With a belief in God there comes the rationale to keep fear, anger and loneliness in check. However, if people were given the proper nurturing environment, then they would not feel the negative emotions, and thus would not need the safety blanket that (blind) faith provides. After all, a relationship with "God" is irrelevant to creating a well-adjusted society since such a society is dependent upon common sense. Nonetheless, I do feel it is pertinent to illustrate that our experiences directly corroborate that a higher power is the underlying foundation behind those experiences; because the underlying fabric of life, nature and the universe is geometric, rhythmical. Such structured patterns could not possibly have arisen by mere coincidence. Structure and design, by definition, implies an intention. So, therefore, logic dictates that there must be a force behind all that is. It's as though God arranged it so that our power to reason would lead us to conclude that a deity must exist.

While I'm on the topic, I have to point out that many people express their devotion to God passively, by attending temples and blowing smoke. That is very easy. Wouldn't it be more fitting to actively show God that you're on His side? There are many of God's creatures who need help, but prayer alone won't provide it; (although a massive group prayer would seriously expedite a lot of improvement).

Don't "take it easy." Take it hard; because, if you take it easy, you'll make it hard.

"God helps them that help themselves." [17]

"Love costs. It takes work and effort." [18]

"Desire is measured by how much effort one is willing to expend to fulfill the desire."

"God needs everyone. I need all the help that I can get."

~ God

Why, as a capitalist society, does the world believe that without the potential for financial gain people will have no motivation or incentive to try their best at everything that they do? When I play racquetball, or read Stephen King, nobody pays me.

Sadly, the only answer I can see is that we've been taught that we've got to prove ourselves; that we're only as valuable as the symbolic worth of numbers, signatures, and material possessions. But, again, the superficial cannot be a cure for low self-esteem and/or loneliness. Ironically, though, we are also a society that claims to believe in God, yet we simultaneously worship the $. Who will claim that God intended us to be measured by our net worth?

"In fact, most students eventually come to believe that the villagers [whom they initially perceived to be living in poverty] are, on the whole, actually more satisfied with their lives than are most Americans." [13]

"When I came back I saw how out-of-control the students here are. It's just crazy. They want so much; they talk about how much money they need to make as if these things are necessities, and you'll never be happy without them. Maybe I was like that, too, but now I know I don't need those things; sure I'd like a new car, but I don't need it. I'm more interested in learning now." [13]

"Most students, upon returning home, said they would no longer take for granted the luxuries, such as hot showers, they had at home." [13]

substantial: having substance (i.e., tangible matter; material), real, actual.

superficial: relating to what is only apparent.

Accordingly, emotions are not substantial. So, unfortunately, being as limited as we are in our perceptions, we rely on the substantial, such as diamond rings, to represent intangibles such as emotion. (Except poor people; they can't afford diamonds, so they must not have love to give.) Ironically, though, this only causes the intangible to become less perceptible. If we were more perceptive (secure), then we would recognize that the imperceptible, such as respect and trust, was actually what is substantial.

Conclusion: Ideally we would all be motivated one hundred percent by our positive innateness. We would then all be one hundred percent honest. Everyone would, automatically and voluntarily, co-operate happily, and strive their best to perpetuate mankind's true desires. "There would be no laziness, and no over-indulgence." [18.5]

Instead, because we are lacking in true motivation, we strive to reach a point where we don't have to strive. That is, the goal is to do enough stuff to enable one to get enough money so that one will never have to do stuff again. The motivation is to wipe out the motivation. So, money is supposed to enable us to survive—yet it's actually killing us.

I-R-O-N-Y

No wonder misery is the norm at old-age homes. They have no motivation left to live. They are completely apathetic. If they were any more apathetic, then they'd have the motivation to commit suicide.

♪ "We give up our sunshine to buy what we need." [19]

standard: anything taken as a basis of comparison; level or degree of excellence considered as a goal or as adequate; model.

We lower (and lower and lower) our standards for money. (To wit: oil spills, the space shuttle disaster, the proliferation of high fructose corn syrup in schools, and the Japanese nuclear crisis.)

"We aim towards lofty heights, but temptation overcomes us. Greed and vanity blind our eyes, envy and arrogance eat into the marrow of our bones, false ambitions bring us bitter remorse, and selfishness dwarfs our souls. We are creatures of haphazard living." [20]

"The most serious flaw in the free-enterprise system, according to Marx, is that it accumulates more and more wealth but becomes less and less capable of using this wealth wisely. As a result, Marx saw the accumulation of riches being accompanied by the rapid spread of human misery."

"Life sucks without bucks."

Reality Check

♫ "When I'm lyin' in my bed at night,
I don't wanna get up
Nothin' ever seems to turn out right
I don't wanna grow up
How do you move in a world of fog
That's always changing things
Makes me wish that I could be a dog
When I see the price that you pay
I don't wanna grow up
I don't wanna be that way
I don't wanna grow up
Seems like folks turn into things
That they'd never want to be
The only thing to live for is today…
I'm gonna put a hole in my T.V. set
I don't wanna grow up
Open up the medicine chest
And I don't wanna grow up
I don't wanna have to shout it out
I don't want my hair to fall out
I don't wanna be filled with doubt
I don't wanna be a good boy scout
I don't wanna have to learn to count
I don't wanna have the biggest amount
I don't wanna grow up
Well when I see my parents fight
I don't wanna grow
They all go out and drinking all night
And I don't wanna grow up
I'd rather stay here in my room
Nothin' out there but sad and gloom
I don't wanna live in a big old tomb
On Grand Street
When I see the 5 o'clock news
I don't wanna grow up
Comb their hair and shine their shoes
I don't wanna grow up
Stay around in my old hometown
I don't wanna put no money down
I don't wanna get me a big old loan
Work them fingers to the bone
I don't wanna float a broom
Fall in love and get married then boom
How the hell did it get here so soon?
I don't wanna grow up" [21]

Life is a riddle/puzzle/game?

Part III: Perceive the puzzle as a whole and go through the "Ah-ha!" effect.

Part II: Put the puzzle together.

Part I: Figure out that the riddle is to realize that it is a puzzle.

Part V: Apply it. Get on the track and go around the circle. Play the game according to the rules that are built in.

Part IV: Help others to get on to the track.

As noted earlier, under initially ideal circumstances, Part V would be the only part since everyone would always and already be applying it (innocently) without even knowing there was such a riddle.

Life is a riddle/puzzle/game.

SOLUTION: Understand that there are those who don't understand that our purpose is to learn, discover, create, play, and challenge others to achieve their best, so that they, and the group, will attain great fulfillment. They need compassion, patience and teaching from those who did receive the proper love and clarified direction during childhood. Counteracting their negativity with anger and rejection will only compound their animosity, thus compelling them to react even more hostilely.

Again, "two wrongs don't make a right" is a cliché—because it's a truism. One doesn't put out a fire with matches, nor by walking away from it. It is in everyone's best interest to help all others since it is in each person's best interest to have people to challenge them to improve. And, being as how the whole is greater than the sum of the parts, the potential achievement and passion to be had, by the individuals and the group, will increase proportionally to the number of people who understand this.

"Love one another as you love yourself." The problem, though, is that we don't love ourselves very much because we feel that no one loves us. So, starting now, everyone is going to start loving everyone, and vice versa.

WE'RE ALL EQUALLY SPECIAL. Living by higher standards and doing what is right doesn't make you better or more deserving than those who had their potential and humanity squelched. It only means that you are more fortunate than those who are not as aware as you are. Living by higher standards should be taken for granted. For example, if someone returns a lost wallet, then a reward should not be expected. It should simply be expected that the wallet will be returned.

SOME ARE MORE IMPERFECT THAN OTHERS. Of course nobody is perfect since we all live with fear and anxiety and we all didn't get clear instructions on how to be a human being. So we all make mistakes. But that doesn't justify wrongdoing or lack of effort. If you make a mistake, follow the three A's: Acknowledge, Accept, Advance. We can all allow the defense, "Honest mistake, won't happen again." But, "But everyone else is misbehaving" is not acceptable."

An error doesn't become a mistake until you refuse to correct it." [22]

"Failure fetishism is good mind-rotting fun, but isn't it time we stopped getting off over the pornography of failure and got naked with the real thing? Rather than simultaneously denying and worshiping failure, wouldn't it be easier on our nerves to come to terms with it? To force ourselves to admit that failure isn't really all that bad—any more than it's all that good?"

There's a song with the great line: "Won't you ever learn? Won't you ever change?" [4] It's great because most of us spend our life refusing to acknowledge, accept and advance. But only a pathetic loser (society) would spend his life noting what a great line it is ("Yeah. What a great line. I *will* never learn, and I *will* never change.") while never taking the words to heart, so that the words will always continue to have weight and truth. Take the sentiment to heart, though, and it becomes more powerful than any ever conceived.

♫ "I won't fall for the oldest trick in the book, so don't sit there and think you're off of the hook by saying there is no use changing 'cause that's just what you are. Always ready to defend your fears; what's the matter with the truth? Did I offend your ears by suggesting that a change might be a thing to try? It would kill you just to try and be a nicer guy? It's not like you would lose some critical piece if somehow you moved point A to point B; maintaining there is no point changing 'cause that's just what you are. So maybe you're right, nobody can take something older than time and hope you could make it better — that would be a mistake. So take it just so far…'cause that's just what you are. It's just argumentative danger to wake you. … Even when it is apparent where your actions will take you." [23]

Mankind has avoided accepting its mistake for so long that we have created a real fear; (you might say that we've avoided looking inside the closet for so long that now it is infested with rats and other vermin). Now, though, if we can be bold we can acknowledge the truth and deal with it. We don't have to continue to behave irrationally, anymore. We now have an opportunity to create what's really supposed to be reality: 100 percent pure, unadulterated honest reality—BULLSHIT FREE.

We can't continue to deny any longer because we now understand that we will inevitably have to face a lot worse bullshit later if we don't face it now. So, let's face it before it faces us. Stop bullshitting/accepting bullshit.

One may cling to the notion that even though you may have a complete understanding of bullshit and the necessity to exterminate it, it doesn't make a difference because the world is buried beneath so many, many layers of bullshit, and is "hopelessly" lost from ever reaching a utopian society which has minimal bullshit, that this understanding won't change the world. So, therefore, it is pointless to even discuss such matters—pointless to even try and escape the bullshit. After all, "It's just not possible." So we may as well just settle for whatever rewards we can scrounge up inside the bullshit while waiting for it to totally collapse. This view is negative, self-defeating and further perpetuates the problem. It's a bullshit attitude.

The positive, problem-solving view would be to realize that, a) if you can understand all of this, then it is also possible for virtually everyone else to, and, b) simply by understanding all of this individually, then individually you will be living in utopia. That is to say, you have the understanding that each individual, and the entire group, has infinite potential, and thereby the capacity to reach it. In other words: WE HAVE THE POWER TO CREATE UTOPIA!

You now understand that utopia, like everything else, is a relative term and, once reached, will only be able to grow and thrive as more and more people also come to understand individual utopia; and these people will perpetuate a greater utopia for the individual and the group.

So, welcome to the first level of utopia; the state of diminishing fear.

THE 5 STEPS TO LIFE:

1) Figure out that there is a question to answer.

1) Figure out what the question is.

1) Answer it.

0) Apply it. Do the math. (Pi is infinite)

2) Show and explain the question/answer you discovered. (Eventually, though, the world will be applying it even though they forgot there was ever a question to answer. But it won't matter since they'll be getting 100 percent, anyway.)

In Arthur C. Clarke's *2001: A Space Odyssey*, the dawning of man—that is, the moment when mankind became separate from the animals—was represented in the moment when one "man" had the "insight" to use a (secret) weapon, a bone, as an "advantage" to defeat another who was his enemy. It is unfortunate that the "man" did not also have the foresight to realize that, although a weapon would be an advantage during the moment it is being used, the very use of the weapon would be giving away the secret. Later on, that same secret would be used against him by his enemies' friends; and the fight would be taken to a "higher" level, but it would still come back to "man" against "man."

Now, since we never even gained hindsight from our lack of foresight, we finally do have the foresight (hopefully) to realize that, regarding nuclear weapons in particular, though not excluding other tools for implementing injury and death, the only way to win the fight is not to. ("The true enemy is war itself.") The duality of the irony is that we've "progressed" to a level where we can simultaneously reveal the infinite potential of the imperceptible, while also potentially destroying the infinite potential of the imperceptible.

Our ironic attitude is, "I might as well do what's wrong since it is inevitable that the other guy will do so, anyway,"—but then the other guy does it for the same reason. If we hit each other back and forth we'll hurt each other, and then incapacitate each other, and then kill each other. Or we could play basketball everyday forever.

"Violence is the last refuge of the incompetent." [25]

Ethologist Frans de Waal found that, among primates, subjects exhibit not only a decided affinity to engage in conflict with each other, but also an equally distinct inclination to re-establish harmony when conflict has broken it. In other words, co-operating to make peace appears to be as "natural" as competing and creating conflict in the primate world. Furthermore, de Waal claims that these behaviors are learned rather than instinctual. [14]

Reality Check

In regards to animals of the same species, they use their individual instinct to survive, thus perpetuating the survival of the species by competitively weeding out those individuals who are the least adaptable, in order to perpetuate the most adaptable group: competition is explicit, (individuals struggle for individual survival); co-operation is implicit, (the group struggles for survival of the group).

In regards to man, we didn't realize, initially, that the trick to properly handling the "secret" weapon was to share it with everyone verbally, instead of revealing it in a practical manner, and should have discussed the catch-22 so that it wouldn't come back in our face the way it did to cause a regressive evolution. (Though how could we have realized it since we weren't actually real men yet since we did not actually have language, yet?)

With regards to ideal man, we should co-operatively use our intellect to survive, and, thus, perpetuate the survival of the species by co-operatively challenging one another to reach a higher potential in order to perpetuate a greater group potential. (**Reminder: According to academia our distinction from the other animals is our supreme ability to adapt*, which stems from our enhanced capacity for reason; which might best be defined as forethought.**) For example, I can't get better at racquetball just by hitting the ball against a wall. Henceforth, co-operation would be explicit, (the group would strive for group enhancement); competition would be implicit, (individuals would strive to be at the forefront).

"No matter how close cultures may find themselves, no two will at all times, and in all ways, exhibit, for example, the same styles of clothing. Thus, while a culture's unique features create inner group cohesion, they also set it apart as distinct from other cultures." [14] These superficial differences are just that; they are not substantial, and are no reason for violent conflict, as they have no bearing on survival. They are just fun and interesting to take notice of and compare.

It is as though we fell into a trap; a very ironic trap. The deeper we fell into it, the more obscured we became from seeing that we were in it, and, yet, at the same time, the more obvious it became that something was not right….

The "obvious" implication, whether it be from the primitive weapon of crude bone, or the primitive weapon of sophisticated science, is that we should not compete to defeat, but co-operate to elevate.

"It's become appallingly clear that our technology has surpassed our humanity." [25.5]

---

*And now we've got to see if the theory will hold true under the utmost challenging conditions. That is, will we be able to re-adapt to the untenable situation we've created, to modify our means of survival, or, in the long run, will we prove to actually be the least adaptable of all the animal species?

Pivot

…Furthermore, as we got closer to the bottom of the trap, it became both easier and harder to go back up and escape it. Easier because we are so much more aware that we need to turn around, since we can more clearly recognize that an abyss lies ahead, and harder because we're so far down that we are no longer even aware that there is a light at the end of the road, let alone see it or know what direction it is. There are just so many, many layers of bullshit that we're buried beneath.

If man had truly been a man at the so-called moment of dawning, then his insight would have gained him foresight before the fact; which leads me back to the concept of time…

If all children were raised to be completely self-secure individuals, then those children would naturally create a world free from suffering, fighting and unjust inequality—and they would create a world that thrived on mankind's better inner half. This is a paradoxical contention since the world already existed before each child was born. To help make sense of this paradox I compare it to the last episode of *STAR TREK: THE NEXT GENERATION*, which was a sophisticated version of "the chicken or the egg" dilemma. Here's my personal analogical paradoxical theory; it regards what anthropologists term "The Missing Link" that should exist between the fossil of the earliest homo-sapien and the fossil of the Neanderthal man, but has yet to be discovered. My speculation is this: it has not yet been found because it does not yet exist. But it will exist after man teaches primates on a grand scale to communicate on a higher level than they can achieve on their own. (A gorilla named Koko has been taught a vocabulary of over a thousand words through sign language. She now has a higher conception, or awareness of, a banana. She is now articulate and has more clarity (of perception). She has reached a higher level.)

That group of children who were raised to remain innocent would always continue on the path of mankind's innate desire to create and discover and play. "Child" and "adult" would become much more relative terms since adults would no longer have the distinction of lost innocence that comes from the awareness of suffering and misery, since such things would be virtually non-existent. I would still define "adult" by "lost innocence," but lost innocence would be the "grasping of the infinite potential within humanity." Perhaps, then, "lost innocence" would be an oxymoron, and it would be more appropriate to call it "found innocence."

Let's not forget the potential reached by the likes of Mozart, and he, too, was "only human." Nor forget the fact that we currently use only five percent of our brain. Obviously we are far from our potential.

We have much room for improvement.

Even if you don't accept the notion of having a spiritual side, which implies a future lifetime to motivate you past your current physical lifetime, you can still conceive the reality that makes it necessary for us to look ahead for our children's children's children's, etc.

Get it? Get it:

We all must have an unlimited perception regarding our concern for future generations because at some point down the line we'll all be the indefinite great grandparents to the same children of a future generation; just as we are all presumably (distant) cousins now.

Reality Check

Do you now grasp why The Golden Rule, (i.e., "The Law of Nature," according to Thomas Hobbes), is such an integral and necessary part to humanity's success? Of course you do. I was just being rhetorical (and needed a segue). It's just amazing, though, that that rule seems so simple and obvious, and it has supposedly been stressed as the number one rule since back in the day, yet, here we are, mired in a sea of vapidity and grief.

If society truly lived by the attitudes that it espouses, then the slogan "JUST DO IT" *would* be an accurate reflection of our collective motto. Perhaps, though, a more apropos slogan would be: JUST SAY IT.

For example: We litter; we destroy the ecosystem as if there's no tomorrow; we condone pepper spraying harmless citizens; we abandon veterans; "the average annual amount the U.S. will spend on nuclear arms programs through the year 2008 is $4,500,000,000"; we play commercials before the movie now; working as a ticket taker is *not* "an exciting career in the motion picture industry" as Sony Theatres would have us believe; nor are Virginia Slims "a woman thing," for crying out loud; we don't wear our seatbelts (nobody ever plans to have an accident); we don't use the turning signal; we rubberneck; we can't handle the right of way, let alone right or wrong; we need to be told to get off at the back of the bus; there are little stickers on all of the fruit; even packages already wrapped in a plastic shell are shipped inside a plastic bag; we unnecessarily age very ungracefully; most people abhor their jobs—even and especially teachers!; Monsanto; the movies "Superman Returns" and "Green Lantern"; the price of movies; we stigmatize "menial" occupations such as trash collectors even though we all need them; we talk about the problems and we talk about the problems and we talk about the problems; even when we come up with a super idea such as midnight basketball, it never materializes; everyone keeps telling me, "So what? It's always been like this. Don't act like it's not supposed to be all screwed up"; the radio is very, very, very, very repetitive; we're so oblivious that we allow the fat kid to be picked last; the economy hinges on tourism, oil, disposable stuff, gambling, junk food, torturing animals, make-up, jewelry, alcohol, drugs (illegal and not), pornography and sugar; it's illegal to be paid for sex unless it is filmed; "In 1992 1,896 individuals and families with incomes above $200,000 filed U.S. tax returns reporting that they owed not one cent in federal income taxes, up from 198 in 1980. The tax-free returns were perfectly legal since filers took advantage of a variety of write-offs and tax shelters that one Congress after another inserted or preserved in the tax code"; "America spends less of its gross national product on education than any other major industrial country," yet we act genuinely confused as to why the general state of affairs is so horrendous; they tried to sell us that Spider Man was all along a space robot; Jon Stewart's job is way too easy; planned obsolescence; 44% of N.Y.C. children live below the poverty line; teachers' salaries versus entertainers'; supermodels' salaries versus everybody else who actually contributes to society; not only do twinkies exist, but they're specifically designed for children!; we outlaw hemp; we outlaw marijuana—even for medicinal purposes—yet alcohol and cigarettes are kosher; we prop up intellectually incongruent bullshit artists, such as Ann Coulter, Laura Ingrahm, Carlson Tucker, Glenn Beck, Tony Snow, Bill Bennett, Joe Scarborough, Daren Kagin, Tammy Bruce, Rush Limbaugh, Sean Hannity, Michael Reagan, Michael Savage, Bill O'Reilley, Bob Novak, Jeanine Pirro, Brett Baier, Britt Hume, Peggy Noonan, Mike Gallagher, Tomi Lahren, Benjamin Shapiro, and Neil Boortz as if they foster any honest debate; we bring guns to school; we bring guns to school; we bring guns to school; we bring guns to school; we bring guns to school; we bring guns to school; we brings guns to school; we bring guns to school; we bring guns to school; we bring guns to school; we bring guns to school; we bring guns to school; we bring guns to school; we bring guns to school; we bring guns to school; we bring guns to school; we bring guns to school; we bring guns to school; we bring guns to school; we bring guns to school; we bring guns to school; we bring guns to school; we bring guns to school; we bring guns to school; we bring guns to school; when I was born, my hometown was the kind of place where you could say that the post office didn't have bullet-proof dividers, but not as of summer of '96; we bring guns to school; we bring guns to school; we brings guns to school; we bring guns to school; we bring guns to school; we bring guns to school; we bring guns to school; we bring guns to school; we bring guns to school; we bring guns to school; we bring guns to school; we bring guns to school; we bring guns to school; we bring guns to school; we bring guns to school; we bring guns to school; we bring guns to school; we bring guns to school; we bring guns to school; we bring guns to school; we bring guns to school; we brings guns to school; we bring guns to school; we bring guns to school; we bring guns to school; we bring guns to school; we bring guns to school; we bring guns to school; we bring guns to school; we bring guns to school; we bring guns to school; we bring guns to school; we bring guns to school; a 6-year-old asked me if I was in a gang; we bring guns to school; we bring guns to school; we bring guns to school; we bring guns to school; we bring guns to school; we bring guns to school; we bring guns to school; we bring guns to school; we brings guns to school; we bring guns to school; we bring guns to school; we bring guns to school; we bring guns to school; we bring guns to school; we bring guns to school; we bring guns to school; we bring guns to school; we bring guns to school; we bring guns to school; we bring guns to school; we bring guns to school; we bring guns to school; we bring guns to school; we bring guns to school; we bring guns to school; we bring guns to school; we brings guns to school; we bring guns to school; we bring guns to school; **"the average number of public school students expelled each school day last year for gun possession: 34"**; we bring guns to school; we bring guns to school; we bring guns to school; we bring guns to school; we bring guns to school; we bring guns to school; we bring guns to school; we bring guns to school; we bring guns to school; we bring guns to school; we bring guns to school; we bring guns to school; we bring guns to school; we bring guns to school; we bring guns to school; we bring guns to school; we bring guns to school; we brings guns to school; we bring guns to school; we bring guns to school; we bring guns to school; we bring guns to school; we bring guns to school; we bring guns to school; the production of *The Simpsons* movie isn't happening because the powers that be can't agree on how to divvy up the "obscene" amounts of money it would generate; we bring guns to school; we bring guns to school; we bring guns to school; we bring guns to school; we bring guns to school; we bring guns to school; we bring guns to school; we bring guns to school; we bring guns to school; a 9-year-old told me that if they don't want to learn, they're told to go to sleep; it's so funny I should cry but we can't cry over others' suffering; we don't know how to laugh at ourselves; **WE STIGMATIZE EDUCATION!;** "In May, 1998, when New York City sixth-grade teacher Ms. Aishad Ahmad, 44, declined to switch the classroom TV set from educational programming to *The Jerry Springer Show*, four girls ages 11 and 12 pounced on her and beat her up, sending her to the hospital. However, a month before that,

Reality Check

Stratford Connecticut High student Joseph Calore filed a lawsuit against the school because it kept the *Springer Show* on in the classroom during an exam. According to Calore, a fight on the show provoked another student to punch Calore and break his jaw"; and we still haven't gotten to the breaking point of declaring, in the immortal words of Popeye The Sailor Man: "I've had alls I can stands, and I can't stands no more!!!"; The United States is home to 2.8 million homeless children; we seem to have no concept of self-discipline, let alone attempt to instill it in children; we're insanely inefficient; we are exceptionally lacking in good judgment.

Billy Joel was right: "We didn't start the fire." We just ignore it and fuel it.

"If you're not part of the solution, you're part of the problem."

Now, getting back to the time-line…In an interview with *Playboy,* Bruce Willis mentioned that Robert Wright, author of *The Moral Animal*, presents the thesis that everything we do is in response to one genetic impulse: to pass on our genes; it's an instinctual urge. Animals do this out of instinct, and the process repeats itself, naturally. They do not need foresight to plan ahead for their indirect descendants who are (will be) the third, or greater, generation. Animals can't make mistakes since that would imply awareness. Therefore, there is no good and bad, right or wrong. We want to have it both ways: to be animals/children and adults at the same time. Children can believe in Santa Claus as long as they have no reason to believe otherwise. That is, if they are not aware of the realities of pain, suffering, oppression and ozone holes. We, though, as adults, know there is no Santa Claus. But we deny reality because to do otherwise would be too overwhelming. Yet, by denying, we further create a world that makes it very difficult for children to remain innocent and carefree; and to believe that all is well.

So, we try to have it both ways, pretending that we're not cheating. We think that we can have freedom without responsibility, equality without everybody, luxury and convenience at the expense of others and the eco-system. But just because we can't see it, or just refuse to, does not mean that the past won't catch up to the future.

In America, the sad fact of statistics is that, black people, in general, tend to be the least successful segment of the population. Well, gee. I wonder why that would be. Why would the institution of slavery, which was implemented several hundred years ago, before anyone alive today was ever born, have anything to do with the world we live in today, especially since blacks were given complete equality, (and treated as such), ever since the distant sixties? And, no matter how poorly the African-American community has been treated in the past, the bottom line is that society these days no longer discriminates against blacks. We've created an even playing field. (Yeah, whatever.)

(The notion occurred to me that "the future" was mankind's first construct conceived to avoid reality: "Let's imagine a place called the future. And in the future, reality has no meaning because we can't perceive it. So, therefore, anything goes. Party time!")

Pivot

Drink and dance and laugh and lie,
Love, the reeling midnight through,
For tomorrow we shall die!
(But, alas, we never do.)

(And neither do our children, nor do the children of the parents whom we spit on; those same children who will live on the same planet as our children.)

"Right" is pursuing our potential; our potential to learn and create and **invigorate** and appreciate. That potential is suppressed in ourselves when we suppress it in others. That potential is suppressed in others when we suppress it in ourselves. (Food and sex are meant to be appreciated, but even an animal can do that.)

I would like to predominantly feel pleasure with only a minimum of pain, instead of primarily living with pain that is occasionally abated with some token pleasure. A path of pain will have pleasure along the way to keep you from seeing that there's nothing to see at the end of it; just as the path of pleasure will have pain to obscure its destination. If we stay on the path we can continue forever— CREATION PERPETUATES CREATION, (and destruction perpetuates nothing).

Remember how I pointed out that a very, very happy person will only get so high before he gets brought back down because he'll have nobody to share his level of happiness with. By the same token, individuals can only proceed a few levels ahead of the pack before hitting a wall.

If we all do our best, then we can all do our best.
If some try our best, then none can do their best.

"My students, in the course of becoming part of the village life, invariably arrive at the notion that, beneath differences in race and culture, Barbidians and Americans are all one. In one student's words:

If I had to sum up my whole trip, it would be this: It was late at night, a full moon, and I sat in the pasture with a local Rastafarian. After hours of talking, about everything from love to politics, the two of us came to an interesting conclusion. Although we lived a thousand miles away from each other, and that our skin color, hair styles and many personal practices were quite different, at heart, we were the same people."[13]

[IGNORE THAT LAST PARAGRAPH....IT'S JUST A BIG CLICHE.]

If we don't all get together voluntarily, then we will all fall together, regardless.

♫ "If it's not love, then it's the bomb that will bring us together." [27]

Reality Check

As I was saying, we pass on our genes out of instinct. Yet, we are not purely instinctual, we are also intellectual: our intellect should tell us that our genes need to survive for an indefinite now. Intellect and instinct are opposite sides of the same coin, so we have to roll the coin in order to balance it on its edge. Remember the explanation of time. Man defines the boundaries of time, so if "now" means ½ a second then that's how long the moment "now" lasts. Or we could define it as ½ a minute, ½ a year, or ½ a century; or we could define it as limitless.

Again, the other major factor that is holding us back from getting through the wall to the next level is fear of the free-ride syndrome. Stop thinking, "Why should I put forth the effort to help someone else that doesn't help himself." That attitude is not going to help anyone. Just constantly remind yourself that no matter how motivated you may be, you are still a product of random chance, just like lesser-motivated people. So, do whatever it takes to help elevate them. (Otherwise they'll wind up relegating you to lower levels without even necessarily trying.)

….what goes around, goes around….

Now, to finish up time… Man became man the moment he gained insight he became man. From that moment he also gained the potential ability to conceive/perceive time. There were two levels of how he could perceive it. He could perceive time/now as both infinitely small and infinitely large, or he could perceive it simply as a scale with a limited range. By perceiving the latter he gave himself decreasingly limited hindsight and foresight, thus giving himself decreasingly limited potential; and potentially forcing his own eradication.

To clarify: the first level is to think of time as three separate parts—before/now/later. The second level would be to just perceive now. That is, to realize that "now" is an indefinite instant. So, we can perceive "now" as a continuous flow, and realize that "now" never begins, nor ever ends. It is always now, and now is always. So, yes, we should live in the "now," and for the "now." And then we will always be happier and happier.

♫ "Lately I've been thinking about how the whole world's come undone. Everybody's got this sinking feeling, the feeling they're on the run. But I know a place where time stands still. I can picture it in my mind. But I'm not sure if we can get there; (there is no reason, reasons rhyme; why can't you see we're almost out of time). It's too late to cover what you've done. It's too late to call for anyone at all. Well I guess I should be so brave to think that I'm the only one who knows it's too late to cover what you've done. Oh no, we need a change. (This world's stranger now.) Now is not the time to run away. (There must be a way.) A way that we could listen to the warning signs, so pay attention; this is my intention to prevent this fate before it gets too late. And as the hands on the clock go 'round and 'round, and the world keeps marching on, can you afford to let it fall now? (The fish in all the streams are dying, fluorocarbons fill the sky, and I don't really want to die before my time has come.) (…Lately I've been thinking, haven't had that sinking feeling now.)" [28]

A study was recently released about self-discipline. About 20 years ago, a teacher of a first grade class gave each child a marshmallow, but with the stipulation that if a child did not eat the marshmallow for one hour then he or she would be rewarded with a second marshmallow. The teacher left the room for an hour and some children did not eat the marshmallow, but some succumbed to the temptation, eventually. Checking up on the subjects fifteen years later revealed that those children who waited tended to be more successful and well-adjusted. Those who didn't wait weren't so prosperous.

"The remaking of character, the achieving of any worthy goal, requires systematic self-control. Self-mastery is needed if we are to be true to our better selves and to develop our capacities for the enrichment of our personalities and for the service of our fellow men."[20]

"To act well on this world one must sacrifice all personal desires. Man is not on this earth merely to be happy, nor even simply to be honest. He is there to realize great things for humanity, to attain nobility and to surmount the vulgarity of nearly every individual."[30]

If you do believe in God, do you think God would be so narrow and demanding as to expect us to attain greatness and nobility in just one lifetime? I expect that God expects us to attain our potential, and that each successive generation can reach a higher potential. Whether or not you believe in God, and also believe in reincarnation, you have to admit that we are falling horribly short of expectations. That is, can you really say we are making progress? Or perhaps you and God have no expectations?

Reality Check

About being cool:

Being "cool" is to act authentically, independent of what others will think of you. I'd prefer not to criticize any particular group, but habitual cigarette smoking is the perfect example to make the point: because smoking only became cool because cool people started it. They started it as a rebellious protest against the oppressive nature of society and parents as a way to say, "Nuts to your rules! If these are your rules, then I will turn my back and stop caring. If you don't like it—tough: I don't care." Ironically, though, that was the message: we care about making you know that we don't care so you'll change into a system that gives us a reason to have enthusiasm.

Being cool also means having a desire for life. Sadly, since we go about in the dark, society offers little to fulfill that desire. We know what activities are wrong, but we don't know what is right; so we offer no alternative. If you tell people, "JUST SAY NO," they're going to say, "JUST GIVE ME A JOB, JUST PAY FOR MY KIDS' HEALTHCARE AND EDUCATION, JUST MAKE SURE THAT THE ONLY FREE PLACES TO HANG OUT AREN'T TACO BELL AND THE MALL, and JUST MAKE SURE MY PARENTS DON'T ALLOW ME TO MAKE TV VIEWING A SPORT, *otherwise*, JUST SHUT UP."

"Maybe if you're truly cool, then you don't need to be told so."

~ Homer Simpson

It's nice to be recognized, but don't let recognition be your motivation.

Throughout history we have frantically attempted to conform to others, and to force others to conform to us. Can we get off of each others' backs already (and get on each others' shoulders) and start realizing that there's plenty of food and shelter for everyone; at least, there will be when we all work as a team. One person's desire for art, and another's desire for sports, and another's desire for science, will not conflict with each other. (It takes several architects to design a structurally sound and aesthetically pleasing gymnasium, many carpenters to erect it, and all of those with passion to share it.)

"What I understand by assimilation is loss of identity." [20]

♪ "It takes a man to suffer ignorance and smile. Be yourself no matter what they say." [24]

"Advertising is the backbone of the American economy."[31] It is also bullshit. All of that effort that goes into it raises prices, when it could, instead, be saved to lower prices, improve quality and increase distribution. If advertising were banned, then the consumer would still purchase, but probably more. There would be an even playing field between competitors, so what would be the problem? Not to mention that all of that time and money and space could be used for art…Not to mention that it implies that we're all a bunch of Homer Simpsons. (Not to mention that advertisers control the "free" press, let alone how obscene it is that the more tragic the news is, the more profitable it becomes.)

"SEINFELD," a television show that many adore because of how true to life it is, is self-proclaimed to be about "nothing"; about day-to-day life. It's about the lives of characters who are shallow, superficial, very self-centered and without any purpose—their lives mean nothing. And that is primarily why it is so funny, because we can all relate to their haphazard struggles to acclimate to life in the society that advocates survival of the fittest and luckiest (and slyest).

On the most insightful episode, Kramer revealed the secret of life when Jerry was hoping and speculating that there must be more to life than the nothing that he was getting out of it. Kramer's reply was: "This is it. There is no meaning [to the bullshit we appropriately call 'nothing']."

My acquaintance Brady sadly confessed that this episode depressed her, but I told her that it was awesome that they were announcing that we are living in bullshit (and that therefore we should stop).

Among that and all its other insightful commentary the most important lesson to take away from it is Mr. Costanza's emphatic reminder that, **"We are living in a society! We're supposed to be acting in a civilized way!"**

These days people tend to offer apologies quite flippantly because you never know who's going to go ballistic just because someone accidentally bumped into them. But the only real time an apology should be necessary, though, is when someone is condescending; being condescending is the epitome of hypocrisy, (unless you're talking to Donald Rumsfeld).

Conversely, the best example one can set is to treat everybody magnanimously. Take Captain Picard of *STAR TREK: THE NEXT GENERATION*. Never has there been a more commanding character than Jean-Luc Picard. Without exception everyone he encounters is made to feel relevant.

The best rule of thumb in life is to set the example.

The best way to set the best example is to follow the best examples.

Reality Check

My initial contention is that we are here to feel positive emotion. If so, then shouldn't we constantly be striving to increase our threshold for emotion?

Here's the situation: the emotions are all linked together. Our fear (almost) conquered us and now our other emotions have been suppressed. We've been numbed. We're not as passionate as we could be. The trick is that the emotion you express will come back to you as either the same emotion, and they will perpetuate each other, or it will come back as the opposite emotion and possibly cancel it out.

If you express anger at any angry person then they'll express anger back and you'll both get angrier and angrier until you're both either dead or hurt and/or lonely. Accomplishment: Zero.

If someone expresses fear, and you express courage, it may give them the self-assurance to give it back. And then you'll both be more courageous. Accomplishment: Unstoppable.

If a person makes a mistake and receives scorn, then he'll become hostile and inhibited. (If you can't say something nicely, what's the point of saying something else?)

Apply the same math to joy/sorrow, love/hate, self-pity/self-confidence, trust/dishonesty.

♪ "And in the end, the love you take is equal to the love you make." [32]

We should not only be happy to be alive, we should be excited! Because being alive means that you can bring happiness to those who are sad; and the more people who are happy then the more people we can play with!! **AND THE GREATER THE THRESHOLD FOR EVERYTHING!!!**

My intention is to try to unite Everyone. Initially, I thought that I had actually found the method and the words to accomplish such a feat without targeting any specific issue that separates us. However, there is one particular point of contention that inevitably polarizes us. So, if I do not acknowledge the abortion debate I would be failing right out of the gate.

Common ground: WE ALL AGREE THAT NO ONE SHOULD BE GETTING PREGNANT WITHOUT INTENTION.

Common ground: The prevalence of parents in America who are very far from being fit parents is barbaric. And, aside from simply being inadequate, parents are not in attendance. As one commentator put it, "We have to be frank: in poor communities we're beyond the problem of one-parent households— we're dealing with *no*-parent households." And even those parents who do have some semblance of understanding about the attention required to create a prosperous human being are falling horribly short of doing so because this horribly disparate system that we like to call a "democracy" does not allow the large majority of citizens the necessary time required to properly be devoted parents.

Personally, I agree with many who believe that life begins at conception. That is to say, upon conception a spiritual life force emerges into a physical host. I also agree with the notion that when the physical body dies the spirit does not; the physical death of a being is separate and distinct from the death of our spiritual energy. That energy is essentially immortal. So, when we abort an unborn fetus we are merely forcing its life-force to relocate into a more viable physical host.

Presuming that we are to apply the Golden Rule, let's look at this predicament from the vantage point of a spirit that is living as an un-born child.

Granted, the bearing of children is a personal, inalienable right. So, unfortunately, we cannot restrict people from pro-creating even when it is blatantly evident that they have been, or will be, shockingly pitiful parents.

Now, if I were a spirit that was destined to be horribly neglected and/or abused, I would certainly hope that my physical being was terminated. Shoot, if my prospective parents had even a touch of uncertainty, then I'd vote to be terminated at the outset so that I could wait for the opportunity to be raised by those who plan to do so with intention. Of course, though, it's impractical to hope for such an ideal when the educated and uneducated alike tend not to make such decisions in a clearly thought out manner. So, let's approach this with an effective and practical strategy; the current one clearly hasn't been.

Let's make certain that, a) people are adequately educated about methods of avoiding conception, b) that we pay men to get vasectomies and women to get their tubes tied, and c) that if this education still doesn't prevent what is not meant to be under precarious circumstances then we make sure that the opportunity to nip the problem in the bud is freely accessible. The alternative is to create dismal situations where parents regret birthing a child and children regret being born. Nothing could be sadder. So, let's make sure that this world doesn't get any sadder than it already is. Please.

Reality Check

Here's another big example of irony we create by trying to have it both ways:

Males have a tremendous instinctual urge to have sex. Deep down they know that it should be restrained, but, instead, they created a double standard; that way they could have lots of sex without remorse, and place the blame on the women, instead.

I speculate that the reason why so many cultures have imposed stringent morés of women being draped in covering is because the men and women knew that the males didn't have the fortitude to rein themselves in—it was a self-fulfilling prophecy. Instead of confronting that challenge, they ran away from it.

("Women, according to Fatma Merniss, a Moroccan sociologist, are seen by men in Islamic societies as in need of protection because they are unable to control their sexuality and, hence, are a danger to the social order. In other words, they need to be restrained and controlled so that men do not give way to the impassioned desire they inspire, and society can thus function in an orderly way." [13])

The "egg" is that they presume women to be inferior so that they, the males, will be able to feel superior in comparison. The "chicken" is that they raise their daughters under this presumption, so then the daughters become fickle women; otherwise they would grow up confident, and then the males would be confronted with the reality of their arrogant fantasy.

So, the women continue to feel inadequate, and, hence, they actually appear to be inferior. (To wit: 43% of women who move near Hollywood to pursue an acting career end up in the porn industry.)

Now, when the women look for intimate relationships they are at the males' mercy. It's a lose-lose situation. More discerning women who look for the males with higher standards are too fickle and insecure to be compatible with them. All they know how to do is be subservient to them. Yet, if the women resort to providing sex in order to attract a male with lower standards, then they are labeled as "sluts." So, when they raise their standards the males label them as "prudes" in order to have their sex. In every case the males complain that they can't find a strong-willed woman because they're all stupid. Of course, when those women do show up, the males become intimidated by the confrontation of their fantasy. So, in order to keep it from collapsing they label the women as "bitches."

Sadly, the women can't ever be satisfied because the men can't.

Of course this is a generalization and doesn't apply to everyone, but if it does apply to you, just be glad that you don't have to feel ashamed about it since most of us are in the same boat. We all got shafted by our predecessors. Never has there been a shorter end of the stick. Just be glad that we don't have to pass it on, anymore, because now we can see land.

♪ "here comes a regular, call out my name….
am I the only one who feels ashamed?
all I know is that I'm sick of everything my money can buy;
a fool wastes his life; God, rest his guts.
opportunity knocks once, then the door slams shut.
everybody wants to be special here,
they call your name out loud and clear:

HERE COMES A REGULAR
CALL OUT YOUR NAME

Am I the only one who feels ashamed?

Everybody wants to be someone's here…

Someone's gonna show up, never fear." [7]

"Now, as love in young men is, for the most part, nothing but fancy, and pleasure its ultimate end, it expires with the attainment of its object; and what seems to be love vanishes, because it has nothing of the durable nature of true affection." [33]

---

strive: to try with painful or strenuous effort.

This world's society doesn't strive because many believe that man is, by nature, inherently sinful, and, thus, can never come to a point in life where he lives without sin. That is some serious Bullshit. It goes hand in hand with, "We're only human." That attitude inherently defeats any motivation to strive for our best. It's an excuse to say, as Bart once ascertained from Homer, "[We] can't win, [so] don't try." COP-OUT.

If we strive for less than perfection aren't we destined to progress backwards? Yes, because striving for less than perfection is an oxymoron—it isn't striving and it really isn't trying.

Why would God create us so that we would be forever condemned to remain at the same level, so that we would have no hope, inspiration, motivation, or incentive to try for the ideal? Some believers of this school of thought told me that after you die, whether it be as an aborted fetus or a repenting murderer, your soul goes up to God. So, then what's the point??? No matter how I live, or whether I barely even get a chance to, I'll spend an eternity in bliss? HOW DOES THIS MAKE ANY SENSE?

Do you think that the challenge that God gave us was to see how fast we could blow up the whole world and at the same time try and create as many people as possible to blow up with it? Because that would be very, very ironic. Although I doubt that God would intentionally create irony since I don't believe that God is irrational. I mean, would God intentionally create irony by creating creation that would create its own destruction—and thus create nothing. Or would He do what He did, and create creation that will perpetuate itself?

Wouldn't it make sense that the whole point of God creating us with inherent "sin" was so that we could exercise our free-will and self-discipline in order to discover the pleasure that comes from reaching one's potential? Yes, that makes sense. Pride, wrath, greed, sloth, gluttony, envy, and lust are instinctual urges and desires. Without self-discipline to moderate them they defeat mankind's true purpose. God gave us our intellectual side of the coin so that we could combat and ascend from those shackles. Otherwise we wouldn't be able to appreciate our attainments.

motivation: something that rouses the mind or spirits, or incites activity.

As I have illustrated we can see that the pursuit of our more animalistic side has a limit to where it can take us. Why would God create us so that there was a limit to what we could achieve? Where's the motivation in that? Where's the fulfillment in something that comes without effort? Where's the so-called glory? God gave us those sinful qualities so that we would have a challenge—a challenge that would give us inspiration to rise to the challenge.

God provoked us to be passionate!

Nothing is more rewarding than overcoming an obstacle through perseverance and hardship. God gave us the biggest challenge so that we could attain the biggest reward.

Stop telling us that God works in mysterious ways. Two hundred years ago biology, physics and electromagnetism were pretty mysterious to us. But we've advanced our understanding of God's creation so that it makes more sense. And through further and further effort we will come to understand God's universe more and more until we can perceive infinity. Then we'll continue to perpetually create more life, and more passion, and more variety.

SURVIVE TO LIVE TO STRIVE TO THRIVE [REPEAT]

So, now the belief that mankind is inherently sinful can no longer be true as long as we stop pretending that it is true. (If you want to believe that it is true, then go ahead and prove it by fulfilling your prophecy.) But we can't believe it's anything but the time we hear at the sound of the beep.

A couple of popular cartoon characters discovered that their lives "suck," so one confidently proclaimed, "Yeah, we're cool." Well, that's dandy if you're imaginary, and temporally stagnant. Of course, though, if time progressed for them, eventually they'd either be forced to change, or their worlds will crumble if nobody is there to take care of them in old age, if not much sooner.

So, if you want to keep pretending that there is a Santa Claus, then I guess you'll prove that my reality and yours are the same when you eventually end up lonely, miserable and in pain at an old folks' home (if you're lucky enough to live that long). You'll have gotten what you expected: disappointment and failure.

There is one other option, though. You can create an even more far-gone reality than the one you/we live in currently. My 92-year-old grandfather lost his wife a year ago. Until recently he was in absolute misery and would cry profusely with every other breath. Now, however, he believes that another woman in the nursing home is his wife and he doesn't understand why they don't call her by her real name. So, now, he is in pretty good spirits, and relatively healthy compared to several months ago. He can afford to live in a fantasy at this point in his life.

Pivot

Finally, the big question: How do we get to the next level? Just talking about what needs to happen is not enough to actually get attitudes to change. But, of course, that's next to impossible since we are creatures who have been telling ourselves since forever that we are only human. However, contrary to popular opinion, we are not incorrigible. Of course, though, since we have made a habit of wantonly indulging in the so-called seven sins because our parents neglected to clearly explain why we should moderate our "sinful" inclinations, giving them up cold turkey would not be a realistic—or even desirable—goal. After all, we have allowed our vices to become so standard that they are commonplace and acceptable. Indeed, as Reverend Lovejoy of *The Simpsons* put it: "Once the government approves something, it is no longer immoral." In fact, our vices have not just become standard, but even admirable. As Morgan Freeman's character put it in the movie *Seven*: "I just can't continue to live in a place that embraces apathy as if it were a virtue." However, I would like to believe that if we acknowledge the ignorance we have been operating under, then we can create the incentive to apply self-discipline in order to overcome our addiction towards the more petty desires that we have become entrenched in.

We should realize that those sins, or indulgences, are not productive. They have gotten us nowhere just in time. The way I see it, it is as though we have been sitting at a roulette table all this time hoping for an easy shortcut while enjoying the free drinks, but we completely lost track of time and failed to realize that a slew of tornadoes had appeared on the horizon, so we just kept tossing the dice as though the real world was the casino. So, it's time to admit that the first step towards making the change that needs to happen is to walk away from the roulette table. (All right, I admit that it is naïve and unrealistic to think that just saying what should be done will actually inspire anyone to adopt a whole new attitude of altruism and nobility. So, if I have at least managed to get you to *want* to change, but not yet accomplished actual change of heart, then here is what I recommend if you want to genuinely renounce an ego-driven, instant gratification-mentality in favor of an Us-driven mentality. Go find a child who lives in fear and in pain, without hope. Hold that child and feel the despair and the plea for help that comes from someone who is so utterly drained the he or she doesn't have any strength left for crying. Empathize with that child, and you will find that you have a much higher threshold for emotion than you thought, and you will be able to do the crying for that child who can no longer do it for herself; that child will already start to feel again, and hope again, just by feeling your feeling. No matter how overwhelmed that you may become, the anguish you will feel will be a positive, life-affirming force that will give us the courage and will to meet the challenge of doing whatever it takes to create a world where there is ***no more misery and suffering***. If that is still not enough to get your heart to do an about-face, then go find one of the downtrodden homeless, or the vengeful convicts, or the hopelessly apathetic nursing home residents that that child will become.)

Ask yourself if you could be happier in life. Then ask yourself how much happier you would be if everyone were completely happy and without fear. Then ask yourself how much happier you would be if you were responsible for helping to bring such a world into being.

…what goes around, goes around….

Reality Check

One day during the early stages of conceiving this work, I was excitedly telling my mother about how I could envision prison reform taking leaps and bounds once this book was circulated and got the collective will to implement unusual politics; politics that was based on treating the cause of the problems, instead of the effects. My mother, with her instinctual need to protect me, tried to diminish my exuberance by warning me that my expectations were excessive, and perhaps unreal, even though she had already agreed from the first draft that she could see it having far and wide influence.

I didn't understand why she would give me such a warning. What was the point? She said she was afraid that I would find disappointment. I assured her that I wasn't delusional. I reminded her that I was well aware that nothing is a sure thing, but that did not mean it was not still imperative, reasonable, and more fun to assume for the best. It was at that point when I had to defend my overzealous ambition that I realized that, by definition, I cannot fail. That is because I earnestly believe that fixing society truly is as simple as flooding the populace with the news that we already have the blueprints for a perfectly good mousetrap, we just need to acknowledge that we are, indeed, being overrun by mice if we are going to be able to deploy that trap. So, I can't fail, because I am so certain that what I am hoping for is attainable that I am never going to stop pushing; and as long as one is trying, then one inherently cannot be failing.

♪ "Ain't lost yet, so I must be a winner." [34]

If you try your best to achieve a goal, but fall short, it is not disappointment as opposed to fulfillment since you still advanced your potential. It just might not be as fulfilling as reaching the goal. But, of course, that is why we have clichés, so that we can get back on the horse. Because it ain't over until you stop trying. And, when you finally need not try anymore because the goal was reached, it will be that much more rewarding since it was earned.

My mother was just afraid to see me get hurt. She overprotected me. So I explained "hope" to her, and that allayed her fears. Now she understands that if you do not try then you will not be disappointed since there were never any expectations in the first place. Ironically, "success" will come from not even trying, because you will get what you wished for.

Pivot

Reality Check

If you want to live without fear, then you have to live right. To me, that means living without regret. If you are, say, 77 years old, and a doctor tells you that you have a month to live, you won't regret being out of time if you are content in knowing that you lived the best life you could; with as few repetitions of mistakes as possible. If you yearn for an extension to life, then be glad that, unlike some people, such as my grandfather, you still have the desire to live. Going out apathetic would be pathetic; if you want an extensive life, then live properly.

The rule of thumb for living properly: BE ACTIVE—IN MIND AND BODY.

Right now the world is scarier than necessary because we haven't been applying ourselves properly or with intent. In the future, though, the potential for death will be exceptionally minimal, since, as our fear decreases, so will the circumstances that increase that fear; and so on.

I say we set ourselves a goal of 55 years to create a world where the only time and place where anyone could experience fear, anger or pity due to a creation of man will be a in a voluntary fictional context such as a roller-coaster, game or drama.

If everyone sets their life expectancy to 105 years, then everyone 50 and younger can expect to see the fruition of this utopia in their lifetime, (assuming that everyone adopts a vegetarian lifestyle). If you are past that age, then at least try to keep us company as long as possible. We could always use the wisdom of experience. Plus, we might get there sooner than expected.

Of course this is easier said than done, but it will become easier and easier as more and more people get on the bandwagon. From the premise of strength in numbers we will exponentially grow and challenge each other to live our best.

Such a tremendous revamping could be quite difficult, so it will take much courage and patience. But don't let that scare you away, because, a) there are many right now who have no other recourse but to muster up every ounce of strength and courage they have to just barely survive, b) if you don't take this chance to rise to the challenge at this age, then you will likely be forced to do so at a later one, anyway, but by then you will be weaker and the challenge will be harder (in other words, consider the alternative), c) getting there is all the fun and, d) that's the point.

"There is not a single noble cause, movement, or achievement that does not call for great sacrifice and martyrdom." [20]

"It's better to die on your feet than to live on your knees."

"We do not truly live for our ideals if we are not ready, if necessary, to die for them."[20]

After reading the first draft of this work, when it was titled *The Biggest If*, Marah remarked that although she believed in it and would wear the shirt I gave her with the Ø symbol on it, the notion of "Let's all get together" is nothing new. Of course not, but that's exactly my point. After all, we're still not together. And we'll never be together until we know who is together and who isn't. That is to say, it takes communication in order to know who is together and who isn't. That's why I'm calling for a representative symbol to accomplish that. So the purpose of the symbol is to communicate that you concede that things are only going to get worse unless we collectively turn things around; and that the first step towards doing that will require us to collectively communicate this to each other. The symbol has several other meanings, as well. Originally, it was designed to negate whatever one particular thing that was behind it that we're not supposed to do. So when "(   )" is behind it, it affirms all general things that we are supposed to do. The symbol represents irony—in five parts: 1) the realization/cessation of it, 2) the irony of this world, 3) the irony of the new and improved world that's on the way, 4) the bridge between the two and of course, 5) the very irony that it is being used to express the opposite of its intended meaning. Lastly, it represents the paradox, "JUST DO IT." Because to say that, or write that, is just that. Second to lastly, it symbolizes the never-ending push towards infinite perfection.

Here are the guidelines to try and follow as a participant of The Initiative Movement:

1. (Wake up and smell.)
2. Wear the symbol on a regular basis of your choosing, and also, to increase unity, wear it on the first and/or last day of the month. (Or, better yet, support **StopLittering.com**!)
3. Don't force the work on others. Just by seeing the symbol they'll read it out of curiosity.
4. Follow the best examples.
5. Don't try to impose your standards upon those who are not so inclined. Just continue to set a better example so they'll see the difference.
6. Share. Give more than you take, then you'll get more than you gave.
7. Allow others to question your judgment without getting defensive.
8. Gradually try to wean yourself from behavior pattens that are not in (y)our best interest. Set standards for yourself and adhere to them.
9. Pick up at least eleven pieces of litter a day when not impractical. It will further promote unity, we'll see that accomplishment is at hand, and before long, the litter will be all gone because people won't litter anymore since littering (and blind indifference in general) will become stigmatized.
10. Initiate and participate in volunteer efforts.
11. Be careful to not become self-righteous in your righteousness.
12. Be happy to be alive; and be alive to be happy.
13. (Don't allow these words to become cliché.)

There's another parameter of this movement that I left out because it's a given, so we'll make it the **rule**: set children as ***THE*** priority. Whether or not you have children or you work with them, take them into consideration with everything you do; recognize when your words and actions will influence them, directly or otherwise. Recognize that for generations people have been taking for granted that we all desire to be happy, but didn't realize that that very simple and "obvious" goal needs to be stated outright and explained to them, because if it isn't, then it will probably be overlooked by them; then they won't be able to recognize when they're being self-destructive, and therefore perpetuate their own fear, apathy, anger and disappointment. If we teach them that everyone wants to simply enjoy themselves, then they will naturally lean in that direction (although it won't work if some people don't have access to these roads), especially if we back it up by directing them to pursue the arts and sciences as livelihoods by the masses.

Or, as Robert Bellah put it: "And since we have believed in the American dream for a long time and worked very hard to make it come true, it is hard for us to give it up, even though it contradicts another dream that we have—that of living in a society that would really be worth living in. What we fear above all, and what keeps the new world powerless to be born, is that if we give up our dream of private success for a more genuinely integrated societal community, we will be abandoning our separation and individuation, collapsing into dependence and tyranny. What we find hard to see is that it is the extreme fragmentation of the modern world that really threatens our individuation; that what is best in our separation and individuation, our sense of dignity and autonomy as persons, requires a new integration if it is to be sustained. The notion of transition to a new level of social integration, a newly vital social ecology, may also be resisted as absurdly utopian, as a project to create a perfect society. But the

Reality Check

transformation of which we speak is both **necessary and modest**. Without it, indeed, there may be very little future to think about at all."

"Children Learn What They Live" [35]

If a child lives with criticism, he learns to condemn.

If a child lives with hostility, he learns to fight.

If a child lives with ridicule, he learns to be shy.

[If a child lives without activity, he learns to be bored.]

If a child lives with shame, he learns to feel guilty.

If a child lives with tolerance, he learns to be patient.

If a child with encouragement, he learns confidence.

If a child lives with praise, he learns to appreciate.

[If a child lives with enthusiasm, he learns to be alacritous.]

If a child lives with fairness, he learns justice.

[If a child lives with trust, he learns to be honest.]

If a child lives with security, he learns to have faith.

[If a child lives with approval, he learns to like himself.]

If a child lives with acceptance and friendship, he learns to find love in the world.

From now on when children ask if there is a Santa Claus, I suggest that if they're over 6 that you tell them the truth. Tell them that there used to be, but people who were non-altruistic took advantage of Santa by being greedy. So, Santa stopped coming around, because his feelings were hurt since he wasn't appreciated; and so we've had to fake it. But we've learned our lesson and now we're going to make it up to him and show him that we would prefer it if we could have the real thing back. It's going to take a while to convince Santa that we mean it since we've been so blatantly unappreciative of his blessings. Earning back trust takes much time and commitment. If everyone continues to be grateful, though, then Santa will come around again for the children of your children. Then he'll never go away again, because everyone will have learned what happens when you get complacent.

When we all believe in Us, everything is possible. If we all grow up, then eventually none will have to. "Always look on the bright side of life." Then eventually there will only be a bright side, so we'll always be looking at it.

Here's my mantra for improving:

WILL. POWER.

I will.
I will do my best.

I will be honest.
I will be trusting.
I will be humble.

Pivot

I will be courageous.

I will be aware.

I will have purpose.

I will be forgiving.

I will have patience.

I will make sacrifice.

I will behave.

I WILL HAVE NO REGRETS.

This is the type of behavior we should practice so that children will emulate it. Then they will just do it without even having to try.

"He who is strong is he who conquers his desires." So the stronger man will gain strength by resisting the temptation that the weaker man offers—and the weaker man will gain strength from witnessing that resistance.

"He who is wise is he who can learn from every person." So the wiser man will gain clarity by teaching the less wise.

"He who is wealthy is he who is satisfied with his lot." So he with the great lot that is not satisfied will gain appreciation in the face of he who is content with a small lot."

Donald Trump once told Charles Grodin that life was just "waiting to die." Sounds like his money is really worth its weight in paper. Hopefully he'll read this and realize with everyone else that "Godot" isn't going to show up. All this time we've been waiting for "Godot," wouldn't ya know it, "Godot" has been here *all the time*.

….It's around…

And if you go around It, We'll be around.

(There's a good reason why the word "I" is capital. (But none why "you" and "we" aren't.))

If you think that life in Utopia will get boring, it won't. Challenges are inherently exciting, and this is the biggest challenge ever. And, if you believe that the beauty of nature, the sweetness of animals, the passion of competition, the wonder of art and science, and the tomfoolery of the Animaniacs®, are boring, well, then I don't know what to tell you. Although it does seem to be the consensus of the homeless community that non-stop anxiety is a thrill a minute; so you could always join them if things get dull.

♪ "What the world needs now is a new kind of tension (because the old one just bores me to death.)." [6]

I ask again: "Do you really want to have fun, or are you just saying that you want to have fun?" [36]

Practically speaking, this isn't going to be as hard as one might think. All it takes is organization. We've got mail, TV, radio, telephone and **favors.org**, and **freecycle**. Once we get a great big lot of us on the bandwagon, then it's just a matter of focus. We all have different capabilities and we all need different help. So, apply yourself in the areas which suit you best. We've got 55 years, so we can take the time that we need to plan out our implementation. And, now that we'll get our priorities straight, we can start thinking efficiently in order to maximize Earth's fun potential (and, once and for all, take up the alarming amount of slack going around regarding the future).

The complete Utopia that I envision is one where there are only 2 broad categories of occupations: artists and scientists; (athletes would probably be a subdivision). Once people reach a certain age, perhaps 66, then we will become teachers of the pre-adolescent. "Menial" occupations, such as trash collectors, road builders and waiters, will be shared by everyone; we'll take turns. A system will be devised where everyone who has no special skills will takes turns managing the more mundane tasks. Maybe each individual will work one week per year collecting trash or maybe one year out of life. Age should likely play a role in determining duration and choice of roles. It will be a complete democracy where the most fundamental decision to vote on will be how much time everyone must devote explicitly to the group before they can engage in more self-indulgent activities. It's the perfect plan for a society comprised of healthy bodies and sharp minds; and, best of all, people will live collectively and use money systems such as The HOURS. Accordingly, we will all live co-operatively. That way, day-to-day living will always be day-to-day thriving. The work will be shared to increase efficiency, and there will always be something to do and people to play with.

And, in this world, people won't understand the concept of dishonesty.

"Happy times, and happy ages, were those which the ancients termed the Golden Age! not because gold, so prized in this our iron age, was to be obtained, in that fortunate period, without toil; but because they who lived were ignorant of those two words, 'Mine' and 'Thine'. In that age all things were common, and all was peace and amity." [33]

(Even if you don't accept that it will be your same spirit living in this glorious future to give you the incentive to achieve this goal, just imagine if this idea had been promoted several hundred years ago. That's what we're missing out on. So let's not let the future down the way it let us down.)

♫   "These are days to remember. Never before and never since, I promise, will the whole world be as warm and whole as this. And as you feel it, you'll know it's true that you are touched by something that will grow and bloom in you.

These are days you'll remember. When May is rushing over you with desire to be part of the miracles you see in every hour. You'll know it's true that you are blessed and lucky. It's true that you are touched by something that will grow and bloom in you.

These are days.

These are days you might fill with laughter until you break. These days you might feel a shaft of light make its way across your face. And when you do you'll know it's true, you'll know how it was meant to be. Hear the signs and know they're speaking to you, to you." [37]

Your sincerely sincere realistic idealist,

~ Pivot

…To paraphrase both Marge and Homer Simpson in one breath:
IN YOUR FACE, HUMANITY!!

Pivot

♫ "Love, I get so lost, sometimes
days pass and this emptiness fills my heart
when I want to run away
I drive off in my car
but whichever way I go,
I come back to the place you are
And all my instincts, they return
and the grand façade, so soon will burn
without a noise, without my pride
I reach out from the inside

In your eyes
the light, the heat
in your eyes
I am complete
in your eyes
I see the doorway to a thousand churches
in your eyes
the resolution of all the fruitless searches
in your eyes
I see the light and the heat
in your eyes
oh, I want to touch the light
the heat I see in your eyes

love, I don't like to see so much pain
so much wasted and this moment keeps slipping away
I get so tired of working so hard for our survival
I look to the time with you to keep me awake and alive
and all my instincts, they return
and the grand façade, so soon will burn
without a noise, without my pride
I reach out from the inside

in your eyes
The light, the heat
in your eyes
I am complete
in your eyes
I see the doorway to a thousand churches
in your eyes
the resolution of all the fruitless searches
in your eyes
I see the light and the heat
in your eyes
oh, I want to touch the light
the heat I see in your eyes

in your eyes" [38]

Reality Check

♫ "I must've dreamed a thousand dreams,
Been haunted by a million screams;
I can hear the marching feet,
They're moving into the street.
Now did you read the news today?
They say the danger has gone away,
But I can see the fire is still alight,
Burning into the night
Too many men, too many people
Making too many problems
And not much love to go around
Can't you see this is a Land of Confusion.
This is the world we live in
And these are the hands we're given
Use them and let's start trying
To make it a place worth living in.
Superman, where are you now?
Everything's gone wrong, somehow
The men of steel, men of power
Are losing control by the hour.
This is the time. This is the place
So we look for the future
But there's not much love to go around

I remember long ago—
When the sun was shining
The stars were bright
All through the night
And the sound of your laughter
As I held you tight, so long ago—

I won't be coming home tonight
My generation will put it right
We're not just making promises
That we know, we'll never keep
Too many men
Too many people
Making too many problems
And not much love to go around
Can't you see
This is a land of confusion.
This is the world we live in
These are the hands we're given
Use them and let's start trying
To make it a place worth fighting for.
This is the world we live in
And these are the names we're given
Stand up and let's start fucking showing just where our lives are going to." [39]

THE ORIGIN OF PIVØT:

Most of my life I've fantasized about becoming a superhero so that I could do the impossible and "save the world" (but primarily so that I could fly). I wished for it to become a reality so regularly that I embarrassed myself; I actually hoped for it. I hoped that if aliens ever decided to grant superpowers to someone—like in some of the science fiction I'd seen—then they would pick me. I believed it was possible, not necessarily probable, or even slightly likely, but still possible. One of my usual daydreams was thinking about how much fun it would be to go to places such as Bosnia and "clean house." I imagined all the possible ways that I could "go to town" on the people who take pleasure in brutally torturing the innocent and defenseless. I was all prepared to SHOW 'EM WHAT IT'S LIKE!!! by getting "medieval on their ass." But, once, while musing over "Green Lantern" and "The Greatest American Hero," it occurred to me that my hope was a very egotistical one. To me, the question of whether or not such an impossibility could ever take place was uncertain. However, I would always assume that if such a thing were ever to happen then it would happen to *me*. It dawned on me, though, that if I lived in those worlds I would be terribly, terribly disappointed to see that someone else, besides me, was getting to have all of the fun. And, recalling that they were picked because of their great integrity, it occurred to me that if there ever were to be such a search, someone with my violent and self-righteous attitude would not be considered. So, I made a promise to God, aloud, that if I were picked, then I would not abuse the power and responsibility, no matter how tempting it might become. I felt pretty darn immature doing this, but I wasn't about to take any chances.

One day, several years later, while I was rollerblading, it came to my mind that "Pivot" would be a cool-sounding name for a superhero. Later that day I told Jarrod, in jest, that I was going to become a superhero named "Pivot." He laughed in agreement that "Pivot" sounded like a clever name for a comic book superhero, and then asked what my powers were. I hadn't actually thought about it consciously yet, but I instantly replied: "I've got superhuman reaction time." I went and told my other friends of my fantasy creation, and they agreed that it was a clever idea. Marah even pointed out how perfectly appropriate it was since it was a self-defense power, and, hence, could only be applied in *reaction* to evil. However, a month later, my friend Josh punched a hole in that ideal by asserting that I could, say, rob a bank by being able to dodge bullets. He also pointed out, though, what he knew we both realized after the fact: that such powers were perfectly appropriate for me since I've always had exceptional reaction time.

Less than two months later I began to conceive of this work. I figured that it would be necessary to keep my identity secret and come up with an assumed name. I kept that idea in the back of my head until the obvious became so. Then the obvious became even more so when I realized just how perfect of a name it is since, as you know, turning points are pivotal.

The obvious finally became complete when I realized that, actually, Pivot *is* inherently good since his reaction-time is not just of the infinitely small, but also of the infinitely large. He has absolute foresight. And, with absolute foresight, such a person couldn't do evil since he would understand the law of cause and domino effect.

If this superhero's tale of destiny before and after the fact doesn't convince you to follow my lead, then how about following another real-life superhero: **S**uperman is confined to a wheel chair with nothing left but two eyes that shine and a mouth to smile with, and that's what he does with it.

Reality Check

The doctors told him that he'd never walk again. He told them that that cannot be true since he believes he *will* walk again. Before his time is up, he's not only going to be walking again, he's going to be flying again: with the rest of us.

The point is that neither of us was born a superhero. We became them because of our parents and true faith in our God-given potential. Even Clark Kent wouldn't have become a superhero if not for such generous parents.

In a discussion incidental to *Reality Check* Marah argued that Christopher Reeve probably wouldn't be smiling if he weren't a celebrity with all of that extra attention. I doubt she would have said that if she had seen the Barbara Walters' special on him that showed us that he was a super man even before he became "**S**uperman," and even before he lost his powers. But, nonetheless, in a perfect world everyone would receive that much attention when it was needed.

What I'm getting at is that we can all become superheroes if we all "call out your name."

♬

"Lend me your ears and I'll sing you a song…
Oh, I get by with a little help from my friends.
Hmmm, I get by with a little help from my friends.
'm gonna try with a little help from my friends."[32]

"You say you've got a real solution, we'd all love to see the plan.
It's gonna be all right, you know it's gonna be all right,
It's gonna be all right. It's gonna be all right, all right, all right…." [32]

"When I find myself in times of trouble Mother Mary comes to me, speaking words of wisdom: 'let it be'
And in my hour of darkness, she is standing right in front of me, speaking words of wisdom, let it be, let it be,
Let it be, let it be, let it be, let it be, let it be, let it be, let it be, let it be. Yeah there will be an answer, let it be
For though they may be parted, there is still a chance that they will see.
Let it be, let it be, let it be, let it be, let it be, let it be, let it be, let it be. Yeah there will be an answer, let it be, let it be, Whisper words of wisdom, let it be. Let it be, let it be, ah let it be, yeah let it be
And when the night is cloudy, there is still a light that shines on me. Shine on until tomorrow, let it be
I wake up to the sound of music, Mother Mary comes to me, speaking words of wisdom, let it be
Yeah let it be, let it be, let it be, let it be. Yeah let it be
Oh there will be an answer, let it be.
Let it be, let it be, let it be, let it be
Let it be, let it be. Ah let it be, yeah let it be
Whisper words of wisdom….let **It** be." [32]

Pivot

Perhaps in the future if society actually learns how to nurture its truest potential instead of nurturing fear, then, if we still feel inclined to want a symbol to represent our collective purpose of maintaining a fearless, or zero-fear, society, then we could drop the line and simply adopt the circle. What could more Universal?

♫

"Why are there so many songs about rainbows, and what's on the other side? 'Rainbows are visions, but only illusions, and rainbows have nothing to hide.' So we've been told, and some choose to believe it; I know they're wrong wait and see….

Someday we'll find it, The Rainbow Connection; The Lovers, The Dreamers, and Me.

Who said that every wish would be heard and answered when wished on the morning star? Somebody thought of that, and someone believed it; look what it's done so far.

What's so amazing that keeps us star gazing? And what do we think we might see?

Someday we'll find it, The Rainbow Connection; The Lovers, The Dreamers, and Me.

All of us under its spell; We know that it's probably magic.

Have you been half asleep, and have you heard voices? I've heard them calling my name. Is this the sweet sound that calls the young sailors? The voice might be one and the same.

I've heard it too many times to ignore it. It's something that I'm s'pposed to be. Someday we'll find it, The Rainbow Connection; The Lovers, The Dreamers, and Me." [40]

"Pi in the Sky"[41]

Sign above the dotted line,
Across the road, beyond the strife;
Cross your heart and hope to shine.

Eat your cake, and have me, too:
I keep awake to wait for you.

Rest above the turning leaves,
Between the stars, upon my honor;
Best of all, upon the dreams.

Check your coat, but leave me mine:
Changed my thought, I'll stay behind.

Sigh beneath the crimson sky,
Across the bridge, beyond the wise;
Cross our hearts and hope to fly.

Pick a nickel from my pocket,
(Make a wish) don't ever drop it.

[in case of fire, turn page]

Reality Check

[IN CASE OF *FIRE*, DUMB-ASS]

But since you're on the page, anyway, have fun!!

(Because there's fun to be done!)

♬ "sometimes you're beaten to the call
sometimes you're taken to the wall
but you don't give in

sometimes you're shaken to the core
sometimes your face is gonna fall
but you don't give in" [8]

♬ "the time has come
to say fair's fair
to pay the rent
to pay our share

the time has come
a fact's a fact
it belongs to them
let's give it back

how do we dance when our earth is turning?"
how do we sleep while our beds are burning?" [8]

♬ "end—your dreamworld is just about to end

fall—your dreamworld is just about to fall

your dreamworld will fall." [8]

Pivot

(…and they said it couldn't be done)

((If you say that "It *can't* be done since there will always be people who don't understand that altruism is for the best and so those people will never get together," then, ironically, *you* are one of those people who don't understand, and so keep us from coming together.))

Welcome to *THE* Real world…

…ain't life grand?

("Now it goes to eleven.")

Are you ready to find out what *THE* Big secret is?

Well, go ahead and turn the page.

[with triumphant theme song from *2001: A Space Odyssey* playing]

(the next page reads from bottom to top, so avert your eyes
as you turn the page, and then re-position them accordingly once you've done
so)

TODAY IS THE FIRST DAY OF THE REST OF POSTERITY'S LIVES

CAKE

OWN

OUR

MAKE

CAN

WE

Part II
The Whole Truth
Divided into just a few brief segments

"The truth must essentially be regarded as in conflict with this world; the world has never been so good, and will never become so good that the majority will desire the truth."

~ Soren Kierkegaard

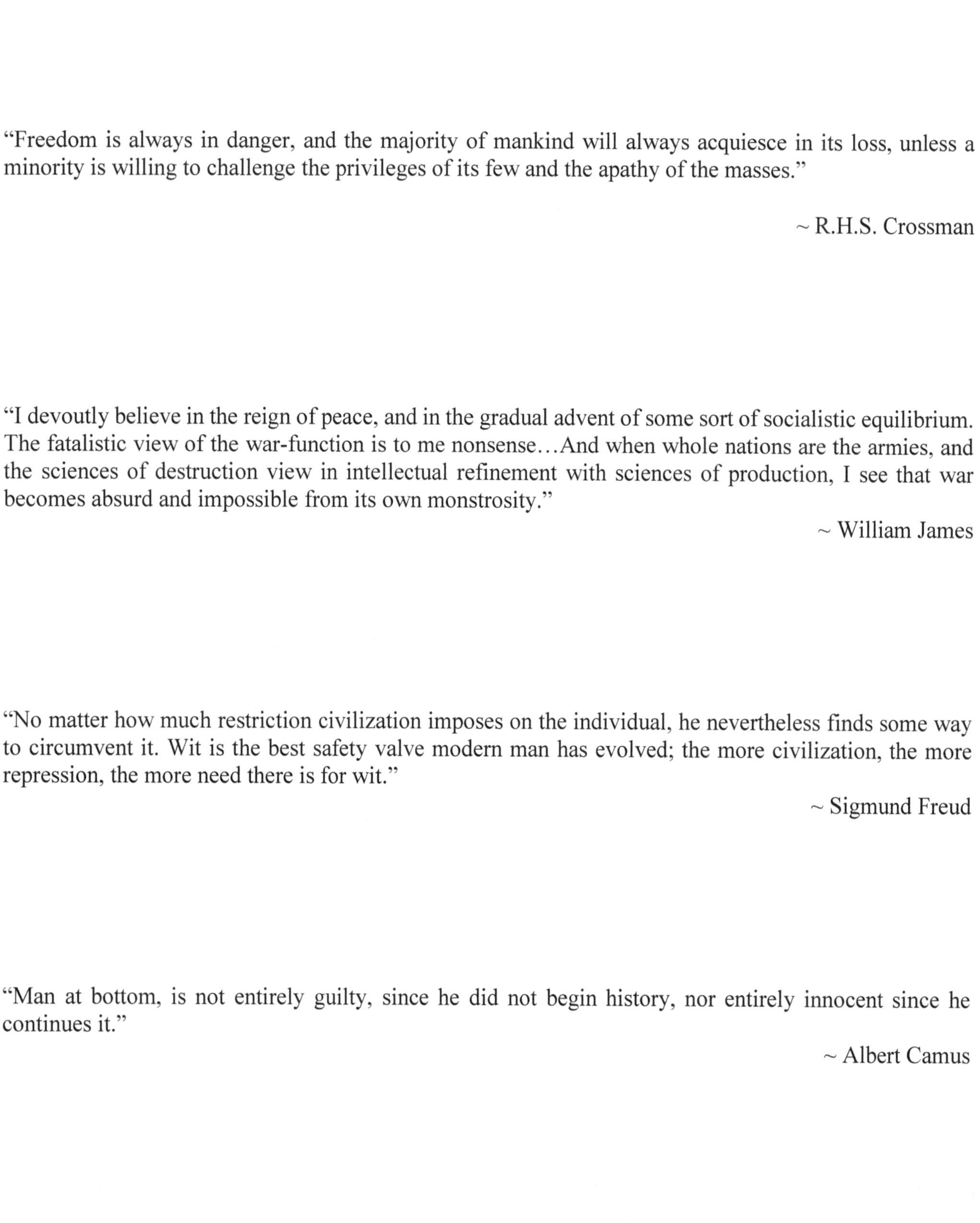

Reality Check

"Freedom is always in danger, and the majority of mankind will always acquiesce in its loss, unless a minority is willing to challenge the privileges of its few and the apathy of the masses."

~ R.H.S. Crossman

"I devoutly believe in the reign of peace, and in the gradual advent of some sort of socialistic equilibrium. The fatalistic view of the war-function is to me nonsense…And when whole nations are the armies, and the sciences of destruction view in intellectual refinement with sciences of production, I see that war becomes absurd and impossible from its own monstrosity."

~ William James

"No matter how much restriction civilization imposes on the individual, he nevertheless finds some way to circumvent it. Wit is the best safety valve modern man has evolved; the more civilization, the more repression, the more need there is for wit."

~ Sigmund Freud

"Man at bottom, is not entirely guilty, since he did not begin history, nor entirely innocent since he continues it."

~ Albert Camus

Reality Check

PROLOGUE

A Homework Assignment I Had To Do in February, 1996:

"Essay #1. Think back to the first time in your life when it hit you squarely in the face that there were people in the world who were culturally different from you, other members of your family, etc. It may have happened when you were a young child, or perhaps you were already a teenager. Describe when it occurred. What was it that drew your attention? How were these people different? What was the experience like for you? What did you think? How did you feel? What did others say? What lasting effect(s) do you believe your first awareness of human cultural differences has had on you? How would you describe your experience in terms of the concepts of 'naïve realism' and 'ethnocentrism'?"

ethnocentrism: 1/ having race [as opposed to a race of aliens?] as a central interest. 2/ based on the attitude that one's own group is superior.

I learned this concept in 9th grade World Culture class. Until this very moment of addressing this question I didn't consciously realize that subconsciously I was confused when I learned this term: Once this concept is defined and explained—how can it continue to exist? I think I just assumed that it only applied to third world nations because they were uneducated.

naïve realism: the assumption that everyone in the world sees things in the same way.

I have been naïve for many years for always assuming that everyone else saw the same reality that I did, although I'm not sure what reality I was seeing my own self, let alone how it may have differed relative to everyone else. But now that I'm forced to consider it, I would argue that everyone should share a common reality based on a certain consensus of what universally matters to everyone. This would be the basis for determining right and wrong, which would be the basis for determining mistakes. This would be the basis for determining when it was necessary to give up certain paths in order to test new paths that at least offered possible hope, instead of paths proven to cause regret. Then we could all "know the good and do the good," as Socrates put it.

I guess "right and wrong" is a very subjective notion when there is no conscious consensus as to what the final "right" is.

Wait a minute; I almost forgot that I actually became aware that I did not share the same reality as those around me when I was in kindergarten. Whenever the teacher was looking for the right answer or a volunteer, all the other kids would flail with "oohs" and "aahs." I, however, knew enough to restrain my enthusiasm by raising my hand with composure and decorum, instead. I noticed the same thing at summer camp. I didn't understand why they didn't see that the teacher was trying to create order. That seemed obvious.

It felt good to get that look of respect from the teacher.

Similarly, whenever there was a disputed call in a game, the kids on the opposing team would ask me to settle it because I had a reputation for calling it against my side if that's what I saw. It felt good to have their trust, but I didn't understand why they didn't see from this that it was better to just be honest.

Pivot

The term "race" is the bigger BIGGEST BULLSHIT. *EVERYONE* is only human. And the first thing they say at alcoholics anonymous is, "I'm an alcoholic," so that they can acknowledge what it is that they are trying to overcome. They are not ashamed of who they are and that they made a mistake. (They didn't come there so that they could all say, "Hey, that's great! I'm an alcoholic too! Now we'll all have someone to get drunk with! We like driving home drunk and killing people and then waking up in the morning feeling like there's a cement mixer in our heads.")

race: human beings, as a group. (<u>The whole concept of race, as it is traditionally defined, may be profoundly modified or dropped altogether, once the genetic approach has been fully exploited.</u>)

Here's another apparent secret regarding right and wrong: when you do something dishonest you are creating fear in yourself because, a) you'll be afraid that those whom you deceive will be suspicious or find out, so you won't have the peace of mind that comes from having their trust, b) when people are deceived they become less trusting, more inhibited and more defensive, so the greater the degree of freedom that is lost to the individuals of the community, i.e., you will have a proliferation of security guards, surveillance equipment, alarms and locks; and not only does this decrease freedom, but it wastes human and material resources. And, c) YOU WILL KNOW THAT THERE ARE PEOPLE WHO CANNOT BE TRUSTED—**BECAUSE *YOU* WILL BE ONE OF THEM.**

"The political liberty of the subject is a tranquility of mind, arising from the opinion each person has of his safety. In order to have this liberty, it is requisite that the government be so constituted as one man need not be afraid of another."

~ Montesquieu

From now on, let's look at life (ourselves) like this: I'M NOT ONLY AN ANIMAL, BUT I'M *ALSO* HUMAN! SO I CAN DO *BETTER* THAN AN ANIMAL!!

I CAN APPRECIATE LIFE TO ITS FULLEST!!!

Reality Check

This page is supposed to have an image of the cartoon "The Far Side"by Gary Larson from January 12, 1984, but permission was denied to use it. Otherwise you'd be looking at a couple of gorillas casually enjoying a bunch of bananas while one says to the other:

"Ya know, Sid, I really like bananas. I know that's not profound or nothin'... Heck! We ALL do. But, for me, I think it goes far beyond that."

Pivot

♫

"As I walk through this wicked world, searching for light in the darkness of insanity, I ask myself: Is all hope lost? Is there only pain and hatred and misery?

And each time I feel like this inside, there's one thing I want to know:

WHAT'S SO FUNNY 'BOUT PEACE, LOVE AND UNDERSTANDING?

WHAT'S SO FUNNY 'BOUT PEACE, LOVE AND UNDERSTANDING?

As I walk on through troubled times my spirit gets so downhearted, sometimes.

So where are the strong? Who are the trusted? And where is the harmony? (sweet harmony)

'Cause each time I feel it slipping away, just makes me wanna cry…

WHAT'S SO FUNNY 'BOUT PEACE, LOVE AND UNDERSTANDING?

WHAT'S SO FUNNY 'BOUT PEACE, LOVE AND UNDERSTANDING!?" [43]

♫ "All together now." ♫

INTERLUDE

From Carl Sagan's *Cosmos*; Ballantine Books, 1980:

The neuro-psychologist James W. Prescott has performed a startling cross-cultural statistical analysis of 400 pre-industrial societies and found that cultures that lavish physical affection on infants tend to be disinclined to violence. Even societies without notable fondling of infants develop non-violent adults, provided sexual activity in adolescents is not repressed. Prescott believes that cultures with a predisposition for violence are composed of individuals who have been deprived—during at least one of two critical stages in life, infancy and adolescence—of the pleasures of the body. Where physical affection is encouraged, theft, organized religion and invidious displays of wealth are inconspicuous, and where infants are physically punished, there tends to be slavery, frequent killing, torturing and mutilation of enemies, a devotion to the inferiority of women, and a belief in one or more supernatural beings who intervene in daily life.

We do not understand human behavior well enough to be sure of the mechanisms underlying these relationships, although we can conjecture. But the correlations are significant. Prescott writes: 'The percent likelihood of a society becoming physically violent if it is physically affectionate toward its infants *and* tolerant of pre-marital sexual behavior is 2 percent. The probability of this relationship occurring by chance is 125,000 to one. I am not aware of any other developmental variable that has such a high degree of predictive validity.' Infants hunger physical affection; adolescents are strongly driven to sexual activity. If youngsters had their way, societies might develop in which adults have little tolerance for aggression, territoriality, ritual and social hierarchy (although in the course of growing up the children might well experience these reptilian behaviors). If Prescott is right, in an age of nuclear weapons and effective contraceptives, child abuse and severe sexual repression are crimes against humanity. More work on this provocative thesis is clearly needed. Meanwhile, we can each make a personal and non-controversial contribution to the future of the world by hugging our infants tenderly.

Pivot

♫

"The whole world's broke and it ain't worth fixing.

It's time to start all over, make a new beginning.

There's too much pain and too much suffering.

Let's resolve to start all over, make a new beginning.

Now don't get me wrong, I love life and living.

But when you wake up and look around at everything that's going down all wrong, you see we need to change it now; this world with too few happy endings. We can resolve to start all over, make a new beginning. Start all over. Start all over. We can break the chain.

We can start all over. In the new beginning we can learn, we can teach. We can share the myths, the dream the prayer, the notion that we can do better. Change our lives and paths. Create a new world, and start all over. Start all over.

The whole world's broke and it ain't worth fixing.

It's time to start all over, make a new beginning.

There's too much fighting, too little understanding.

It's time to stop and start all over. Make a new beginning.

There's too much fighting, too little understanding.

It's time to stop and start all over. Make a new beginning.

Start all over. Start all over.

We need to make new symbols, make new signs, make a new language.

With these we'll redefine the world. And start all over.

Start all over…" [44]

\

I think I think for all of us when I write:

DO OVER

(We need to make new clichés.)

Reality Check

EPILOGUE

From *Path of the KABBALAH*, by David Sheinkin, M.D. Paragon House, New York, New York. Copyright, 1986:

"God said, 'the earth shall send forth vegetation, seedbearing plants and fruit trees that produce their own kinds of fruit with seeds shall be on earth.' It happened.

What kind of tree does God mention? The Bible states, 'seedbearing plants and fruit trees.' Thus, we care hearing about fruit trees. But do we see in the next sentence 'fruit trees'? No, we see 'trees producing fruit.' What is the difference between a fruit tree and a tree which produces fruit? Kabbalists insist that even such a minor distinction in the text must be taken quite seriously. God says that there shall be a fruit tree, but the next sentence relates that the earth brought forth a tree which produced fruit.

Jewish mystics have explained this seeming contradiction in the following way. A fruit tree is a tree which is literally fruit. Certainly such a viewpoint is not how we would think of a fruit tree, but rather as one that produces fruit. But the traditional notion is that people could literally eat the tree; the tree itself was the fruit. Thus, God said, 'Let there be fruit trees' meaning the trees would themselves be fruit, but what resulted was something different—trees producing fruit. In other words, a violation of God's plan occurred on the third day of Creation. The spiritual forces that controlled the earth brought forth something divergent from the deity's wishes.

Somehow, life on this day of Creation exercised its own freedom of choice and changed God's plan. Of course, the sin that will pertain to humans will come from a tree and fruit. So the stage had already been set, in some sense. There was already a disobedience to God at this level and it will be compounded later with Adam and Eve.

Bear in mind that even with this violation of God's wishes, [God] said that 'it was good' on this third day. If it was part of God's plan that evil be introduced into the earth to allow free will to exist, then obviously from God's perspective the day was 'good.' Even after the sin of Adam and Eve on the sixth day God said 'it was good.' From God's perspective, remember, there is not true difference between good and evil; it is only from our vantage point that such a difference manifests itself.

A chief highlight of the third day of Creation is that for the first time God's decree is not actualized. Somehow, God's plan was for the tree itself to be the fruit—the Hebrew expression is *etz pri* ('tree-fruit')—but nature did not co-operate. It is almost as if the tree said to God, 'Wait a minute, this is my space. I am going to have a bark to protect myself. I'll give you fruit you can eat, but you're not going to eat me.'

How the tree would perpetuate itself is an issue that we cannot even comprehend. This is because had it done what God had asked, then the entire universe would obviously have been different. The later scene with the fruit tree and Adam and Eve would never have taken place. So the whole universe took a turn right there. When life was introduced, somehow it exerted its own will on Creation."

I really didn't want to get this deep into it but watching the news made me realize that it's very easy for us to sometimes get confused and contradict ourselves while trying fervently to uphold the value of life and God's will. Specifically, I am referring to the debate over the legality of suicide in the case of people who are terminally ill and constantly suffering in agony while waiting hopelessly to die.

Some argue that, according to the seventh commandment, THOU SHALT NOT MURDER, suicide is an act which contradicts God's will, therefore we ought to prevent others from disrupting God's wishes, regardless of circumstances.

Lest we not forget what "mercy" is about. Nor lest we forget the phrase: DO UNTO OTHERS AS YOU WOULD HAVE THEM DO UNTO YOU. Does not this phrase supersede the seventh commandment?

Perhaps the act of suicide is something which God frowns upon, whether a person is terminally ill and in constant agony or not. But that is between God and the individual. It's nice of you to seek to preserve life and uphold God's laws but be careful not to break other laws in the process and behave in a manner which could be considered inconsistent. Determine for yourself if your actions are contradictory by going to a hospital to have them hook you up to electrodes, put the setting a notch below that which would render you unconscious, flip the switch, and then see how long you can last before screaming "MERCY!!!"

Make sure that you stop eating and using all forms of life. Don't eat any meat, any plant life, and any bread that uses yeast. Don't wear clothing that has been made from any animals or plant life. And make sure that any time you get sick with any kind of infection you don't do anything to kill it.

Language is an agreement. In order for language to function we must have an agreement as to what the words of a language mean. For this purpose, "murder" should be defined not simply as "the taking of life," but as "the taking of life against another's will."

The reason I expounded on the third day of creation, and the author's interpretation of it, is to demonstrate the most important point.

There's a father who is teaching his 16-year-old son to drive. Before the third lesson, after the son has displayed great self-reliance and maturity, the father tells him for the first time to drive the car alone, just down to a nearby gas station, and, "fill up the car with gas." Does the son fill up the entire car with gas, or does he just fill up the gas tank?

He uses his intelligence.

As Captain Picard once proclaimed to an apparent deity, while pleading for absolution for breaking his own cardinal rule, "There can be no justice as long as laws are absolute!"

He was absolved.

Public Citizen
@Public_Citizen
Jeff Bezos
2010 net worth: $12 billion
2019 net worth: $112 billion
Mark Zuckerberg
2010 net worth: $4 billion
2019 net worth: $76 billion
Larry Page
2010 net worth: $28 billion
2019 net worth: $61 billion
2010 federal minimum wage:
$7.25
2020 federal minimum wage:
$7.25
GUYS I SWEAR
I swear you just gotta wait for it to trickle down

Meet Betsy DeVos,
Trump's Secretary of Education
• Billionaire
• No education degree
• No teaching experience
• No experience working in a
school environment
• Never attended public school
or state university
• Never put her own children in
public school
• Does not believe in or support
public education
• Believes that public school
teachers are overpaid
• Supports for-profit education
• Invested $200 million in
Christian schools and
organizations
• Doggedly advocates
funneling money out of public
education and into for-profit,
Christian-based education
I have no experience, but I donated
$9.5 million to Trump's campaign!
I work hard to
dismantle public
education in the U.S.
#Unqualified

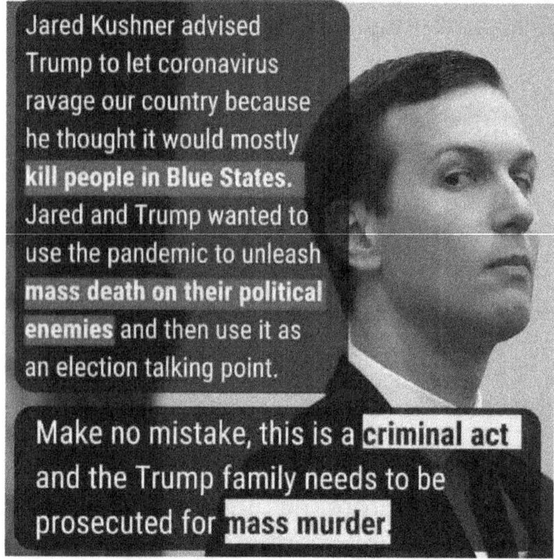
Jared Kushner advised
Trump to let coronavirus
ravage our country because
he thought it would mostly
kill people in Blue States.
Jared and Trump wanted to
use the pandemic to unleash
mass death on their political
enemies and then use it as
an election talking point.
Make no mistake, this is a criminal act
and the Trump family needs to be
prosecuted for mass murder.

"STOP BREAKING THE LAW, ASS-HOLE!!!"
AMERICA TO TRUMP

Republicans claim we can't afford
to help Americans struggling to
make ends meet in the pandemic
HAZMAT
AMERICA
These are the same people who
gave a $2 trillion tax cut payoff to
wealthy donors and corporations

In 1984 I lowered the top income
tax rate from 70% to 28%.
Then I imposed the first ever
income tax on social security
benefits to make up for it.
PATRIOTIC
MILLIONAIRES

SUPPLEMENTAL

Believe it or not, I didn't begin to read George Orwell's *1984* (Copyright 1949) until after writing all of the above….

"The book [within *1984*] fascinated him, or, more exactly, it reassured him. In a sense, it told him nothing new, but that was part of the attraction. It said what he would have said, if it had been possible for him to put his scattered thoughts in order. It was the product of a mind similar to his own, but enormously more powerful, more systematic, less fear-ridden. The best books, he perceived, are those that tell you what you know already."

"Indeed, so long as they are not permitted to have standards of comparison they never even become aware that they are oppressed."

"<u>Crimestop</u> means the faculty of stopping short, as though by instinct, at the threshold of any dangerous thought. It includes the power of not grasping analogies, of failing to perceive logical errors, of misunderstanding the simplest arguments if they are inimical to Ingsoc [the prescribed doctrine], and of being bored or repelled by any train of thought which is capable of leading in a heretical direction. <u>Crimestop</u>, in short, means protective stupidity. But stupidity is not enough. On the contrary, orthodoxy in the full sense demands a control over one's own mental processes as complete as that of a contortionist over his body. Oceanic society rests ultimately on the belief that Big Brother is omnipotent and that the Party is infallible. But since, in reality, Big Brother is not omnipotent, and the Party is not infallible, there is need for an unwearying, moment-to-moment flexibility in the treatment of facts."

"And if it is necessary to rearrange one's memories or to tamper with written records, then it is necessary to *forget* that one has done so. The trick of doing this can be learned like any other mental technique. It *is* learned by the majority of Party members, and certainly by all who are intelligent as well as orthodox. In Oldspeak it is called, quite frankly, 'reality control.' In Newspeak it is called <u>doublethink</u>."

"<u>Doublethink</u> means the power of holding two contradictory beliefs in one's mind simultaneously, and accepting both of them. The Party intellectual knows in which direction his memories must be altered; he therefore knows that he is playing tricks with reality; but by the exercise of <u>doublethink</u> he also satisfies himself that reality is not violated. The process has to be conscious, or it would not be carried out with sufficient precision, but it also has to be unconscious, or it would bring with it a feeling of falsity and hence of guilt. <u>Doublethink</u> lies at the very heart of Ingsoc, since the essential act of the Party is to use conscious deception while retaining the firmness of purpose that goes with complete honesty. To tell deliberate lies while genuinely believing in them, when it becomes necessary again, to draw it back from oblivion for just so long as it is needed, to deny the existence of objective reality and all the while to take account of the reality which one denies—all this is indispensably necessary. Even in using the word <u>doublethink</u> it is necessary to exercise <u>doublethink</u>. For by using the word one admits that one is tampering with reality; by a fresh act of <u>doublethink</u> one erases this knowledge; and so on **indefinitely**, with the lie always one leap ahead of the truth. Ultimately, it is by means of <u>doublethink</u> that the Party has been able—and may, for all we know, continue to be able for thousands of years—to arrest the course of history."

"If one is to rule, and to continue ruling, one must be able to dislocate the sense of reality."

Reality Check

"If human equality is to be forever averted—if the High, as we have called them, are to keep their places permanently—then the prevailing mental condition must be controlled insanity."

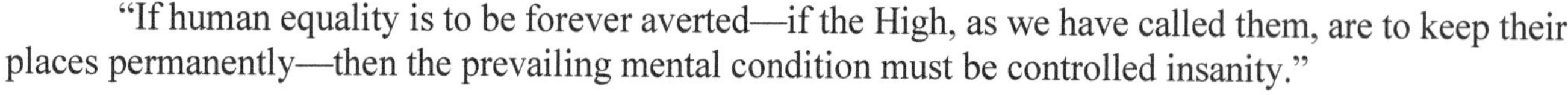

The following is taken from Erich Fromm's AFTERWORD, which was written after the year 1984 for the re-issue. …What's it going to take to get this kind of stuff to become mainstream?

"*1984* is a warning. The mood it expresses is that of near despair about the future of man, and the warning is that unless the course of history changes, men all over the world will lose their most human qualities, will become soulless automatons, and will not even be aware of it.

"The philosophy of the Old Testament assumes that man develops his powers of reason and love fully and thus is enabled to grasp the world, being one with his fellow man and nature, at the same time preserving his individuality and his integrity.

"[…] Four hundred years later, when all these hopes are realizable, when man can produce enough for everybody, when war has become unnecessary because technical progress can give any country more wealth than can territorial conquest, when this globe is in the process of becoming as unified as a continent was four hundred years ago, at the very moment when man is on the verge of realizing his hope, he begins to lose it. It is the essential point of all the three negative utopias not only to describe the future toward which we are moving, but also to explain the historical paradox.

"The question common to Orwell and similar works is: can human nature be changed in such a way that man will forget his longing for freedom, for dignity, for integrity, for love—that is to say, can man forget that he is human? Or does human nature have a dynamism which will react to the violation of these basic human needs by attempting to change an inhuman society into a human one? Orwell and the like assume that man has an intense striving for love, for justice, for truth, for solidarity.

"[…] It is one of the most characteristic and destructive developments of our own society that man, becoming more and more of an instrument, transforms reality more and more into something relative to his own interests and functions. Truth is proven to be the consensus of millions; to the slogan 'How can millions be wrong?' is added 'and how can a minority of one be right?' Orwell shows quite clearly that in a system in which the concept of truth as an objective judgment concerning reality is abolished, anyone who is a minority of one must be convinced that he is insane.

"Another important point in Orwell's discussion is closely related to 'doublethink,' namely that in successful manipulation of the mind the person is no longer saying the opposite of what he thinks, but he thinks the opposite of what is true. Thus, for instance, if he has completely surrendered his independence and integrity, if he experiences himself as belonging either to the state, the party or the corporation, then two plus two are five, or 'Slavery is Freedom,' and he feels free because there is no longer any awareness of the discrepancy between truth and falsehood. Specifically, this applies to ideologies. Just as the Inquisitors who tortured their prisoners believed that they acted in the name of Christian love, the Party 'rejects and vilifies every principle for which the socialist movement originally stood, and it chooses to do this in the name of socialism.' Its content is reversed into its opposite, and yet people believe that the ideology means what it says. In this respect Orwell quite obviously refers to the falsification of socialism by Russian communism, but it must be added that the West is also guilty of a similar falsification. We represent our society as being one of free initiative, individualism and idealism, when in reality these are mostly words. We are a centralized managerial industrial society, of an essentially bureaucratic nature, and motivated by a materialism which is only slightly mitigated by truly spiritual or religious concerns. ["**SHOW ME THE MONEY!!!**"] The reader will find many other features of our present Western society in Orwell's description in *1984*, provided he can overcome enough of his own 'doublethink.'

"Certainly Orwell's picture is exceedingly depressing, especially if one recognizes that as Orwell himself points out, it is not only a picture of an enemy but of the whole human race at the end of the twentieth century.

"One can react to this picture in two ways: either by becoming more hopeless and resigned, or by feeling there is still time, and by responding with greater clarity and greater courage. All three negative utopias [presented by other authors] make it appear that it is possible to dehumanize man completely, and yet for life to go on. One might doubt the correctness of this assumption, and think that while it might be possible to destroy the human core of man, one would also in doing this destroy the future of mankind. Such men would be so truly inhuman and lacking in vitality that they would destroy each other, or die out of sheer boredom and anxiety. It is quite obviously the intention to sound a warning by showing where we are headed for unless we succeed in a renaissance of the spirit of humanism and dignity. Orwell is simply implying that the new form of managerial industrialism, in which man builds machines which act like men and develops men who act like machines, is conducive to an era of dehumanization and complete alienation, in which men are transformed into things and become appendices to the process of production and consumption. Orwell wants to warn and to awaken us. He still hopes—but it is a desperate hope. The hope can be realized only by recognizing the danger with which all men are confronted today, the danger of a society of automatons who will have lost every trace of individuality, of love, of critical thought, and yet who will not be aware of it because of 'doublethink.' Books like Orwell's are powerful warnings, and it would be most unfortunate if the reader smugly interpreted *1984* as another description of Stalinist barbarism, and if he does not see that it means us, too."

♪ "Who sucked out the feeling?"

"I never use the words *Republican* and *Democrats*. It's *liberals* and *Americans*."

~ James G. Watt, Reagan's Secretary of the Interior

I DON'T KNOW WHAT THE DEAL IS,
BUT Y'ALL HAVE GOT TO STOP LEAVING THESE HUGE GAPS AT RED LIGHTS. IT TREMENDOUSLY EXACERBATES TRAFFIC CONGESTION.

Pivot

Part II's AFTERWORD

From the introduction to *A TREASURY OF THE WORLD'S GREAT SPEECHES*:

"Ralph Waldo Emerson, master of the lecture and a life-long student of public speaking, began one of his late essays with these words: 'I do not know any kind of history, except the event of a battle, to which people listen with more interest than to any anecdote of eloquence; and the wise think it better than a battle. It is a triumph of pure power, and it has a beautiful and prodigious surprise in it.' This book is a record of such triumphs and near-triumphs, with scores of anecdotes throwing light and color on scores of speeches, from the ancient Hebrews, Greeks and Romans, to MacArthur, Stevenson and Eisenhower.

"In a broader sense this book depicts the crises and cruxes of history as seen from the platform and interpreted to a deathless audience. For 'it is the peculiarity of some schools of eloquence,' said Rufus Choate, 'that they embody and utter, not merely the individual genius and character of the speaker, but a national consciousness—a national era, a mood a hope, a dread, a despair—in which you listen to the spoken history of the time.'"

"[…] These facts are no solace to those who would abolish the whole art of eloquence as a magical art, a black art, which has always misled mankind. Why is it not possible to get along with simple, clear, truthful statements, without elaboration or ornament? Cicero gives the quick, obvious answer: 'If truth were self-evident, eloquence would not be necessary.' But as truth is not ordinarily self-evident and a human being is a complicated mixture of reason, feeling and impulse, with stores of knowledge and stores of ignorance, all wonderfully related, speakers who would move audiences must play on many strings, must appeal to hope and fear, anger, mercy, pity, as well as to pure truth and the laws of logic. While some speakers have been too loftily logical, many more have been viciously irrational. But emotions are not necessarily opposed to reason. Anger and indignation may be righteous, disgust may be justifiable, fear may be rational, and mercy and pity the greatest wisdom. As long as human nature is what it is, eloquence will remain a double-edged sword, to be used for noble and ignoble purposes—but used inevitably.

"Of course, I do not mean to suggest that every speaker captures his audience, changes the vote or sets in motion a new train of events. All too often many speeches have been weak in substance, all too many have been badly delivered. Some have fallen on deaf ears, only to weave a spell on later generations. In going through a collection of speeches, the reader to some degree joins the audience. But what kind? There are apathetic, sleeping audiences that must be awakened; there are hostile audiences that must be defied and conquered; there are alienated or sullen audiences that must be won back; there are frightened audiences that must be calmed. There are loyal, affectionate audiences that must be further inspired. There are cool, skeptical audiences that must be molded into some kind of unity.

"In line with Webster's dictum that true eloquence exists not merely in the speech but 'in the man, the subject, and in the occasion,'…

"Here then are prophets, warriors, preachers, lawyers, authors, scientists and agitators. Here are ruthless demagogues and unworldly saints. Here is the tense courtroom and the buoyant banquet hall, the battlefield and the burial ground, the mass meeting and the street crowd. Here are subtle and purple passages, the conversational and vehement styles. Here are even a few instances of near gibberish proclaimed with magnetism, eternal truths uttered with disarming humility. Here are audiences hostile and friendly, sleeping and skeptical, alienated and alert. Here are the ears of humanity open to the mighty voices."

♫ "DE DO DO DO, DE DA DA DA" ♫

Reality Check

Being as how the printed word is (potentially) more productive than the blank page, I give you the speech that was appropriately given first order:

I appeal to any white man to say if ever he entered **Logan**'s cabin hungry, and he gave him not meat, if ever he came cold and naked, and he clothed him not. During the course of the last long and bloody war Logan remained idle in his cabin, an advocate for peace. Such was my love for the whites that my countrymen pointed at me as they passed, and said: '**Logan** is the friend of white men.'

I had even thought to have lived with you, but for the injuries of one man. Colonel Cresap, the last spring, in cold blood and unprovoked, murdered all the relations of Logan, not sparing even my women and children. There runs not a drop of my blood in the veins any living creature.

This called on me for revenge. I have sought it. I have killed many. I have glutted my vengeance. For my country, I rejoice at the beams of peace. But do not think that mine is the joy of fear. **Logan** never felt fear. **Logan** will not turn on his heel to save his life. Who is there to mourn for **Logan**? Not one!

Isn't love about sharing experience? Isn't sharing about intimacy? The potential for intimacy is directly proportional to the depth of our consciousness. So, if we allow circumstances to exist that inhibit the potential elevation of our consciousness, then we are inadvertently inhibiting love and the other beneficial emotions.

Aside from physical barriers, fear is the only barrier that exists to inhibit potential. We should do whatever is necessary to break down all of those unnecessary barriers.

In the first draft of this work I melodramatically declared that if no one could reasonably refute my assertions that society is going to hit the fan if we continue to passively and actively promote the status quo, then it looked as if this show was finally going to get on the road. But, then again, the show has always been on the road. It's the never-ending story. But even a never-ending story must evolve; otherwise the audience will walk out.

Perhaps, then, it is about time that we raise the curtain for the next act.

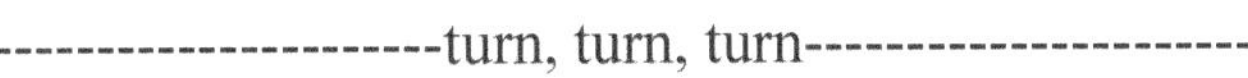

----------------------turn, turn, turn----------------------

"But you don't know what it's like for me."

"Nobody ever knows what it's like for anybody else. That's always the problem."[45]

But it's not a problem, anymore, because now we can recognize how much alike it is for everyone, and how interdependent we are. Now we can get together to mutually say to each other: "I, too, am mad as hell and am not going to take it, anymore! I may not like you, fellow citizen, nor even know you, for that matter, let alone agree with your politics or religion, but, for the sake of our mutual appeasement I will join in publicly communicating that I will no longer contribute to the culture of exploitation, indifference, self-destruction and willful blindness. In so doing I do not necessarily imply that I agree with all of the arguments put forth in this document, but I do concede that, the United States in particular, as well as the world in general, is too scary and precarious to bear any longer. Therefore, I am going to renounce any role I may have in promoting a divide-and-conquer approach towards survival; such as by pitting parents against children, for instance, by targeting kids to get them to pester their parents for sugar disguised as food, both for the body and the mind. I recognize that this sounds extreme to the point of being fanatical, but that is only because I am acknowledging that the state of affairs is extremely dysfunctional and not conducive to posterity's congruity. Therefore, I am pledging to conform to policies that adopt a mentality that embraces the long-term success of humanity instead of the current approach that primarily disregards the laws of nature. Because, now, I know that it is the same time for everyone; and I understand that it is always now—and that **now** is the best time to be alive."

♫ "A good day is any day that you're alive." [4]

Start reading this sentence now.

Pivot

♫

Instant Karma's gonna get you,
Gonna knock you right on the head.
You better get yourself together,
Pretty soon you're going to be dead.
What in the world are you thinkin' of? Laughin' in the face of love.
What on Earth you tryin' to do? It's up to you; yeah, you!

Instant Karma's gonna get you,
Gonna knock you right in the face.
You better get yourself together, darlin', join the human race.
How in the world you gonna see? Laughin' at fools like me.
Who on Earth do you think you are? A superstar?
                                        Well all right you are!

Well we all shine on, like the moon and the stars and the sun
Well we all shine on, ev'ry one come on!

Instant Karma's gonna get you, gonna knock you off your feet
Better recognize your brothers, ev'ry one you meet
Why in the world are we here?
Surely not to live in pain and fear
Why on Earth are you there? When you're everywhere
                          Come on and get your share!

Well we all shine on, like the moon and the stars and the sun
Well we all shine on, like the moon and the stars and the sun

Come on
On and on and on and on

Well we all shine on
Yeah,
We all shine on
Yeah,
We all shine on
And on and on and on and on and on and on….

                                                ~ John Lennon

Boy, that guy sure had some crazy imagination. You might say he had a dream. And you might say that "I have a dream." [46] Or you might say that I have a reality, a reality that "we will be able to transform the jangling discord of our Nation into a beautiful symphony of brotherhood." [46]

Reality Check

Pivot

♫

"Why are there so many songs about rainbows?
--that's part of what rainbows do.

Rainbows are memories; sweet-dream reminders.

What is it you'd like to do?

All of us watching and wishing we'd find it.
I've noticed *you're* watching too.

Someday you'll find it, the Rainbow Connection; the Lovers, the Dreamers and…

Life's like a movie

So write your own ending

Keep believing
Keep pretending

We'll do just what we set out to do.

Thanks to the Lovers, the Dreamers and

You." [47]

One for all…

Pivot

AND ALL FOR LOGAN.

Reality Check

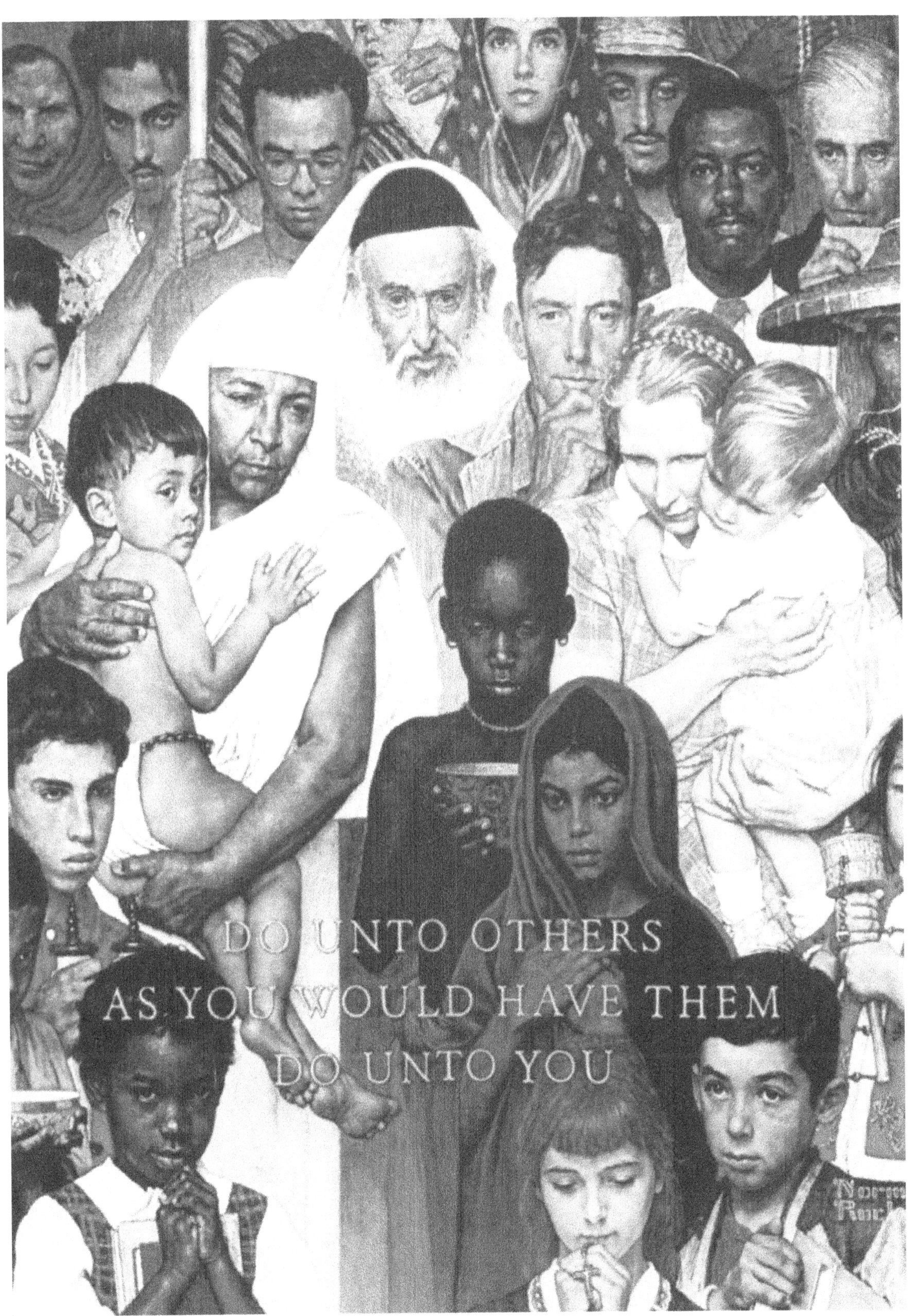

DO UNTO OTHERS
AS YOU WOULD HAVE THEM
DO UNTO YOU

Reality Check

♫

If it's a temporary law, why am I bored right out of my skull?
And I'm dressed up sharp and feelin' dull.
Lonely, I guess that's where I'm from. I was from Canada.
And if it's just a game, then I'll break down just in case.

Hurry up (hurry up)
We're runnin' in our last race

A dream, too tired to come true, left the rebel without a clue.
And I'm searchin' for somethin' to do.
If it's just a game, then we'll hold hands just the same.
So what. We're bleedin' but we ain't cut.

And I could purge my soul perhaps for the imminent collapse.
Oh yeah! (oh yeah!)
I tell ya what we could do….

You be me for a while
….and I'll be you.

A dream, too tired to get to, left the rebel without a clue.
Won't ya tell me what I should do.

If it's just a law, why am I bored right out of my skull?

Oh yeah! (oh yeah!)
Help keep me from feelin' so dull.

If it's just a game, then we'll break down just in case.
Then again, I'll tell ya what we could do.
You be me for a while…

And I'LL BE YOU." [7]

"And, after all, isn't that what life is all about, the ability to go around back and

come up inside other people's heads to look out at the damned fool miracle and say: so

that's how you see it? Well, now, I must remember that." [48]

Pivot

To Me (Or Not To Me?)

(For what did I learn to earn silver and gold?)
I always thought that money would make me,
But up to now, all that I've gotten is dollars and cold.
Just must admit that it's not gonna please me.
(Guess I'll just be, and watch more TV.)

> Is it just me, or is everyone lazy?
> (I don't know, so I just lie so.)
> Is it just me, or is everyone hazy?
> (I don't guess, so I just nod yes.)

Does anybody worry over what they will bury?
"Nobody blink while we try not to think."
Does anybody weep over what we will reap?
So body still tries, and, so, please, dry my eyes.

> Is it just us, or is everyone crazy?
> (I don't think, so I just wait the week.)
> Is it just you, or are we both done and through?
> (I don't care, so I just leave it there.)

If you'll read me the quote that I left in your coat, then
Perhaps, now and then, we could please try again
If you send up some hope or drop me a rope when,
Perhaps change in time will perfect us this time, then,
Perhaps, never again

> Is it just me, or is everyone lazy?
> (I don't know, so I just lie so.)
> Is it just me, or is everyone hazy?
> (I don't guess, so I just nod.)

Guess I'll be me,
('Cause we're something to be.)
Yes, wait and see.
('Cause I'm someone, to me.)

CARICATURE OF PIVØT
TO BE ADDED LATER

BORROWED WISDOM AND POETRY

51. "Superman"

50. S.E. Hinton (p. 192)

49. Oscar Wilde (p. 169)

48.5. from *PrairyEarth*, by William Least Heat-Moon

48. from *Dandelion Wine*, by Ray Bradbury (p. 90)

47. Everyone. (p. 85)

46. Dr. Martin Luther King, Jr. (p. 83)

45. from the movie *A Family Thing*

44. Tracy Chapman, from the album A NEW BEGINNING (p. 71)

43. Elvis Costello (p. 69)

42. Peter Townsend (p. 68)

41. Pivot ((co)incidentally, I wrote it and *To Me…Or Not To Me?* a year prior to having   the epiphany)

40. Kermit the Frog (Paul Williams and Kenny Ascher) (p. 57)

39. Genesis; Anthony Banks, Philip Collins, Mike Rutherford (p. 54)

38. Peter Gabriel (p. 53)

37. 10,000 Maniacs; Rob Buck and Natalie Merchant, off the album OUR TIME IN EDEN (p. 50, 197)

36. "Cosmo" (p. 49)

35. Dorothy Law Nolte (p. 47)

34. The Replacements, from the song, "I Will Dare," off the album LET IT BE (p. 42)

33. from *The Adventures of Don Quixote De La Mancha*, by Miguel De Cervantes (p.   38, 50, 68)

32. The Beatles (p. 35, 56, 69)

31. David Letterman (p. 34)

30. Joseph Ernest Renan (p. 32)

29. from *A Brief History of Time*, by Stephen Hawking (p. 32)

28. Bob Mould (p. 31)

27. The Smiths; Johnny Marr and Stephen Morrissey (p. 31)

26. Dorothy Parker (p. 30)

25.5. Albert Einstein (p. 25)

25. from *Foundation*, by Isaac Asimov (p. 24) (Wow, what a parallel, eh?)

24. Sting (p.33)

23. Aimee Mann (p. 22)

22. John F. Kennedy (p. 22)

21. Tom Waits (p. 20)

20. from the Jewish High Holiday Prayer Book (p. 19, 45, 33)

19. Harry Chapin (p. 19)

18.5. from *The Celestine Prophecy*, by James Redfield; (I only read it after Part I was done.)

18. from the move *Seven*, (p. 18, 192)

17. Ben Franklin (p. 18)

16. Billy Bragg (p.16)

15. "Mr. Pink" (Quentin Tarantino) (p. 14)

14. from *Competition & Co-operation: A Cross Cultural Perspective*, by Janice Morrison

13. *Conformity & Conflict: Readings in Cultural Anthropology*, Eighth   Edition/Copyright 1994, by Spradley and McCurdy

12. "Kramer" (p. 8)

11. **The World Book Encyclopedia**, Copyright 1981, W.T. Jones

10. Michael Penn (p. 8, 12)

9. Talking Heads (p. 7)

8. Midnight Oil (p. 6, 58)

7. The Replacements (p. 5, 37, 90)

6. David Lowery (p. viii, 49)

5. Michael Stipe (p. viii)

4. Paul Westerberg (p. iv, 22, 81) (Sooner or later, "eventually" has to become now.   C'mon, I'll help ya burn 'em to the ground (if ya want it that badly.)) In other words: hold your own life, you bastard; because you're gonna use it…...Are you really   achin' to be, or are you just sayin' you're achin' to be?

3. Joan Osborne (p. iv)

2. from the opening to A *TREASURY OF THE WORLD'S GREAT SPEECHES*, Houston Peterson, Simon and Schuster, 1954/1965

1. Andy Partridge (p. i)

  1) "Buzz Lightyear"

Excerpts from Robert Bellah's **Habits of the Heart: Individualism and Commitment in American Life,** used with permission, (with Richard Madsen, William M. Sullivan, Ann Swidler and Steven M. Tipton, University of California Press, 1985; paperback, Harper & Row, 1986).

Recommended:

1. *The Shocking Truth About Our Money System And How We Can Break Free*, by Ellen Brown

2. *Confessions of an Economic Hit Man*, by John Perkins

3. "Money as Debt" on YouTube

4. *Ishmael*, by Daniel Quinn

6. *Howard Kunstler Dissects Suburbia,*
https://www.ted.com/talks/james_howard_kunstler_the_ghastly_tragedy_of_the_suburbs

5. *Smart Communities*, by Suzanne Marse

7. "Parenting the Strong-Willed Child," presented by John Rosemond; available through P.B.S.

8. "How to Meditate," by Deepak Chopra

9. *The Post Corporate World: Life After Capitalism*, by David Korten

10. The documentaries: "Ghetto Physics," "Hot Coffee—The Movie", "The One Percent," "The Union: The Business of Getting High," "Who Killed the Electric Car?", "Inside Job" and "Food Matters" and "Capitalism: A Love Story" and "SICKO"

11. *Why We Suffer: A Western Way to Understand and Let Go of Unhappiness*, by Peter Michaelson

"We're a species out of context." [48.5]

Chris Christie vetoed raising the minimum wage while giving $4 billion in tax cuts to corporations
NEW JERSEY NOW HAS THE 2ND WORST JOB GROWTH IN THE US AND THE HIGHEST POVERTY IN 50 YEARS

25TH AMENDMENT!
MSNBC.COM
Diplomat: Trump's ambassador took steps to 'line the president's pocket'
TRUMP MUST GO NOW!!!

THE GREATEST REPUBLICAN OF THE 20TH CENTURY
WEALTHIEST CLASS TAXED AT 91%
BUILT INTERSTATE HIGHWAY SYSTEM
SENT U.S. MARSHALS TO ENFORCE CIVIL RIGHTS
PROSPERITY AT ALL TIME HIGH
U.S. WAS GREATEST NATION ON EARTH
PLAYED 800 ROUNDS OF GOLF

THE U.S. HAS BLOWN $400 BILLION ON ITS LATEST FIGHTER JET
THAT'S ENOUGH TO BUY EVERY HOMELESS PERSON IN AMERICA A $664,000 MANSION.
OCCUPY DEMOCRATS

Reality Check

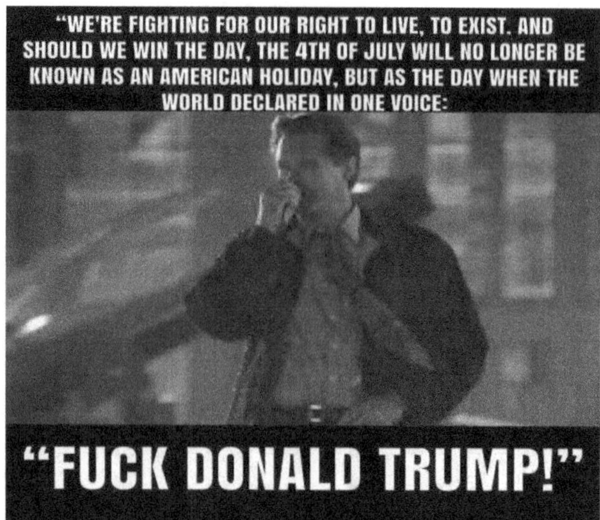

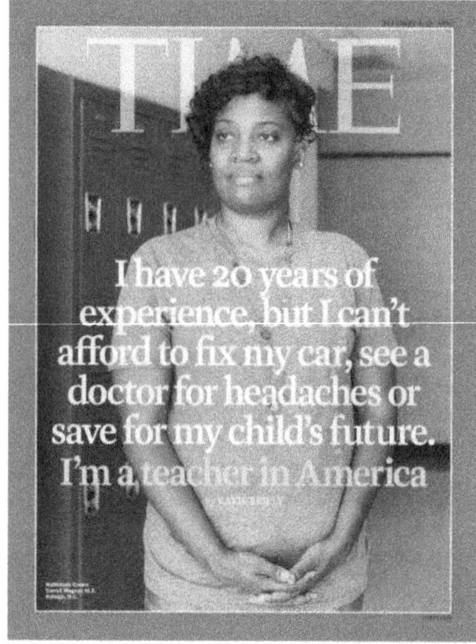

Pivot

"Deep Thoughts," an intermission

"Words do not describe reality, they create it."

~ William Shakespeare

"Good writers define reality; bad ones merely restate it."

~ Edward Albee

"By deliberately changing the internal image of reality, people can change the world."

~ Will Harman

"A man's mind stretched by a new idea can never go back to its original dimensions."

~ Oliver Wendell Holmes

"Imagination is more important than knowledge, because knowledge tells what was, whereas imagination tells what will be."

~ Albert Einstein

"Because they have so little, children must rely on imagination rather than experience."

~ Eleanor Roosevelt

"What the mind can conceive and believe, it can achieve."

~ Napoleon Hill

"No real social change has ever been brought about without a revolution… Revolution is but thought carried into action."

~ Emma Goldman

"Without revolution no new history can begin…History has already broken through the closed circle of slavery. The revolution is the break from captivity, from the condition of bigotry and oppression in which the spirit found itself before it became self-conscious."

~ Moses Hess

"I want to do away with everything behind man, so that there is nothing to see when he looks back. I want to take him by the scruff of his neck and turn his face toward the future!"

~ Leonid Andreyev

"History is the torch that is meant to illuminate the past, to guard us against the repetition of our mistakes of other days."

~ Claude G. Bowers

"That men do not learn very much from the lessons of history is the most important of all lessons of history."

~ Aldous Huxley

"I believe more in the dreams of the future than of the history of the past."

~ Thomas Jefferson

"This is the seal of the absolute and sublime destiny of man—that he knows what is good and what is evil; that his **destiny** *is* his very ability to will either good or evil."

~ George Hegel

Where there is a will, there is a way.

"A moral being is one who is capable of reflecting on his past actions and their motives—of approving of some and disapproving of others; and the fact that man is the one being who certainly deserves this designation, is the greatest of all distinctions between him and the lower animals. The moral sense follows, firstly, from the enduring and ever-present nature of the social instincts; secondly, from man's appreciation of the approbation and disapprobation of his fellows; and thirdly, from the high activity of his mental faculties, with past impressions extremely vivid; and in these latter respects he differs from the lower animals. Owing to this condition of mind, man cannot avoid looking both backwards and forwards, and comparing past impressions. Hence after some temporary desire or passion has mastered his social instincts, he reflects and compares the now weakened impression of such past impulses with the ever-present social instincts; and he then feels that sense of dissatisfaction which all unsatisfied instincts leave behind them, he therefore resolves to act differently for the future,—and this is conscience."

~ Charles Darwin

"There is no such thing as failure, only feedback that what you're doing is not working.

~ Joseph P. Thompson

"The only thing necessary for the triumph of evil is for good men to do nothing."

~ Edmund Burke

"Only one thing is ever guaranteed, that is that you will definitely not achieve the goal if you don't take the shot."

~ Wayne Gretzsky

"We cannot be complacent until everyone is treated equally and everyone is allowed equal opportunity at modest prosperity."

~ Thomas Jefferson

"Democracy is the most difficult of all forms of government, since it requires the widest spread of intelligence…"

~ Will Durant

"Let no man imagine that he has no influence. Whoever he may be, and wherever he may be placed, *the man who thinks* becomes a light and a power."

~ Henry George

I think, therefore I expound.

"We are not going to be able to operate our spaceship Earth successfully nor for much longer unless we see it as a whole spaceship and our fate common. It has to be everybody or nobody…."

~ Richard Fuller

Perspective and pacing are everything.

The mind learns, the body does, the spirit Becomes.

"Truth is a torch, but a terrific one; therefore we all try to grasp it with closed eyes, fearing to be blinded."

~ Johann Wolfgang Von Goethe

"That men are divided into leaders and the led is but another manifestation of their inborn and irremediable inequality. Men should be at greater pains than heretofore to form a superior class of thinkers, unamenable to intimidation and fervent in the quest of truth, whose function it would be to guide the masses dependent on their lead."

~ Sigmund Freud

"…but no pleasure is comparable to the standing upon the vantage ground of truth."

~ Lucretius

"No."

~ Rosa Parks

Pivot

"I'll never understand people!"   ~ Elaine Benes

"Irony is really only hypocrisy done with style."

A classless society is preferable to a society lacking class.

"If I criticize somebody, it's because I have higher hopes for the world, something good to replace the bad. I'm not saying what the Beat Generation says: 'Go away because I'm not involved.' I'm here, and I'm involved."   ~ Mort Sahl

"Serious humorists try to jolt you with humor into looking with a fresh eye at something bizarre in our daily environment that was previously taken for granted."   ~ William Zinsser

"Since childhood is a time when kids prepare to be grown-ups, I think it makes a lot of sense to completely traumatize your children. Gets 'em ready for the real world."   ~ George Carlin

Shouldn't the expression be: "Welcome to the real world, SUCKER"?

Parents are natural-born hypocrites.

"[What qualifies as 'funny', you ask?] The relief from pain; that's what's funny."   ~ Buddy Hackett

"Laughter is a common denominator among the enlightened."   ~ a friend of Tim Allen's

"People's brains are like sieves; only with comedians' brains the holes are smaller."   ~ Jerry Seinfeld

"The problem with the French is that they have no word for 'entrepreneur.'"   ~ "President" G.W. Bush

"Success is the sole earthly judge of right or wrong."   ~ Adolph Hitler

It takes one to know one.

I've known people who exhibited symptoms of insanity, yet weren't insane, per se.

"Regarding the fitness craze: America has lost its soul; now it's trying to save its body."   ~ George Carlin

"Traditional American values: Genocide, aggression, conformity, emotional repression, hypocrisy, and the worship of comfort and consumer goods."   ~ George Carlin

"I don't believe there's any problem in this country, no matter how tough it is, that Americans, when they roll up their sleeves, can't completely ignore."   ~ George Carlin

"I told you guys: Never underestimate the power of a free hat."   ~ Eric Cartman

"Trust in Allah, but tie up your camel."

Rome didn't collapse in a day.   All bad things must come to an end.

In Your Faith!

"Believe" is ironic,
The word's a mistake.
If you believe in that word,
Then you might be a fake.

If convincedness is honest,
The belief from inside,
Then you don't have to tell us,
That God's on your side.

The sky is called blue;
It's accepted as fact.
We all know it is true;
None would argue on that.

No matter where that you go,
Even out into space,
The Earth, we all know,
Is blue in the face.

We take this as given,
There's no talk of this.
Our belief in the heaven,
Is quite hard to miss.

From the day I could see,
I assumed in the sky.
It was that color to me,
No one had to imply.

If one believed it was green,
We'd expect a discussion.
There'd be a big scene,
On how light hits the ocean.

So, if conviction is there,
Your belief could be quiet.
Because, God is aware.
So, like…don't try to buy it.

…and for my final act:

Part III
Nothing But The Truth

"I am a firm believer in the people. If given the truth, they can be depended upon to meet any national crisis. The great point is to bring them the real facts."

~ Abraham Lincoln

This page was supposed to have an image from the cartoon strip "The Far Side," by Gary Larson, but permission was denied. Otherwise you'd be seeing a full-page color cartoon of a chicken standing on the side of a highway looking at a billboard just across the other side of the road which read: "WHY DO YOU NEED A REASON?"

♪ "Miracles always happen when they have to happen." [4]

Reality Check

April 26, 1996

Prior to today, I had actually thought that this manuscript was complete after Part II. Since finishing it I have been anxiously waiting for a literary agent's response. In the meantime, my wheels have kept turning and I have kept getting more feedback. Last night it occurred to me that in the first part I made a mistake that needs to be corrected. (Plus, I have subsequently found more fodder that needs to be pondered by everyone.)

I just finished reading Dennis Miller's *The Rants* and found that he shares many of my views. However, some of his opinions contradict mine; I bet that after he reads *Reality Check* he'll have to admit that he is wrong about some things. (And I don't just mean every positive thing he's ever said about "President" George W. Bush, Jr.)

Fair warning: Miller's book contains some very graphic language. (Quite frankly, he's a very disgusting man.) So, for those of you who think that such language is inherently offensive and gratuitous, let me explain the terms "vulgarity" and "context."

As I said before, there is no such thing as an inherently vulgar word. The reason we label certain behaviors or words as "vulgar" is so that we have an "eloquent" way to express ourselves when we are upset over wrongdoing; things that are destructive. The purpose of vulgar language is to express disgust over vulgar, offensive and disgusting behavior. That is why we're offended by it—it brings to our attention that which is offensive. The purpose of bringing it to our attention is to move our emotions in order to persuade us to re-direct our actions against the behavior that caused us to be offended in the first place; and that way there will be no need to get upset again in the future.

So, how come we try to hide all of the vulgar language from children?

Because most of the language we consider crude and vulgar stems from our shame and embarrassment over our animalistic nature, i.e., sex.

Fornication

Under

Consent of

the **K**ing

That's where the word comes from. In ye olden days, when people were even more ignorant than we are today, a couple who wanted to procreate needed permission from the king.

I'm pretty sure that the king was "special" because of some (bullshit) religious rule that granted him such prerogative. I bet that somewhere down the line people finally got smart and realized that he was a regular guy just like everyone else, so he had no right commanding appropriate behavior. Men probably started to say, "The king can go fuck himself! If I want to fuck, then I don't need his goddamned permission!" (Unfortunately, the king was probably laughing behind their backs, saying, "Yeah, but now they call it 'fucking' instead of fornicating, so I still get credit for it.")

…"But while I was sitting down, I saw something that drove me crazy. Somebody'd written, 'Fuck you' on the [elementary school hallway] wall. It drove me damn near crazy. I thought how Phoebe and all the other kids would see it, and how they'd wonder what the hell it meant, and then finally some dirty kid would tell them—all cockeyed, naturally— what it meant, and how they would all *think* about it and maybe *worry* about it for a couple of days.

"I went down a different staircase, and I saw another 'Fuck you' on the wall. I tried to rub it off with my hand again, but this one was scratched on, with a knife of something. It wouldn't come off. It's hopeless, anyway. If you had a million years to do it in, you couldn't rub out even half the 'Fuck you' signs in the world. It's impossible."

(Oh, ye of little faith.)

I would explain it to the kids.

I would explain to them that animals, including human ones, have a built in need to make more of themselves in order to ensure that they will be around indefinitely. In fact, the desire is so strong that if it's not controlled properly it will actually cause the problem it was supposed to help avoid; in one of two ways.

One way is to allow ourselves to fully satiate the desire by under controlling it. We will then neglect other important aspects of ourselves and, additionally, we will make so many more of us that we won't have enough space for everyone. The second way occurs if we over control it. That is, if we don't allow ourselves to indulge this need, then there will be a backlash. We will get frustrated and antsy and take that frustration out in destructive ways.

What happened a long time ago, kids, was that they tried to over control it and under control it at the same time. They tried to over control it by making people ashamed of it, by making them believe that they were bad for doing what came naturally. People began to believe that anything having to do with it was wrong, and so should be avoided and not discussed. So, any words that had to do with it became "bad words." Now, in this day and age, we try to keep kids from seeing and hearing these words. Some of us do this because we don't want you to get confused when you see words like "fuck" and be misled to think that sex is "dirty" and shameful in and of itself just because adults still have a tendency to use sex-related words to represent vulgarity; and we don't want you to use vulgar words out of context since that reduces their power and debases the entire language. And, since language is a reflection of our thoughts, it is important to not get lazy and careless with how we use language because then our minds will become weak. When our minds become weak our capacity for appreciating life becomes diminished. But, if we can express our thoughts directly, clearly, and with intention, then the littlest details of experience can become quite…remarkable.

So, basically, kids, language is like weightlifting for the mind. Language is a tool to enhance the clarity of our thoughts.

Simply put, it is fun to communicate; and that fun is directly proportional to how articulate a person is.

…What was I saying?

Oh, right: "Fuck"….

Reality Check

Others of us try to keep kids from seeing the word "fuck" by banning books such as J.D. Salinger's *The Catcher in the Rye* because we're afraid that if you see the word you will want to know what it means, and if you find out what it means then you will want to do it; and if you do it too soon….then things could get kind of hairy.

…. "[You see,] Scout, 'nigger' is just one of those terms that don't mean anything—like snot-nose. It's hard to explain—ignorant, trashy people use it when they think somebody's favoring colored folks over and above themselves. It's slipped into usage with some people like ourselves, when they want a common, ugly term to label somebody."

"You aren't really a nigger-lover, then, are you, [Atticus]?"

"I certainly am. I do my best to love everybody…I'm hard put sometimes—baby, it's never an insult to be called what somebody thinks is a bad name. It just shows you how poor that person is, it doesn't hurt you."

But, again, I digress…see, lately, people have been fornicating each others' brains out as if there were no tomorrow, so now we don't really have enough room or supplies for everyone, and many of us are messed up in the head because we were taught that if we didn't suppress and deny this instinct then we should be punished. Many of us don't have the wherewithal to understand that absolutely uninhibited physical expression and gratification diminishes intimacy and can lead to feelings of worthlessness. All of this confusion has caused the adults to not know how to relate to the opposite sex, (or maybe I'm just projecting, l o l). Adults have trouble figuring out when to draw the line between platonic friendships and intimate partners. Basically, we are taught that we are "man and woman" instead of human and human. By defining ourselves by our sexual characteristics we see each other according to our differences instead of our similarities—and then that's what we focus on. This causes us to dwarf the rest of our being. If we were to focus on each other as a whole, then the whole being would come into focus—very sharply. And then all other aspects of a relationship would be that much more engaging.

So you see, kids, it is important to remember that while adults are here to help guide and direct you, we usually don't have a fucking clue. So, make sure that you always question everything we tell you until you get an answer that makes sense. And, if you ever ask "why?" and someone tells you, "Because I said so," remind them that you will probably not do what they say next time if you don't understand why they said "so."

"Mr. Pivot," said young Johnny Appleseed, "I think I understand what you're saying. When people are ignorant and confused they make themselves scared, and vice versa; and so on. So, now, we kids have to pay for all your fucked up shit. But, there's one thing that I still don't get. I have an uncle who has a boyfriend instead of a girlfriend; the government says that they can't get married and have the same rights as a couple of the opposite sex; plus, sometimes they get beat up because they can't make babies. So, then, shouldn't we be beating up old heterosexual couples, too? You said that something was wrong if it suppressed someone else's potential, or was destructive, but my uncle and his boyfriend aren't suppressing anyone's potential."

"Well, Johnny, everyone gets scared when they see someone living a different lifestyle because it could mean that their own way isn't as good, or could even possibly be wrong. But their fear would vanish if they understood that a different way of living isn't necessarily better or worse, but just weird, uhm, I mean, different."

"But, Mr. Pivot," queried some kid on the right side of the room, "why do you say that they should be allowed to get married and thus be entitled to all of the legal benefits that go along with that?"

"I should ask you why you say that they should be denied that, especially in light of the Fourteenth Amendment which says that 'No State shall make or enforce any law which shall abridge the privileges or immunities of citizens of the United States; nor shall any State deprive any person of life, liberty, or property, without due process of law; nor deny to any person within its jurisdiction the **equal protection of the law**.' What is it exactly that you hope to accomplish or avoid with that denial, anyway? Perhaps if you could provide some rationale for that, then we could come to a meeting of the minds on this."

"Because it says in the Bible—"

"According to the First Amendment it is unconstitutional to base legislation on the Bible. The government can only maintain laws pertaining to citizens between each other, not between citizens and God."

"But, still, Mr. Pivot, you have to admit, it's kind of disgusting behavior, ya know? Do you really think that society should formally condone such onerous behavior?"

"Just because the government doesn't prohibit something, that doesn't necessarily mean that it is condoning it. Besides, who are you or I to call it disgusting? 'Disgusting' is in the eye of the beholder. You may find some people's styles of expressing love repulsive, or certain forms of entertainment infantile, crude, shocking and offensive, such as that Howard Stern fella, but, right or wrong, obnoxious or enlightening, people have a right to live according to their heart and conscience as long as they don't undermine the happiness and long-term survival of others. Moreover, people have to make a living; and you can't very well expect people to voluntarily curtail less than noble standards as long as we're living under the auspices of to-the-victor-goes-the-spoils/to-the-loser-goes-the-shaft capitalism.

"And, to underscore the point about how homosexuality can hardly be synonymous with ignominy, kids, that is, to illustrate just how irrelevant who a person does (or doesn't) make babies with is, listen to some of the people from history who did it their way despite, or even because of, being into the same sex: Alexander the Great, Horatio Alger, Hans Christian Anderson, Aristophanes, Marie Antoinette, Susan B. Anthony, W.H. Auden, St. Augustine, Caesar Augustus, Joan Baez, Sir Francis Bacon, Josephine Baker, Tallulah Bankhead, Beethoven, Leonard Bernstein, Captain William Bligh, Lord Byron, Julius Caesar, Calamity Jane, Lewis Carroll, Fredric Chopin, Montgomery Clift, Noel Coward, Stephen Crane, E.E. Cummings, Salvador Dali, James Dean, Ellen Degeneres, Emily Dickinson, Amelia Earhart, T.S. Eliot, Ralph Waldo Emerson, Errol Flynn, The Fonz, Frederick the Great, Cary Grant, Alexander Hamilton, Howard Hughes, Henry James, Joan of Arc, Janis Joplin, D. H. Lawrence, Leonardo Da Vinci, Carson McCullers, Herman Melville, Michelangelo, Valentine, Walt Whitman, Tennessee Williams, and Virginia Woolf.

"And, I'll let you in on a little secret of mine, kids. Sometimes, when there's a new moon on a Monday I like to come out of the closet, put on a cape, and go dancing with the rest of my superhero friends who like to wear capes and tighter-than-skin-tight tights. And, when Pivot comes out of the closet, he is no longer Pivot. He becomes…

Swivel!!

(caricature of Swivel to be added later)

Actually, that's just a joke. Pivot "prefers" Supergirl and Catwoman, et al. (Not that there's anything wrong with that, per se.)

Pivot

Context – Part II

America is supposedly supposed to epitomize the principles of freedom and democracy; a place beholden to the free flow of ideas for the purpose of establishing intellectual autonomy in the belief that such autonomy will ultimately lead to the fruition of said freedom so that it is no longer merely an aspiring ideal or an illusionary reality, but a bona fide manifestation. Ironically, it is a very far cry from it if you critique it according to its politicians' behavior. Politicians don't **debate** according to the first part of the definition of the word, i.e., "to exchange views about something in order to arrive at the truth," but only according to the second part: "to convince others." They try to convince others based on their conclusion that their truth is the truth. But, of course, they tend to neglect to acknowledge that even if their truth is actually the truth, it isn't actually accepted as the truth, so, therefore, should not be asserted as definitive. It's fair to say that politicians, as well as many of those they represent, do not engage in debate because that would entail *exchange,* and exchange would entail *listening.* Yet listening isn't what happens when the goal is no longer to arrive at the truth, but only to remain at your own personal truth: what is right for you, but not necessarily for others. If listening were to happen, then the debater, even if it is actually the one with the reality-based point of view, would seek to arrive at the other person's truth. That way they would then be able to find the unquestioned assumptions and premises that are subtly causing the discrepancy, thereby make reconciliation possible.

An example of this is the attempt to make flag burning unconstitutional. The reason some folks want the desecration of the flag prohibited is because it represents the country and everything that makes the country great: freedom of speech and expression, the right to peaceable assembly, the right to burn the American flag as a protest against any injustice, or hypocrisy, or failure to uphold the bedrock values that make the country great.

My father was sympathetic to the people who were against flag burning because he understood that many of them have many emotional memories over the flag or, rather, what the flag represents. He said that if someone is upset with the government then they should write a letter.

Let's see...how about:

Dear Senator Lieberman,

I think our involvement in Iraq is a travesty of the highest order!!! I am disgusted at you for all you've done to facilitate these crimes in my name!!!! And for every time that you've ever had a positive thing to say about "President" Bush I hold you in contempt to the Nth degree, you feckless, self-serving, hypocritical, Shmo!!!!!

Sincerely,

Pivot

Reality Check

Now, do you think I said that forcefully enough, or should I add some more exclamation points to get his attention and prove how serious I am? Although, at the same time, I don't want to unnecessarily offend anyone, or have them think that I'm not a proud American who believes in standing up for American values and principles. Yet, if I don't take a stand against this injustice, this corruption of democracy, then I might not have anything to stand up for in the future. I really don't want to allow any more lives to be pointlessly lost if I can help it. How can I and others really get their attention so that they'll know that we mean business and refuse to tolerate such atrocities?

Hmmm?

…I know! It's a shame that it has to come to this, but if I burn the flag as a symbolic protest, then it will be the most compelling thing that I could do to show my conviction. Luckily, this isn't a communist nation where they exile you for disagreeing with the government. That way, all the ideas can be expressed, and then we'll be assured of getting the best possible solution for the greatest good. I'd hate to live in a communist nation and have reason to disagree since then they might threaten me and tell me that if I don't love my country unconditionally and without question, then I should leave. The implications of that would be frightening.

"The price of freedom is eternal vigilance."

When all is said and done, the most powerful and eloquent words are no match against the desecration of a revered symbol. (And, after that, the expression of extreme anger and disgust through the use of the loftiest words in the dictionary are no match against the most vulgar and debase words a language has to offer, assuming that the society has treated the language with the proper respect and vigilance to reserve such words for such appropriate occasions. For example, if this were 1809, and I publicly declared at the top of my lungs that "THIS SOCIETY IS SO MUCH FUCKING BULLSHIT THAT I SHOULD CRY!!!", then it would really strike a chord. Yet, these days nobody would give a shit.)

JUST BURN IT (if necessary)

(Actually, a few days after I first wrote the above, while I was watching a Dateline episode about adoption, I discovered the most eloquent sentiment to ever befall a language. One adoptive mother said that when they were picking up her 3-year-old daughter from the orphanage she shouted with glee, "Mommy! Mommy! Mommy! Now I have my own mommy!!")

Speaking of vulgarity, here's a riddle: What's more disconcerting than separating people by skin color, more appalling than flagrantly destroying Mother Nature, more disheartening than guns in schools, and more embarrassing than the kids (and their parents) all wearing their pants halfway down their butts, and crasser than Time Square?

The commercial where the announcer says, "Scientists tell us that the earth is getting warmer…

"Guess we're gonna need some cooler drinks!!"

How dare they?! How fucking dare they capitalize on their own dying planet!!

Pivot

Incidentally, that reminds me of another bumper sticker I'm planning on marketing:

PLEASE, I'M TRYING TO GIVE A SHIT.

Speaking of Holden Caufield, a.k.a. "Catcher"…

"Ah, but a man's reach should exceed his grasp…or what's a heaven for?"

~ Robert Browning

Or, in other words….

"…the only way of discovering the limits of the possible is to venture a little way past them into the impossible."

~ Arthur C. Clarke

Reality Check

When my father was in his early sixties I once asked him if he would like to do it all over again by adopting a boy to raise if someone gave him a million dollars. "No way," he instantly replied. "I'd love to do it, but the strain of having to keep up financially would just make it too much of a burden." (Financial strain caused it to be so much of a hassle the first time that he immediately said "no" in his head and blocked out the rest of what I said.)

"But," I repeated, "what if money was not a factor this time and you could just give the kid complete attention without all the other aggravation?"

"Well, sure. Then I'd definitely do it again."

Raise your hand if you'd gladly adopt an unwanted child and/or animal if only you could afford it.

Raise your hand if you're so loaded that you could financially sponsor an orphan by funding his or her adoption with another family without even noticing that the money was gone.

Fill in the ______.

"Mommy! Mommy! Mommy! Now I have my own mommy!"

Back in Part One I tackled abortion. I patted myself on the back after writing that because of how well I put the issue into perspective. However, that was actually a revision of the way I had addressed it in all of the previous drafts. One of the reasons I was so pleased with it is because it no longer had a contentious, as well as condescending, tone. Well, yesterday (1996) I came upon a couple of folks in Times Square preaching that abortion is an abomination, so I asked the woman to read my perspective. (This actually was not the first time that I had engaged her on the subject; and it was that last time that made me realize how I could clarify my argument and make it more magnanimous. It also made me realize that we're all on the same side. Nobody wants this to be an issue. So, even if we disagree on the best way to address the problem of unintentional pregnancies, we can at least appreciate the fact that the other side cares enough to also address it.)

So, with that in mind, the following may come across as patronizing, as well as a little redundant, but it would be a mistake if I risked not making the most compelling argument just to save the face of the "opposition." And I hope this woman accepts my apology for shouting at her that she stopped using her f%&*ing brain. I know it was harsh to speak that way, but it's difficult to contain oneself when addressing the unnecessary plight of babies abandoned in garbage cans who are addicted to crack and infected with A.I.D.S.

Anti-abortionists, most of you share my belief that life begins at conception in the sense that it has a spirit. I further believe that since a spirit does not die when its physical host does, the spirit merely moves on to another physical host at its conception. This is my belief; I do not personally know it to be true. But I do know some who do know it to be personally true, so if they say that it is so, then it is.

Regardless, I can't stress enough how much more effective your efforts would be spent aiding people (and animals (also God's creatures)) who have actually been born, and who are in dire need of help and compassion and education. These people may also be the products of parents who were not ready to be parents, yet these parents chose to have the baby, anyway. Let's give these parents and their children the support that they need so that they don't regret having the baby/being born—and so those children don't get themselves into the same situation.

Your strategy is putting the cart before the horse. People are coming to this crossroads because they weren't given the proper education. If a conception has occurred when the parents weren't prepared, then the damage is already done, regardless of whether they abort. If someone fires a gun with the intent to inflict harm, then, even if the bullet misses, the damage is already done since there's someone attempting to inflict injury. You can't stop the bullet once it is fired, but you can teach that person why he shouldn't do it again.

And, to all of the pro-abortionists: don't let yourselves resort to their methods by counter-demonstrating. Instead, you, too, should devote your time by helping the needy families. Besides, can you really say that protesting against fanatics is fruitful? You're already an effective organized force, so direct your focus in ways that would be productive, and possibly the confused will follow your example. And maybe in fifteen years there'll be no more need to fuss. The way that we're going now, the problem is not going to go away. (Especially if the dumb-fuck Republicans like Steve King have their way; …this is beyond moronic on so many levels!!)

Reality Check

P.S. On second thought, several years after writing the above I changed my mind: abortion should be illegal, with the stipulation that RU-86 should be free to all and all prenatal care must be free and accessible, as well as the care for the first 18 years. Plus, there needs to be the most accessible adoption programs in place. I figure that with RU-86 being that readily available the type of people who'd prefer not to have an accidental pregnancy after the fact would find it too convenient to nip any such accident in the bud, therefore, there would be no good excuse for anyone to ever to need an abortion.

My basic rationale for changing my mind is that the law is meaningless if it's not consistent. And the so-called "right to privacy" doesn't apply to a mother with a one-day-old baby.

"If the people knew what we had done, they would chase us down the street and lynch us."

~ George H.W. Bush to journalist Sarah McClendon

Pivot

After

Start reading this poem, now,

Wait until I say "stop."

Begin on line three,

Then after line four,

Go back to line three,

Or go on to "Before."

Before

Stop reading this poem, now,

Wait until I say "start."

Begin on line four,

Then after line three,

Go back to line four,

Or just leave this be.

Reality Check

Gratuitous

(This poem is silly,

And quite in excess.

To pull off such a poem

Would be meager success.)

The purpose of verse

Is a means to purport,

But this poem is pointless,

It is merely for sport.

When writing a poem

Where anything goes,

I could get away

With calling it prose.

The goal of this poem

Is to press all my luck,

So you'll pardon my style

If I end it with "fuck."

With that poem being said, I'd like to use the opportunity to give you my impression of comedian Stephen Wright hitting on a woman:

"There's a fine line between pornography and your butt cheeks."

Pivot

I've had a lot of fun spotting irony the last few months, but this next observation is my favorite.

A couple of nights ago, on "60 Minutes," there a was a story regarding the dispute over prayer in schools because, in one particular community, three siblings new to the town found themselves bombarded by the religious fervor of the other children and faculty: the school had religion structured into daily activities. The parents of these three brothers were forced to seek legal protection of their sons' civil liberties.

It's flustering that this is even a point of contention requiring legal intervention. After all, it was declared unconstitutional to allow prayer in schools over 30 years ago; and with very good reason. ("Neither can the Federal Government pass laws which aid one religion, aid all religion or prefer one religion over another.") But, unfortunately, the community at issue with the ruling has become so drunk with God's love that it has clouded their judgment and common sense.

The reason the new family was opposed to this is because, as we know, a fundamental principle regarding the founding of the U.S.A. was the idea of separation of church and state so that people would be free to choose the faith that suits them best.

At any rate, the community in question insisted that prayer is essential and necessary to instilling good moral values, although that is not the relevant point of discrepancy between opposing points of view. The necessity for prayer *in school* is the relevant point of discrepancy that still begs to be supported with a logical argument. And when some of the people were asked by the feckless Leslie Stahl if they would like it if their children were being subjected to Jewish prayers one of the people answered "no," although no expressed acknowledgment of the double standard was given.

The townspeople's sole argumentative justification for ignoring this bedrock principle that the United States was founded upon is that prayer is a necessary part of getting people to help their fellow man and to properly worship God. But, if this is so, HOW COME THIS FAMILY THAT IS FIGHTING TO KEEP PRAYER OUT OF SCHOOLS HAS BEEN OSTRACIZED WITH DEROGATORY NAME-CALLING AND THREATS OF VIOLENCE? Which version of the Bible are these people reading, anyway?

Remember my slogan, "JUST SAY IT"? Well, in the tradition of ubiquitous dramatic ironical confusion everywhere, for without which there would be no reason to cross the road, I have one don't-forget-that-life's-too-important-to-take-seriously reminder for these folks:

DON'T TALK WITH YOUR MOUTHS FULL.

("And let that be a lesson to the rest of you…nuts.")

Reality Check

I'm watching TV one day and a promo for "What Makes a Woman Beautiful?" comes on and one model who is asked that question says, "If you're a beautiful person inside." Unfortunately I forgot to watch what must have been a very enlightening discussion about how women have become sex objects and their self-esteem is stolen if they don't live up to Greek Goddess standards. I wonder if the model who made that comment knew to attribute any of her brimming self-confidence to all the tremendous attention she must have received throughout life for just looking super pretty. Anyhow, a week later I happened to catch Barbara Walters discussing the insecurities women go through when their breasts are subpar.

In my opinion, they didn't handle the problem very well. They didn't confront it. Instead of giving the women they talked to firm recommendations on overcoming their worry, they coddled them. "If it makes them feel better to have breast enlargement surgery, then we're glad that they feel better," was essentially the message.

It's very unlikely that they'll feel better in one year or ten after pursuing men who are so perfect that they can insist on only accepting women who are independent thinkers as well as particularly easy on the eyes.

"64% of people in the fashion business say that they are pressured to make female readers and viewers feel ugly about themselves."

A while back I started going bald and was quite distressed about it. Life as I knew it was coming to a horrible and humiliating finish. I panicked and resorted to hair transplants, thanks to a loan from my mother.

Biggest mistake of my life.

The point of the transplant was so that I wouldn't have to be embarrassed over what other people would think when they saw me. But, now, because of how obvious the transplants are it's mortifying to be seen without a hat. If someone had sat me down and just told me to shave my head every day and forget about it, I could be walking around oblivious to those who might look at me askew with pity for going with the current Bruce Willis look.

Sigh.

Once, while I was watching "STAR TREK: THE NEXT GENERATION" in a dorm lounge, someone pointed out how ridiculous it was that Captain Picard was bald. "I mean, come on, it's 300 years in the future and they're traveling faster than the speed of light, yet they couldn't find a cure for baldness?"

It's not that they couldn't find one, it's just that somewhere down the line they stopped looking for one because somewhere down the line they learned not to let fear get the better of them. If they hadn't, then they wouldn't have gotten so far in the first place. (Or maybe Picard was just too cool to request the treatment.)

ONE WEEK SUBSEQUENT TO WRITING THE ABOVE....

Another one of my subconscious thoughts finally surfaced. Yay.

Think of all the insecurity and waste and heartache that stems from vanity. Think of how it gets there.

Ask yourself: Are blind people vain? Do they even know that it means? How would a blind person describe what "ugly" and "pretty" mean?

I bet they'd say that "ugly" spoils things that represent nature and innocence and purity.

We all learned from those who came before us that our own physical beauty is determined by what others see, as opposed to how we feel.

How often do we tell children how pretty and handsome they are?

How much public scrutiny do we give to presidents' adolescent daughters? (I'm lookin' at you, U.S.A. Today.)

taboo: banned as immoral or dangerous.

We should make words that represent scales of aesthetics taboo for any context that applies to humans and animals when in the presence of children. (Though that doesn't preclude complimenting them on their cheerful smiles.)

If children don't think that we are attracted to them because of their looks, then as adults they'll be much less likely to believe that how they look matters (when it comes to procuring a sexual partner)— and then they won't think that how others look matters. (And maybe then the fools will just find everybody attractive.)

Yes, perhaps it's true that this would cause children to grow up and not be able to appreciate the physical beauty in people since they won't have standards of comparison. That is, they won't be able to say, "She is so pretty, [as opposed to that other girl who is not very easy on the eyes]."

That is the implication we have been making all of this time.

I could over explain this some more.

"85% of 10-year-old girls say that they feel ugly; and that they wish that they could look like the teen stars they see on TV."

Reality Check

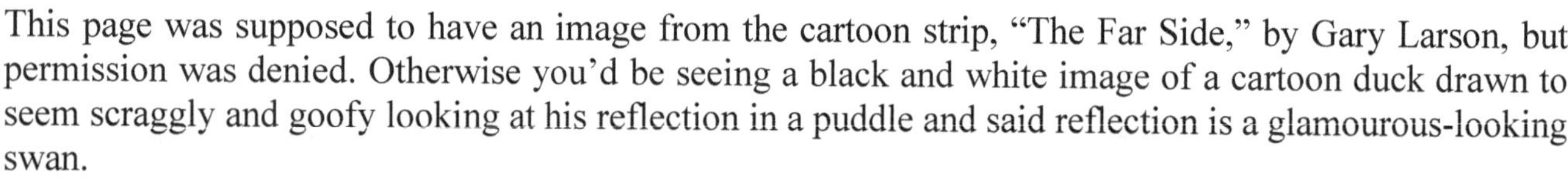

This page was supposed to have an image from the cartoon strip, "The Far Side," by Gary Larson, but permission was denied. Otherwise you'd be seeing a black and white image of a cartoon duck drawn to seem scraggly and goofy looking at his reflection in a puddle and said reflection is a glamourous-looking swan.

The Flaw in "Rudolph the Red-Nosed Reindeer"

Rudolph was an average guy,

Loved, by everyone he knew,

But their love was just a lie!

(Took just looks to say he's through.)

This observation is one big shot in the dark, but I think I can shed some light on the problem with "race." We are always saying that we need to talk about race and our differences, but it's a waste of time since we are obviously not listening to each other. The people who are willing to sit down and have an open-minded discussion are already open-minded, so they don't need to discuss this. So, let's stop talking about what we already know: When we meet a person whose résumé with photo qualifies him to fit into a particular stereotype we think, "Nice to meet you, Blank Slate. At first glance my memory bank of experience can't help noticing that you appear to be eligible for that stereotype. However, I don't assume that your behavior will also qualify you to be a member of said stereotype since stereotypes are derived from groups, and you are an individual. If I should find that you *do* happen to fit it, then I won't be surprised. But if I find that you don't fit it, then I won't be surprised, either."

There are two groups of people:

Group A—those who fall into the minority; and

Group B—those who fall into the majority.

Within group A are two groups of people, those who think of themselves as in the minority, and those who don't.

Within group B are two groups of people, those who think of themselves as in the minority, and those who don't.

You say majority, I say minority.

Let's call the whole thing off.

And let's all say Humanity.

It's probably not possible to say the following without sounding corny, but it needs to be said for the record. It's a mistake to dignify this issue with our attention. If you believe that those people who don't share your ethnic heritage are less human than yourself, then the rest of us won't hold that against you. You're entitled to your opinion. In fact, who am I or anyone else to say with absolute certainty that you're not right? Maybe if we get together and discussed it we could figure out why there's a discrepancy between the two opposing points of view. Maybe God actually does have the audacity to categorize some of us as less deserving based on who our grandparents were. All I know for sure is that I don't like tension and strife, and I assume that all racists and all non-racists alike would agree with that sentiment. So, if we can't see eye to eye on this, let's at least find a way to co-exist without conflict.

"Just because I'm aware of our differences, doesn't mean that I care."

Reality Check

Orange

Long before man made history,
The rainbows and fruit already existed,
But then names came along to create a blind mystery.

When naming this fruit the people got lazy,
So they hired a poet so they'd know what to call it.
…And he wrote us a joke so as to drive the blind crazy.

"If this fruit be a color, by day or by night,
Then I canst help to wonder….
Are the rest black and white?"

We reference to color, and light all around,
Yet the blind see no difference…
(They can only see sound.)

Pivot

Music

To those who can hear it,
This should be a song,
But this poem is silent,
So you can't sing along.

To the deaf it is confusing,
This doesn't make sense:
"Is there something we're missing,
Besides a fifth sense?"

I'll try to explain it,
To those who can't hear,
Though, that's probably stupid,
Since they can't lend an ear, anyway.

See, some poems work without any words…
Just like babies and actors:
In some other language they still can be heard.

Symbols and words can impress an idea,
But, smiles and laughter go beyond any signs.
So, we also have music to express things like fear.

This poem is called "Music" so that the deaf can compare.
Yet, to give that impression, is mighty unfair.

Reality Check

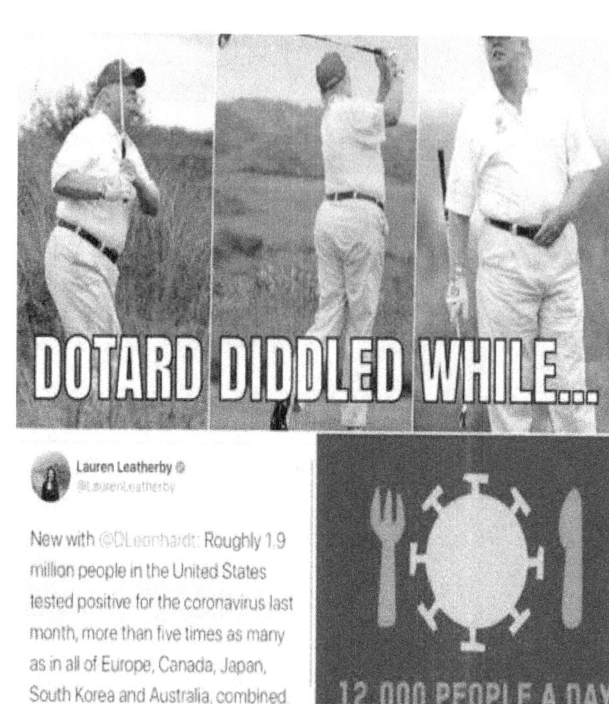

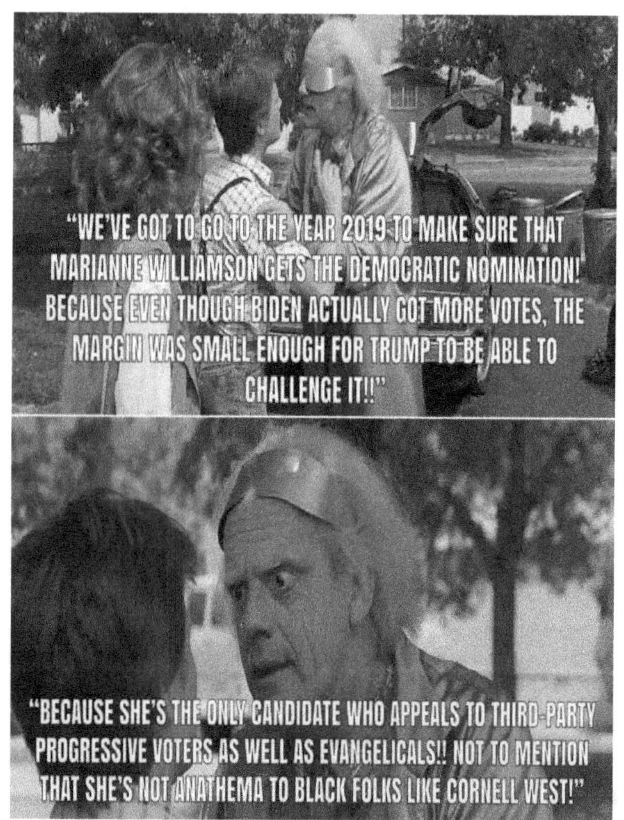

Supplemental No. 2

A few months after I finished Part II I picked up Jane Goodall's *Through a Window*, the 30-year-in-the-waiting follow up to her landmark *In the Shadow of Man*. You tell me if you don't think that the following excerpts shouldn't be read far and wide:

"[…] Thus it is fascinating as well as shocking to learn that chimpanzees show hostile, aggressive territorial behavior that is not unlike certain forms of primitive human behavior. Long before sophisticated warfare evolved in our own species, pre-human ancestors must have shown pre-adaptations similar—or identical—to those shown by the chimpanzees today, such as co-operative group living, co-operative territoriality, co-operative hunting skills, and weapon use. Another necessary pre-adaptation would have been an inherent fear or hatred of strangers, sometimes expressed by aggressive attacks.

"Among humans, members of one group may see themselves as quite distinct from members of another, and may then treat group and non-group individuals differently. Indeed, non-group members may even be "dehumanized" and regarded almost as creatures of a different species. Once this happens people are freed from the inhibitions and social sanctions that operate within their own group, and can behave to non-group members in ways that would not be tolerated amongst their own. This leads among other things, to the atrocities of war.

"What of the other side of the coin? Where do chimpanzees stand, relative to us, in their expression of love, compassion and altruism? Peaceful interactions are far more frequent than aggressive ones; mild threats are more common than vigorous ones; threats per se are much more frequent than fights; and serious, wounding conflicts are rare compared to brief, relatively mild ones. Moreover, chimpanzees have a rich repertoire of community members. The embracing kissing, patting and holding of hands that serve as greetings after separation, or are used by dominant individuals to reassure their subordinates after aggression. The long, peaceful sessions of relaxed social grooming. The sharing of food. The concern for the sick or wounded. The readiness to help companions in distress, even when this means risking life or limb. All these reconciliatory, friendly and helping behaviors are, without doubt, very close to our own qualities of compassion, love and self-sacrifice.

"[…] Little Bee's behavior was not only a demonstration of entirely voluntary giving, but it also showed that she understood the needs of her old mother. Without understanding of this sort there can be no empathy, no compassion. And, in both chimpanzees and humans, these are the qualities that lead to altruistic behavior and self-sacrifice.

"As the ancestors of chimpanzees (and, incidentally, ourselves) gradually evolved more complex brains, so the period of childhood dependency became longer and mothers were forced to expend more and more time and energy in raising their families. Mother-offspring bonds became ever more enduring. The offspring of the most caring, supportive and successful mothers thrived and became themselves good and caring mothers who tended to produce large families. Loving and nurturing characteristics thus competed successfully, in the genetic sense, with more selfish behaviours. Over the aeons, tendencies to help and protect, which were originally developed for the successful raising of young, gradually infiltrated the genetic make-up of chimpanzees. Today we observe, again and again, that the distress of a non-related but well-known community member may elicit genuine concern in a companion, and a desire to help.

Reality Check

"Compassion and self-sacrifice are two of the qualities we value most in our own western society. In some cases—as when someone risks his or her life to save another—the altruistic act is probably motivated by the same inherent complex of helping behaviors that cause a chimpanzee to aid a companion. But there are countless instances when the issue is clouded by cultural factors. If we know that another, especially a close relative or friend, is suffering, then we ourselves become emotionally disturbed, sometimes to the point of anguish. Only by helping (or trying to help) can we hope to alleviate our own distress. Does this mean, then, that we act altruistically only to soothe our own consciences? That our helping, in the final analysis, is but a selfish desire to set our minds at rest? One can speculate endlessly on human motives for helping others. Why do we send money to starving children in the Third World? Because others will applaud and our reputation will be enhanced? Or because starving children evoke in us a feeling of pity which makes us uncomfortable? If our motive is to advance our social standing, or even to alleviate our own mental discomfort, is not our action basically selfish? Perhaps, but I feel strongly that we should not allow reductionist arguments of this sort to detract from the inspirational nature of many human acts of altruism. The very fact that we feel distressed by the plight of individuals we have never met, says it all.

"We are, indeed, a complex and endlessly fascinating species. But while chimpanzees have, to some extent, an awareness of the pain which they may inflict on their victims, only we, I believe, are capable of real cruelty—the deliberate infliction of physical or mental pain on living creatures despite of, or even because of, our precise understanding of the suffering involved. Only we are capable of torture. Only we, surely are capable of evil.

"But let us not forget that human love and compassion are equally deeply rooted in our primate heritage, and in this sphere too our sensibilities are of a higher order of magnitude than those of chimpanzees. Human love at its best, the ecstasy deriving from the perfect union of mind and body, leads to heights of passion, tenderness and understanding that chimpanzees to the immediate need of a companion in distress, even when this involves risk to themselves, only humans are capable of performing acts of self-sacrifice with *full* knowledge of the costs that may have to be borne—not only at the time, but also, perhaps, at some future date. A chimpanzee does not have the conceptual ability to become a martyr, offering his life for a cause.

"Thus although our 'bad' is worse, immeasurably worse, than the worst conceivable actions of our closest living relatives, let us take comfort in the knowledge that our "good" can be incomparably better. Moreover we have developed a sophisticated mechanism—the brain—which enables us, if we will, to control our inherited aggressive hateful tendencies. Sadly, our success in this regard is poor. Nevertheless, we should remember that we alone among the life forms of this planet are able to overcome, by conscious choice, the dictates of our biological natures. At least, this is what I believe.

"But the question [of how much further chimpanzees will evolve] is purely academic. It could not be answered for countless thousands of years, and even *now* it is clear that the days of the great African forests are numbered. If the chimpanzees themselves survive in freedom, it will be in a few isolated patches of forest grudgingly conceded, where opportunities for genetic exchange between different social groups will be limited or impossible. And, unless we act soon, our closest relatives may soon exist only in captivity, condemned, as a species, to human bondage.

"Today, striding the face of the globe, humans clear the trees, lay waste the land, cover mile upon mile of rich earth with concrete. Humans tame the wilderness and plunder its riches. We believe ourselves all-powerful. But it is not so.

"Relentlessly the desert inches forward, gradually replacing the life-sustaining forests with barren and uncompromising harshness. Plant and animal species vanish, lost to the world before we have learned their value, their place in the great scheme of things. World temperatures soar, the ozone layer is depleted. All around us we see destruction and pollution, war and misery, maimed bodies and distorted minds, human and non-human alike. If we allow this desecration to continue we shall, ourselves, be doomed. We cannot meddle so greatly in the master plan and hope to survive. Thinking of this whole terrible picture, the magnitude of our sin against nature, against our fellow creatures, I was overwhelmed. How could I— or anyone—make a difference in the face of such vast and mindless destruction?

"A fig dropped close by, startling me. Fifi climbed from the tree and lay near me with closed eyes, replete. Here, at last, was perfect trust between humans and animals, perfect harmony between creatures and their wild environment. Faustino, tottering a little, moved close to me and, with his wide-eyed stare, reached to touch my hand, then wandered back to Fifi. Trust. And freedom. I thought of the countless chimpanzees who have lost their forest homes, and of the prisoners in zoos and labs around the world. I remembered the story of Old Man and how he had responded to the need of a human friend.

"The will to fight, to fight to the bitter end, flared up. The chimpanzees need our help now more than ever before, and we can only help if we each do our bit, no matter how small it may seem. If we don't, we are betraying not only the chimpanzees but also our own humanity. And we must never forget that, insurmountable as the environmental problems facing the world may seem, if we all pull together we have a good chance of bringing about change. We must. It is as simple as that!

"Evered, Freud and Frodo climbed down and, with Fifi and Faustino, moved away deep into the peace of the forest. I watched them go, then looked back. And where the sun shone through a window in the dense vegetation, a rainbow had appeared, spanning the spray-cloud at the foot of the waterfall.

"[…] Sometimes, when watching the chimpanzees, I have felt that, because they have no human-like language, they are trapped within themselves. How much more they might accomplish if only they could *talk* to each other.

[Yeah, because then they could say things like, "Let's get them before they get us!" or, "You *better* run!" or, "I'll sue you for everything you've got!" But, then again, they could also say things like, "Look at this pretty flower I found," or, "Good game," or, "Hey, me and my pals are getting together to beat the living hell out of those upright opposable-thumb-wielding klutzes that kidnapped our families. You wanna come?" or, "Can I trust you not to hurt me?" "Can I trust YOU not to hurt me?" "Well, of course, because we both know that neither of us wants to get hurt, and if I try to hurt you then you will try to hurt me. So, if I try to hurt you I will only be hurting myself."]

"Cruelty is surely the very worst of human sins. To fight cruelty, in any shape or form—whether it be towards other human beings or non-human beings—brings us into direct conflict with that unfortunate streak of *inhumanity* that lurks in all of us. If only we could overcome cruelty with compassion we should be well on the way to creating a new and boundless ethic—one that would respect all living beings. We should stand at the threshold of a new era in human evolution—the realization, at last, of our most unique quality: humanity."

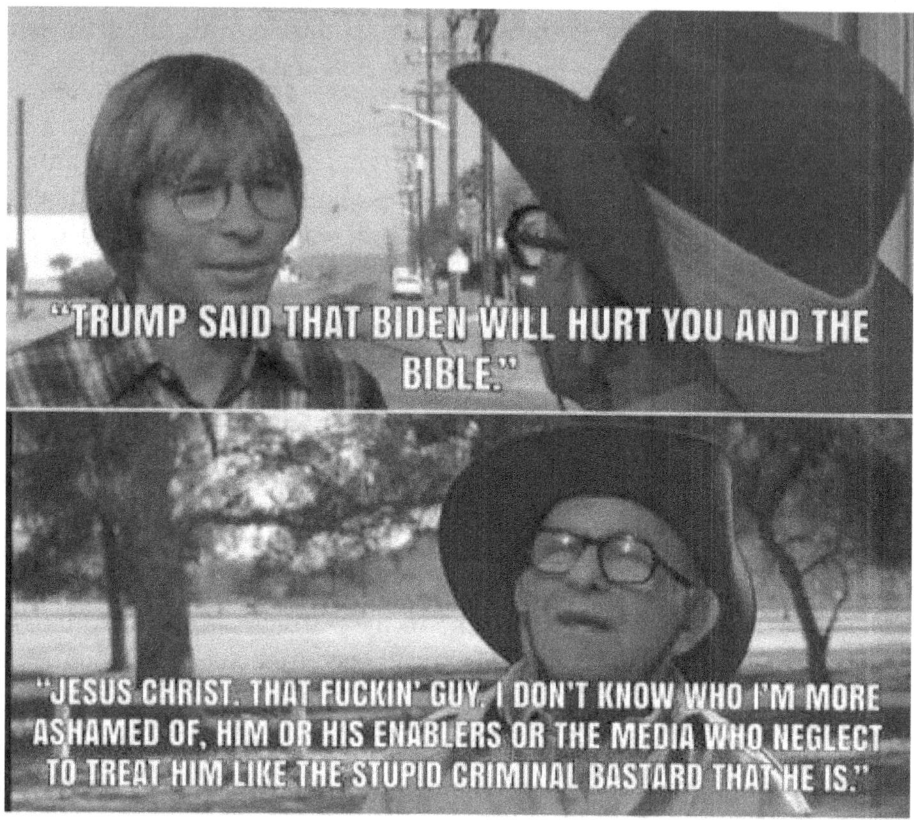
"TRUMP SAID THAT BIDEN WILL HURT YOU AND THE BIBLE."
"JESUS CHRIST. THAT FUCKIN' GUY. I DON'T KNOW WHO I'M MORE ASHAMED OF, HIM OR HIS ENABLERS OR THE MEDIA WHO NEGLECT TO TREAT HIM LIKE THE STUPID CRIMINAL BASTARD THAT HE IS."

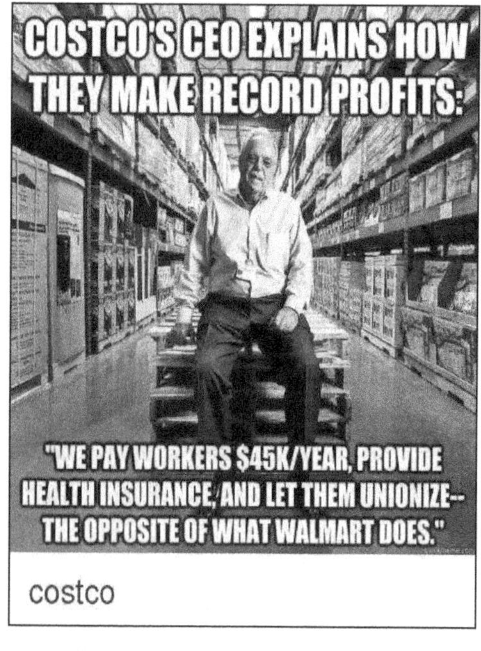
COSTCO'S CEO EXPLAINS HOW THEY MAKE RECORD PROFITS:
"WE PAY WORKERS $45K/YEAR, PROVIDE HEALTH INSURANCE, AND LET THEM UNIONIZE-- THE OPPOSITE OF WHAT WALMART DOES."
costco

2016
2019
I Will Eliminate The Federal Debt In 8 years
Increased The Federal Budget Deficit By 77%

This page was supposed to have 3 images from the cartoon strip, "The Far Side," by Gary Larson, but permission was denied. Otherwise you'd be seeing:

1. A scene with a man and son standing beside a large tree they had, evidently, just cut down with the saw on the ground. The father is pointing at the rings, saying, "And see this ring right here, Jimmy? … That's another time when the old fellow miraculously survived some forest fire."

2. A scene of 4 animals sitting on a log who show signs of injuries with bandages and a neck brace and crutch facing a bear who is missing half his harm and ostensibly giving them a pep talk, saying: "Listen. You want to be extinct? You want them to shoot and trap us into oblivion? … *We're* supposed to be the animals, so let's get back out there and *act* like it!"

3. A scene of a house on the edge of the forest in which a large pipe is flowing from the forest into the window of the home whereby some liquid is oozing out into the living room and the homeowner is standing there looking outraged and disgusted, while on the other end of the pipe in the woods two bears with hard hats appear to be monitoring the pipe. And the caption at top reads: "Animal Waste Management."

"It's not pollution that's harming the environment, but impurities in the air and water."

~ George W. Bush

Reality Check

From Carl Sagan's *Pale Blue Dot*, Random House N.Y. 1994:

[…] More of us flee from war, oppression, and famine today than at any other time in human history. As the earth's climate changes in the coming decades, there are likely to be far greater numbers of environmental refugees.

[…] From your alien orbital perspective, you can see that something has gone unmistakably wrong. The dominant organism, whoever they are—who have gone to so much trouble to rework the surface—are simultaneously destroying their ozone layer and their forests, eroding their topsoil, and performing massive, uncontrolled experiments on their planet's climate. Haven't they noticed what's happening? Are they oblivious to their fate? Are they unable to work together on behalf of the environment that sustains them all?

[…] Of course we must keep our planet habitable—not on a leisurely timescale of centuries or millennia, but urgently, on a timescale of decades or even years. This will involve changes in government, in industry, in ethics, in economics, and in religion.

[…] And so, due to the almost mythic powers of our technology (and the prevalence of short-term thinking), we are beginning—on continental and on planetary scales—to pose a danger to ourselves. Plainly, if these problems are to be solved, it will require many nations acting in concert over many years.

"Just like a sunbeam can't separate itself from the sun, and a wave can't separate itself from the ocean, we can't separate ourselves from one another [or the Earth]. We are all part of a vast sea of love, one indivisible divine mind."

~ Marianne Williamson

Pivot

Irony

It's another word for "comedy,"

Though, ironically, if not spotted out,

Too soon becomes monotony.

It's another word for "tragedy,"

But, ironically, once figured out,

At least provides us poetry.

It's another word for "duality,"

Because, ironically, we laugh and cry,

When mistakes collide with destiny.

There's no other word for "irony,"

Yet, ironically, once pointed out,

Can no longer arise unintentionally.

In the animal world it can't exist,

Since that would imply expectedness,

(Although I doubt we ever expected this).

Reality Check

If your child has asthma and it's getting worse, then news about the White House's recent retreat on ozone (that is, smog) standards for the air over your city wasn't exactly cause for cheering. Thank our environmental president for that, but mainly of course the Republicans, who have been out to kneecap the Environmental Protection Agency since the 2010 election results came in. We may be heading for an anything-blows environmental future, even though it couldn't be more logical to assume that whatever is allowed into the air will sooner or later end up in us.

With a helping hand from that invaluable website Environmental Health News, here's a little ladleful of examples from the chemical soup that could be not just your air, soil, or water, but you. It's only a few days' worth of news reports on what's in our environment and so, for better or mostly worse, in us: In Dallas-Ft. Worth, there's lead in the blood of children, thanks to leaded gasoline, banned decades ago, but still in the soil. In New York's Hudson River, "one of the largest toxic cleanups in U.S. history" (for PCBs in river sediments) is ongoing. Researchers now suspect that those chemicals, already linked to low birth weight, thyroid disease, and learning, memory, and immune system disorders," are also associated with to high blood pressure. Then there's mercury, that "potent neurotoxin that is especially dangerous to the developing brains of fetuses and children." If allowed, it will enter the environment via a proposed open-pit gold and copper mine to be built in Alaska near "one of the world's premier salmon fisheries."

And speaking of fish, there is ancient DDT, plus more modern PCBs and spilled oil in ocean sediments off California's Palos Verdes Peninsula, a toxic superfund site, whose cleanup is now being planned. And don't forget that uranium mill near Cañon City, Colorado, which "has the state's backing to permanently dispose of radioactive waste in its tailings ponds, despite state and independent reports over a 30-year period showing the ponds' liners leak." Or consider bisphenol-A, a chemical most of us now carry around in our bodies. It is used in the making of some plastic containers and "may cause behavior and emotional problems in young girls" according to a new study (as older studies indicated that it might affect "the brain development of fetuses and small children"). Or think about the drinking water tested recently by the University of Tennessee Center for Environmental Biotechnology from six of 11 Tennessee utilities statewide that "contained traces of 17 chemicals found in insect repellent, ibuprofen, detergents, a herbicide, hormones, and chemical compounds found in plastics." And that's just to dip a toe in polluted waters.

~ Chip Ward

♫ "What good is a used up world—and how could it be worth having?" [24]

If permission hadn't been denied, you'd be seeing an image of a cartoon child and his tiger looking with dismay at a tree stump surrounded by trash; the boy says, "Sometimes I think the surest sign that intelligent life exists elsewhere in the universe is that none of it has tried to contact us."

Reality Check

Tag!

Left to our own devices,
Two months of the year,
Our objective was decisive,
But our reasons never clear.

My backyard was auspicious,
Once the darkness had renewed;
And we never were suspicious
As our innocence pursued.

"How long until they find us?"
(The future was unstill.)
"Hope they don't 'never mind' us,
Then perhaps they never will."

Pivot

Ineffable

This poem is impossible…

But, then again,

Man's poetry is unstoppable.

Reality Check

A new friend of mine, Pauline, brought to my attention that which is the attitude of those under my zodiac sign. I'm making it my epitaph.

I feel it very aptly applies to me, but it seems foolish, to me, to presume it is not an attitude which we all share. I mean, wouldn't it be foolish not to subscribe to the notion that "It doesn't matter who wins or loses, as long as everyone has a good time?"

(Not that winning doesn't matter, per se: if it didn't, then games wouldn't be any fun.)

Several months after Pauline told me about my sign I met an astrologist who informed me that Sagittarians are flaky and philosophical. "Boy," I said, "if you only knew how much that makes sense of my entire life." (If I hadn't experienced "en spirit d'escalier," then I would have said something witty, instead.)

The other inscription I'd like on my tombstone….

BORN TO POET

A Poem

Instead of just having a point to convey,

I wish I had words to indulge,

This feeling within, so vaguely intense,

A poem cannot begin to divulge,

The gnawing impulse that won't go away,

Some need to get traction through thoughts on a page,

(Is it real or imagined?)

Our fear and our hope that we're all on a stage,

Is why we write poems, day after day,

Creating more reason to look up for fun,

May be part of the reason we've made it thus far,

Is to remind everyone that our star is the sun.

If we take light for granted, May after May,

Our poems and songs won't mean all that much,

When we don't know our fellows despite all the words,

We are left in the dark with no one to touch,

With no one to sleep with each Saturday,

We believe in the poems as something to hold,

But, like rumors and ice cream…

A Circle

A Circle

A Joke

This poem is a joke.

A Joke

Quality

This poem is written
With *Pirsig in mind,
To back up his claim
That it can't be defined,

Because it's not absolute,
So it can't be conclusive,
Because when something's abstract,
It's forever elusive.

But, if we use common sense,
It will always persist;
Though, in a formalized fashion,
It should not exist.

Yet, rhetorically speaking,
It is inherently square:
If you need to define it,
Then, you're just not aware, man,

That this poem has proven,
That you can't draw a line,
Between feeling and meaning,
So long as words can combine.

*Robert M. Pirsig, author of *Zen and the Art of Motorcycle Maintenance*

Pivot

And since I'm on the subject of quality I figure it's incumbent upon me to formulate a standard by which we can "definitively" measure, and thereby enhance, the quality in our art and culture. Otherwise we won't be able to prune out all of the poor quality that is polluting the spotlights. (We can't draw *the* line until we draw *a* line.)

Rules of thumb for creating and measuring quality (and whether something merits being broadly shared):

1. Ask yourself: "Is the work of enduring interest?"

2. Does the work's (potential) existence have any correlation to the creator's goal of survival?

3. How often has it been done?

4. [this line unintentionally left blank for no apparent reason]

5. Curb your curiosity.

6. Apply the time-machine test: If you could send a note to yourself in the past, would you tell yourself to not experience the work "again"?

7. Parents, it's your responsibility to direct your kids towards the higher caliber, more sophisticated material, and to restrict them from the wasteland.

8. Don't piss in the glass.

9. Don't be disingenuous. That is, don't necessarily let your ego fuel your creativity.

10. Leave them wanting more, as they say.

"Art is a great tester of the fake."

~ Sister Wendy Beckett

"When a form of 'art' is primarily personal, [as opposed to arising from the spirit and heart of mankind], it deserves to be treated as if it were a neurosis."

~ Carl Jung

When a form of "art" is primarily political, i.e., serving an agenda, it deserves to be treated as if it were reactionary.

"As soon as any art is pursued with a view of money, then farewell, in ninety-nine cases out of a hundred, all hope of genuine good work."

~ Samuel Butler

"When creativity becomes useful it is sucked into the vortex of commercialism, and when a thing becomes commercial, it becomes the enemy of man."

~ Arthur Miller

"If you're not breaking new ground, why even bother?"

~ James Cameron

"Definition of Culture: The effort to build a House of Life where man will be able to attain the highest development that his animal nature will permit, taking him ever further away from the jungle and the cave, and bringing him nearer to that humanistic society which under the name of Paradise, Elysium, Heaven, City of God, Millennium, has been the cravings of all good men these last four thousand years and more."

~ Bernard Berenson

"Civilizations collapse when the people lose their creativity."

~ Arnold Toynbee

Standards exist for a reason.

Reality Check

A Good Reason

I like to write poems,
But they've got to have sake;
If it's born of my ego,
Then that would be fake.

That is to say,
It shouldn't be easy;
If anyone could do it,
Then that would be cheesy.

It's been a long time
Since I last wrote in verse,
I've not been impulsed
To compose such a birth.

I know I've got talent,
It's come out before,
But without a true motive,
It comes out no more.

But as you can see,
I've finally found cause:
This poem is written
To get a girl to take pause.

We call ourselves "friends,"
And that's pretty great,
But more would be better,
So I'm deterring that fate.

I'm not talkin' marriage,
And 'till death do us part,
But at least for the moment,
On my sleeve there's my heart.

If you say that my motive
Is to get to first base,
Well, then I won't deny
That my thoughts are unchaste.

But in my defense,
That wasn't the prime,
That gave me a reason
To make a bona fide rhyme.

The reason of course,
After all of this while,
Was to harness my power,
And get Barbara to smile.

That girl Pauline whom I mentioned a few pages ago is a young woman that I met at a NY Cares bi-annual cleanup day. I was impressed by how genuine she was, but because of our age difference and her educational deficiency (her school never even taught her the Big Bang theory) I figured that I shouldn't expect any surprises from her. But on the second day of hanging out, she says to me, "You remind me of this story I just read for class about this guy, I forget his name. I think he was Plato's teacher."

"You mean Socrates?"

"Yeah, him. In this story an oracle tells him that he is the wisest man in the land, which he finds hard to believe. So he goes around to all of the men who are reputed to be wise to see if he can find fault with their wisdom; and it turned out that he really was the wisest man."

I was stunned. Retracing the only two times we had hung out I didn't recall any diatribe of mine really directed in the direction of debunking. Man, call me glass.

"Wow," I said. "I can't believe that you said that. Wait'll I show you what I wrote."

So I show it to her, and after only reading up to the moon analogy on page two she says, "It's not like we haven't all thought this before, but you actually wrote it down."

"Wow, you have no idea how perceptive that is. The first quote I lifted from *1984* is that same sentiment."

Anyway, for the time being she had to postpone further reading.

A couple of weeks later she asked me if I had ever tried marijuana. She said that she had twice, but it had no effect. So, we ended up having some, and when I asked her if she felt it, she says, "I don't know. I've got nothing to compare it to."

Man, that's essentially the same sentiment as the second quote I pulled from *1984*.

Well, after some more time hanging out she reveals to me a tremendous revelation: "Ya know, if I had met you six months ago, before starting college, I would've thought that you were just trying to show off how smart you are by a lot of the things you talk about. But now that I've been in school I can see that it's just what you talk about because it's stuff you know. Like how I knew about Socrates and the oracle."

Yes!

"That's great! Can you see now the difference? Now you're going, 'Oh, there's more.'"

"Yeah, actually, I didn't realize it until just now, but I'm not just more aware, but I'm aware of my new awareness."

The next level.

So, I went on to explain to her that that's exactly what *Reality Check* is an attempt to do: get everyone who hasn't had the opportunity to see what they're missing to understand that there's more.

Then she reminded me of the most important cliché of all:

KNOWING IS HALF THE BATTLE.

(A few days later I met her brother and asked him if he thought that a Utopian society was possible. Not only did he believe it possible, he didn't even hesitate in saying so. He defined a Utopian society simply as one that was non-reactionary. To illustrate the point he gave an example that was basically the same example I gave just before the moon analogy about the two black fellows I knew who wouldn't compromise space for white folks on the street.

"[....]And when the chain comes around to me, that's where it stops.")

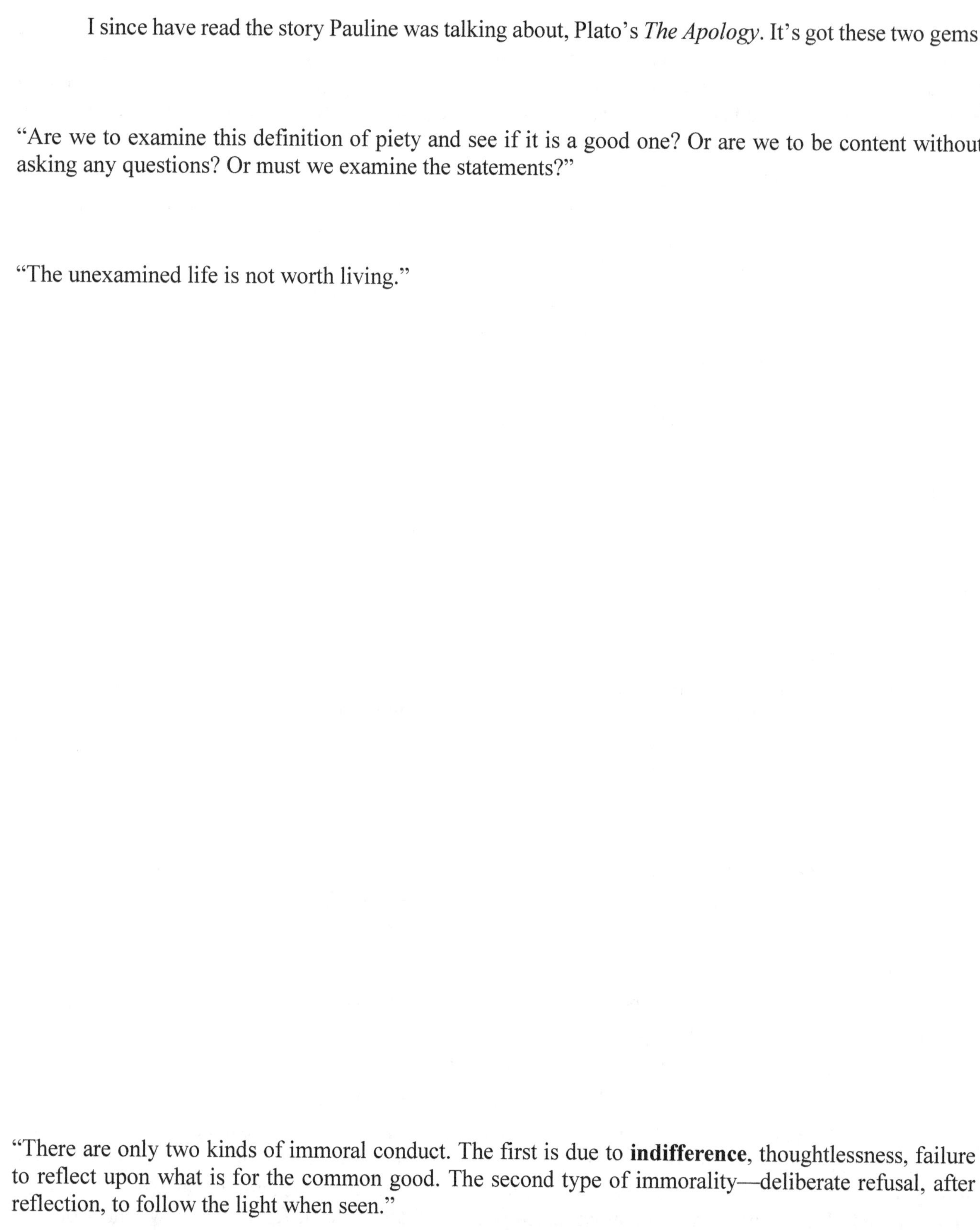

Reality Check

I since have read the story Pauline was talking about, Plato's *The Apology*. It's got these two gems:

"Are we to examine this definition of piety and see if it is a good one? Or are we to be content without asking any questions? Or must we examine the statements?"

"The unexamined life is not worth living."

"There are only two kinds of immoral conduct. The first is due to **indifference**, thoughtlessness, failure to reflect upon what is for the common good. The second type of immorality—deliberate refusal, after reflection, to follow the light when seen."

~ Robert Millikan

Just for fun one day I went to school with Pauline at her community college. In the first class that I attended the teacher, for no apparent reason, introduced me to the class as, "Our visitor. You're like that prophet, what's his name…Elijah."

After that was Pauline's sociology class, and, would you believe, on that day the teacher was explaining the differences between capitalism, democratic-socialism, and Soviet-style socialism. He asked the students to vote for which system they would like to live in. He then asked for volunteers to debate in the next class why they chose the system that they did.

I was the only one to vote for democratic-socialism.

Needless to say, I returned on Thursday.

The following text is what I learned to complement my theories for the ideal society. It's from Ian Robertson's *Sociology*. As I go through it I will point out the bunk.

Capitalism: In its **ideal** form capitalism contains two essential ingredients. The first is the deliberate pursuit of <u>personal</u> <u>profit</u> as the goal of economic activity. The second ingredient is <u>market</u> <u>competition</u> as the mechanism for determining what is produced at what price, and for *which* [emphasis added] consumers.

Why is the pursuit of profit and an atmosphere of unrestricted competition so necessary for capitalism? The theory [operative word] is that under these conditions, the market forces of supply and demand will ensure the production of the best possible products at the lowest possible price. The profit motive will provide the incentive for individual capitalists to produce the goods and services the public wants. Competition among capitalists will give the public the opportunity to compare the quality and price of goods, so that any producers who are inefficient or who charge excessive prices will be put out of business. The "invisible hand" of market forces thus ensures the greatest good for the entire society. [*Entire* society? When did those who got put out of business stop counting?] Efficient producers are rewarded with profits, and consumers get quality products at competitive prices. [This assumes that the consumer is wary enough to pursue with a long-term perspective to maximize resources, as opposed to the frivolous way we do it now by ignoring Mother Nature and the seventh generation.] For the system to work, however, there should ideally be a minimum of political interference in market forces. The government should therefore adopt a policy of <u>laissez-faire</u>, meaning, "leave it alone." [Yeah, really good idea to not impose restrictions on business. Left to their own devices I'm so sure that they'd seek to ensure employees' equity and respect for Mother Nature.]

However, in the United States at least, the federal government supervises much of the economic activity. [And it's no secret that they pay special attention to those businesses with the firmest handshakes; if you catch my drift (wink, wink, nudge, nudge).]

Modern American capitalism is thus unlike the classical model in many respects. It has certain drawbacks, too, [(gee, you don't say)], that are common to all capitalist systems: marked social inequality, a large and impoverished lower class, and repeated cycles of prosperity and recession, employment and unemployment. No capitalist society has yet found a way out of these dilemmas. [Why would they want a way out? They call that "ideal".] Nevertheless, for those who can afford them, American capitalism has certainly delivered the goods. With just over five percent of the world's population, the United States accounts for over 20 percent of its output. ["Nevertheless"?! "Delivered the goods"?! In other words, what they are saying is that you don't count unless you can afford to buy a ticket into the inhuman Monopoly game that is the epitome of BULLSHIT!!!]

Democratic-Socialism: In its ideal form, socialism also contains two essential ingredients: the fulfillment of <u>social needs</u> as the goal of economic activity, and reliance on <u>centralized planning</u> as the mechanism for determining what is produced, at what price, and for which consumers. Socialism thus rests on entirely different assumptions from those of capitalism. The pursuit of private profit is regarded as fundamentally immoral, because one person's profit is another person's loss, and the ultimate result of capitalism is social inequality. In addition, competition among different firms producing similar products is regarded as a waste of resources.

Socialism proposes that production should be designed to serve social needs, and whether it is profitable or not is of secondary importance. It is therefore necessary for the means of production to be taken into public ownership and run in the best interests of society as a whole. Similarly, the means of distribution of wealth must be publicly owned to ensure that goods and services flow to those who need them rather than only to those who can afford them. To this end, the government must regulate the economy in accordance with long-term national plans, and it must not hesitate to establish artificial price levels or to run important industries at a loss if necessary.

Soviet-Style Socialism: Soviet-style socialism exists in the Soviet Union and other communist nations. Although they are ruled by communist parties, they consider themselves to be in a stage of socialism, a preparatory step toward their true goal. That goal is **communism**, a hypothetical egalitarian political and economic system in which the means of production and distribution would be communally owned.

Since no communist society has ever existed, and since the writings of Marx and other advocates of communism are somewhat vague in their vision of one, it is not entirely clear what a communist society would look like. In general, however, it would have some of the characteristics of the communal ownership pattern that is currently found only in primitive societies. The role of the state would shrink, there would be an abundance of goods and services, people would no longer regard property as "private," and wealth and power would be shared in harmony by the community as a whole. Under socialism people are paid according to their work, but under communism individuals would contribute according to their abilities and receive according to their needs. The history of human alienation and strife would be over, and each person would be able to fulfill his or her human potential to the full. [Can we say "WOW!"] The major problem with such a society is that nobody seems to know quite how to arrive there. It is now clear that the Soviet Union and other communist-ruled societies are "stuck" in the socialist stage and have virtually no idea of how to get beyond it.

It is important to recognize that when Marx advocated communism, he had in mind the concept of communism outlined above, not the Soviet version of socialism. Much of the antagonism to Marxist thought in the United States stems from a confusion between Marx's ideas and contemporary Soviet practice. On the basis of his writings, however, it seems highly unlikely that Marx would have regarded modern Soviet society with much enthusiasm.

Pivot

After arguing for my society with the above ammo in conjunction with my own, most of the students still didn't go for it. The general points of contention were that, a) I was arguing for something that didn't and couldn't exist because it was ideal, b) capitalism promotes freedom, choice and opportunity and, c) "I don't want someone telling me that I can't be a doctor if society already has enough doctors."

Well: A) It's that kind of attitude that has kept it from existing. B) "freedom"? Where's my freedom if I can't go to the park at 3 a.m. and feel safe? And where's my freedom if I can't swim in the Hudson River? "Choice"? Yeah, don't you just feel so blessed to be able to say that you can choose from 352 kinds of toothpaste, more than one kind of cola, dozens of sugar-laden garbage for children's most important meal, and 500 channels of quality programming? "Opportunity"? Yeah, it's great to be able to have the opportunity to get the best education, healthcare, and justice that money can buy. C) so you're saying that you'd like to become a doctor even if you won't be needed?

I also pointed out that we need to examine where the line should be drawn between cost/profit and discretionary income. This can be done by categorizing professions/salaries in a hierarchy of the most productive at the top, and the most counterproductive at the bottom; a.k.a. prioritizing. For example, presently, C.E.O.s of major banks and insurance companies, and folks such as Wolf Blitzer and Matt Laur and Brian Williams and Drew Carey and Al Roker and David Letterman and Piers Morgan and Ryan Seacrest and Anderson Cooper and Glenn Fucking Beck and John Paulson and the Koch brothers are paid obscenely exorbitant salaries, yet their occupations add no actual value to the universe. Teachers, however, are obscenely underpaid, yet they're the most valuable resource that a society has.

To wit: "In 2009, the worst economic year for working people since the Great Depression, the top 25 hedge fund managers walked off with an average of $1 billion each. With the money those 25 people 'earned,' we could have hired 658,000 entry-level teachers. Those educators could have brought along over 13 million young people, assuming a class size of 20. That's some value. …The wealthy will have placed an estimated $2 trillion into hedge funds by the end of this year." Not to mention that in 2010 Goldman Sachs bankers received $15.3 billion in bonuses alone.

"**Waste**": any human activity which absorbs resources, but creates no value.

~ Taiichi Ohno

"What we want and what we need has been confused."

~ Michael Stipe

"We can have a democratic society or we can have a great concentrated wealth in the hands of a few. We cannot have both."

~ Justice Louis Brandeis

"Every empirical study of both historic and contemporary cultures finds that the 'leisure time' state of 'freedom' is enjoyed by only a very small class of people within the city/state: its economic and political rulers."

~ from Thom Hartmann's *The Last Days of Ancient Sunlight*

"Free enterprise and the market economy mean war; socialism and planned economy mean peace. We must plan our civilization or we must perish."

~ Harold Laski

"Capitalism….is not intelligent, it is not beautiful, it is not just, it is not virtuous—and it doesn't deliver the goods."

~ John Maynard Keynes

Reality Check

I thought that I should defer to a professional economist to further clarify the economic situation, but, on second thought, why would the average so-called economics expert side with me and common sense? After all, they believe in the G.D.P. as the definitive measure of prosperity, yet the minimum wage today is lower, in inflation-adjusted dollars, than in 1979. Not to mention that today's worker works 160 hours longer per year than 25 years ago. The G.D.P. also registers things like the Exxon-Valdeze oil spill and its cleanup as increasing the G.D.P.; and if a person takes a bicycle to work, but his neighbor takes a car, then the person in the car boosts the G.D.P. (while contributing to pollution and congestion).

So, I'll put it into a perspective that includes repercussions and consequences in the equation. Plus, I found the perfect analogy to underscore the potential backfire we're heading for.

In any system where energy is produced there must be an equal amount of energy being fed into the system, or else the system will eventually collapse. My representation of why the "trickle down" theory doesn't work is because two percent of the population has virtually all of the wealth (and most of that is literally virtual). That two percent is holding buckets and buckets of water. Sometimes a little bit trickles down to the rest of the 98%. Overall, though, since it takes money to make money, the buckets of water at the top perpetually get exponentially fuller and fuller, while the buckets at the bottom keep getting relatively emptier. (To wit: In 1980 CEOs made 42 times as much as workers, in 1990 they made 85 times as much, and in 2000 they made 531 times as much.)

The problem is that we look at every situation and ask, "What will be the (immediate and direct and numerically measurable) return on my investment?" Unfortunately, under the current system and mentality, there is little or no return in most areas where the money is needed, i.e., cleaning up the environment and changing systems that harm it, schools, parks, daycare centers, boys' and girls' clubs, and addressing poverty.

Well, money isn't going to protect you if farmers can't do their jobs because too much ultra-violet light is getting through the ozone holes. Money isn't going to protect you if the majority of children get neglected, and then grow up angry and without self-esteem, let alone direction and ethics. It's not that those who are rich necessarily did so surreptitiously and with willful disregard for the environment and the general welfare of others (though of course there is also a lot of that going around), but even though the affluent citizens may be technically entitled to their fortunes, we're all going to be feeling it just as badly as those at the bottom if there isn't a resurgence of generosity and community spirit. To actually make that resurgence materialize the investment strategy for the future would need to give up the front door approach of directly handing your leftover discretionary income to your children to guarantee they have money and, instead, realize that you'd be providing for their safety and survival more effectively by investing in the institutions that support posterity now. Because the only true protection from deranged madmen is to eliminate the circumstances that produce them. That means treating the world as if it were everyone's oyster.

I remember an after-school TV special about four high-schoolers from Nevada whose plane crashed in the desert on the way to a band conference. They survived the crash okay but needed to make it out of the unforgiving desert sun.

One guy who thought he was a big-shot know-it-all kept insisting that they conserve their water; save it for later. But the shy girl who happened to have done a report on survival in the desert said that it wasn't uncommon for people trapped in the dessert to utilize such a strategy. Nor was it uncommon for people to be found dead with lots of water left.

Several months after writing the last few pages I came across James A. Michener's new book, *This Noble Land—My Vision for America*. My first thought was, *boy, do I have a problem with that title. By what terms is he defining "noble"?* My handy-dandy electronic dictionary defines "noble" as: 1) illustrious; 2) aristocratic; 3) stately; 4) of outstanding character. Michener must be referring to the second definition—government in which the "nobles" or a privileged upper class rules.

On the back cover he writes that, "We are an outstanding success."

Last week I came across this notable quip: Someone once said to Voltaire, "Life's hard." Said Voltaire, "Compared to what?"

I didn't read Michener's whole book, but just skipped right to the chapter titled, "The Distribution of America's Wealth." I immediately knew that I would have to hit you over the head some more with the evidence from someone of his stature....

"The figures of inherited and accumulated wealth that I have listed at the beginning of this chapter are interesting and indicative of a major problem in our society, but even more meaningful to the average observer are the grotesque amounts of yearly income being acquired today by many of our nation's new millionaires.

"[....] In late June 1996 a study group at the University of Michigan, which has been conducting an ongoing analysis of how the wealth of America is distributed, released data proving conclusively that the rich families in America were indeed getting richer by the hour, while the people at the bottom of the economic ladder remained in dire poverty. More specifically, as reported by *The New York Times*, the Michigan data found that 'The most prosperous 10 percent of American households held 61.1 percent of the nation's wealth in 1989 and 66.8 percent in late 1994.'

"My own prediction based on the Michigan data is that year by year the discrepancy between rich and poor will grow wider until finally it will become intolerable. If my extrapolations are correct, I would expect that some time in the next century something will snap and there will be a violent upheaval. The grossly unequal distribution of wealth is felt most brutally in the family incomes of the very poor. The government's 1993 definition of the poverty level for a family of three is a family income of less than $11, 422 a year; in the United States in that year 15.1 percent of the nation's population fell below the official government poverty level. Only government intervention in the form of food stamps, rental allowances and aid for the children of deprived families enabled these very poor to continue to function even at a very low level.

"The plight of our very poor today is similar to what the dispossessed suffered in medieval Europe or what they experienced in Dickensian Britain a century and a half ago. We have made some progress in caring for our poor, but not nearly what a great industrial nation should have achieved.

"*Forbes* magazine, in its issue of November 21, 1994, revealed a nasty secret about how some of the very rich handle their wealth. The magazine listed six American multi-billionaires by name and business affiliation who had discovered a clever trick for avoiding taxes on the yearly income from their investments. A billion dollars prudently invested can yield many millions of income every year without invading the principal. According to *Forbes*, these six billionaires simply left the United States, legally renouncing their American citizenship, and enjoyed millions of dollars of tax-free income.

Reality Check

"Self-expatriation to avoid U.S. taxes on fortunes earned in the United States widens the gap between rich and poor, and sends a dangerous message to the less affluent, who often feel heavily burdened by the taxes that they conscientiously pay. Such an action is so offensive that I find it difficult to express the full extent of my condemnation. [i.e., THEY'RE OUGHT TO BE A GODAMN RETRO-FUCKING-ACTIVE LAW!!!]

"[…] It is preposterous that a national tax program should be so complicated that even an individual with an advanced college degree such as myself has no chance whatever of filing his own tax return and, therefore, has to hire an accountant.

"[…] Looking carefully at the distress of the very poor and the severe financial discomfort of many in the middle class, I regretfully conclude that these imbalances in income will continue in American life indefinitely. But we shall have to alleviate the problem one way or another.

"The United States can feed itself and much of the rest of the world using much less than 60 percent of our present farm workforce. And our manufacturing genius can, with no more than 60 percent of our present factory workers, provide all the consumer goods we need.

"For many years now I have pondered this almost insoluble problem, and no reasonable solution seems practical…and even now, sixty years later, I cannot think of a better way to support the unemployed, and neither can our nation's leaders. I would certainly regret seeing a gratis dole—that is, the indiscriminate distribution of unearned money—established in our country. But I need not worry—the general public would not allow it. [Right, God forbid that every child be guaranteed three good meals per day and a bicycle and all necessary healthcare.]

__"Recommendations__

1. We should immediately abandon our juvenile faith in the trickle-down theory, which preaches that if you structure your tax system so that a few fortunate people can grow very rich, out of the goodness of their hearts they will allow some of their wealth to trickle down to those less fortunate below.

2. We must remind our more affluent citizens that taxes are the contribution they must make to prevent revolution from below."

[I excluded 3-5.]

****

Capitalism is pure irony. The reason Michener can't find a reasonable solution is because he's attempting to find solutions within an unreasonable system. He's trying to solve the problem by thinking about it the usual way when a new way of thinking is needed. He's also just not looking in the right places.

If he wants alternatives he should consult with The Henry George School of Economics. There he will find the innovative and realistic single land tax theory that would be a great leveler of economic inequality. And I'll have to assume that he would condemn democratic-socialism since he neglects to include it in the discussion.

Without going much further into the benefits and intricacies of socialism let me just add that, to me, a large degree of the problem in our economic society stems from our general misconception of the institution of government. We seem to have the attitude that the government is a separate entity from the community; as if, for instance, our taxes don't go to the general welfare of all, but directly to the employees of the I.R.S. Or that The Post Office is a living creature out to get you, when in fact it is merely a collection of individuals trying to get the job done within a determined budget.

"We, the people of the United States, in order to form a more perfect Union, establish Justice, insure domestic Tranquility, provide for the common defence, promote the general Welfare, and secure the Blessings of Liberty to ourselves and our Posterity, do ordain and establish this Constitution for the United States of America."

Of course that's easier said than done, but it sure can't be done without being read, and then deeply examined; as well as being taken into consideration when determining all legislation.

What makes these ideals so difficult to achieve is that the government is not supposed to infringe on anyone's liberty, yet it is also supposed to protect everyone's liberty—and what is inherent in protecting one person's liberty is the restriction of another person's freedom. To achieve Justice between the two is to achieve **BALANCE** because freedom, inherently, cannot be absolute.

When courts make their rulings it always comes down to the question of, "What is constitutional?" And since what is constitutional should be what is just, they must weigh the potential restriction of one group's freedom versus the protection of another group's. And the pre-amble to the Constitution is what must be considered when trying to find that balance.

My 10th grade history teacher, Mr. Chaitoff, explained it very clearly with a cut and dried example: "The right to swing your fist stops at my nose." Granted that that scenario doesn't require great wisdom to know where freedom ends and justice begins, but, nonetheless, the principle applies to all situations.

One of the most common grounds for debate in America is the first amendment, which says that Congress is not allowed to abridge the freedom of speech. At face value that would mean that it would be unconstitutional for a law to restrict someone from yelling "fire!" in a crowded theatre (when there isn't actually a fire), yet, obviously, that would be akin to punching everyone in the theatre in the nose. The reason it *is* within the bounds of Congress to prohibit such an act of speech is because of Article I, Section 8—the Elastic clause: **"To make all Laws which shall be necessary and proper for carrying into Execution the foregoing Powers, and other powers vested by this Constitution in the Government of the United States. The Congress shall have Power To lay and collect Taxes, Duties, Imposts and Excises, to pay the Debts and provide for the common Defence and general Welfare of the United States; but all Duties, Imposts and Excises shall be uniform throughout the United States."** Which means, in part, that "Corporations are a creature of the law, and may be molded to any shape, or for any purpose, that the Legislature may deem most conducive for the general good." It also means that, according to Hamilton, "Every power vested in a government is, in its nature, sovereign, and includes, by force of the term 'necessary and proper,' a right to employ all the means requisite and fairly applicable to the ends of such power."

A current example of contention revolves around a Supreme Court ruling made in 1976 (*Buckley v. Valeo*) in which the court struck down the limits on citizens' expenditures towards politicians. They ruled that it would be an infringement on the First Amendment to set such limits. But, by the very nature of what it means to achieve balance, it should be clear that a ruling that allows for *unrestricted*…expression must inherently be lopsided, and, therefore, not balanced, nor just. Because, again, by definition, balance requires restriction, or limitation. Yet Sean Parnell of the Center for Competitive Politics would have us believe that, "Money enables free speech; and if you're going to limit the ability of money to be spent to promote political speech, then you are necessarily limiting political speech."

Actually, Sean, since it is called FREE speech one doesn't need any money for one's speech to be enabled. Hence, if we are going to limit the amount of money that can be spent on political speech, it does not necessarily limit political speech. It merely limits the medium by which (every)one can express it. Because if you really think about it, the right to not have our speech abridged refers to the content of our speech, not the medium by which we express it. And, if you think about it a little more, since Bill Gates et al. have no political spending limits on their speech the amount of speech that I have IS necessarily limited, by comparison. Moreover, thanks to highly duplicitous Supreme Court rulings, the right of so-called corporate personhoods to invoke constitutional protections has led to corporations overriding the protections that individuals are supposed to have. For example, although pleading guilty to causing deaths due to fraudulent marketing, pharmaceutical company Pfizer merely had to pay a steep fine—but nobody in the decision-making process actually had to go to jail the way normal citizens do when held accountable for murder, ironically.

Leaving the extreme nature of the ruling of *Buckley v. Valeo* aside, we might simply ask: Is it fair that a small minority of the citizens can afford to have a very direct influence in politics while the very large majority doesn't have such privileges?

Although not official documents of government, <u>The Federalist Papers</u>, penned by Alexander Hamilton, James Madison and John Jay, play an integral part in critiquing the complexity of achieving a free and just society amidst so many varying and conflicting interests. In Federalists No. 10 Madison points out that the disparate distribution of wealth, or property, inherent in society is a major reason for there arising parties with conflicting interests. He notes that the creation of an objective judiciary body to intervene between opposing factions is what is necessary to "secure the public good and private rights, against the danger of such powerful factions, and at the same time to preserve the spirit and the form of popular government." Simply put, this means that it is to be expected that some people will have more than others, and this will lead to struggles between the rich and the poor—and the rich will have the upper hand. The *point* of government is to act as an equalizer of sorts so that no one group can have too great of an advantage. Government's responsibility is to minimize such discrepancies; to "PROMOTE THE GENERAL WELFARE." And, although the "objective" judicial body required to act as mediator between conflicting interests is presumably wise enough to truly exhibit prudence there is no way to know which men are truly wise enough (or at least capable of feeling shame) to wield such authority. (To wit: the Wisconsin State Supreme Court and Clarence Thomas) Moreover, Madison points out, it is not possible for any man to truly act objectively and without bias since every man has his own interest at heart; most rulings extend to the entire society, which those same members of the judiciary belong to. This was the reason for setting up separate branches of government, in order that they would keep checks on each other. Unfortunately, all members of all three branches of government benefit from laws favoring those of wealth, so such partitions between the federal branches are often ineffective; just as was the case before the constitution was adopted: "…the public good is disregarded in the conflicts of rival parties; and measures are too often decided, not according to the rules of justice, and the rights of the minor party, but by the superior force of an interested and overbearing party." The only difference after the adoption of the Constitution is that the overbearing money-hoarding parties no longer need to resort to force since they are the ones to write the laws—so they write them in their own favor.

As the cliché goes, you can't buy happiness. After all, there are plenty of uber-rich who are unhappy, and vice versa. But, ALL OTHER THINGS BEING EQUAL, as a person's wealth goes up, so does his happiness. So, is it money that makes one potentially happier, or the opportunity it provides?

If I were told that I could never have access to money again and was asked what I would want to be provided to me in order to be happy, I would say that I want what is necessary to have fun in life. That would include the following: clothing for all kinds of weather and comfortable shelter for myself and my possessions. I would want to possess the usual amenities that most industrialized societies enjoy: a small assortment of art, access to a racquetball court and skiing locales, access to books and education, access to healthcare, access to healthy food, access to parks 24/7, adequate transportation, and the opportunity to feel useful and needed. And maybe some women if you don't mind.

"For over a hundred years," as Robert Bellah has written, "a large part of the American people, the middle class, has imagined that the virtual meaning of life lies in the acquisition of ever-increasing status, income, and authority, from which genuine freedom is supposed to come. We have committed what to the republican founders of our nation was the cardinal sin: we have put our own good, as individuals, as groups, as a nation, ahead of the common good. And if we are to transform this misguided approach we should, in the words of Christopher Jenck's, 'reduce the punishments of failure and rewards of success.'" Because the current system gives so much reason to be terrified of not succeeding that we are forced to strive for excess in order to achieve financial security, even if it means ignoring the consequences of pollution and the adulteration of children and the standards of culture. After all, the safety net we have for those who do not manage to assimilate to the culture of success is quite flimsy and narrow and callous.

"Reducing the rewards of ambition and our inordinate fears of ending up as losers would offer the possibility of great change in the meaning of work in our society and all that would go with such a change. To make a real difference, such a shift in rewards would have to be a part of a re-appropriation of the idea of vocation of calling, a return in a new way to the idea of work as a contribution to the good of all and not merely as a means to one's own advancement. Because when education becomes an instrument for individual careerism, it cannot provide either personal meaning or civic culture.

"It should be clear that we are not arguing that a few new twists in the organization of the economy would solve all our problems. It is true that a change in the meaning of work and relation of work and reward is at the heart of any recovery of our social ecology. But such a change involves a deep cultural, social, and even psychological transformation that is not to be brought about by expert fine tuning of economic institutions alone."

And the transformation that is needed is for everyone to recognize that just as a doctor can't say to someone, "Your heart is in very bad shape, but otherwise you're in very good health," the society and the economy and the government cannot be separated into individual compartments.

"The sum of the whole is greater than the sum of the parts." This means that a hundred people working collectively is infinitely more effective than 100 people working individually. The point of organizing a society/government is to organize the collective into a structure that will maximize the efficiency and output of the collection of individuals. The key to achieving our maximum potential is to consolidate corporations.

Robert Bellah eloquently expressed the essence of what I'm talking about in *Habits of the Heart: Individualism and Commitment in American Life* as regards to, "a recovery of older notions of the corporation. As Alan Trachtenberg has written: '…the assumption was widespread that a corporate charter was a privilege to be granted only by a special act of state legislature, and then for purposes clearly in the public interest.' Re-asserting the idea that incorporation is a concession of public authority to a private group in return for service to the public good, with effective public accountability, would change what is now called the 'social responsibility of the corporation' from its present status, where it is often a kind of public relations whipped cream decorating the corporate pudding, to a constitutive structural element in the corporation itself."

In essence, this transformation would mean that those who control the corporations would not be able to continue defrauding Americans as much as they can get away with to the point that Mark Zepezauer and Arthur Naiman had to document it in books such as *Take the Rich Off Welfare*. They would not have to document that "Back in the 1950's, U.S. corporations paid 31% of the federal government's general revenues. Today, they pay just 15%. If businesses paid taxes at the same rate that they did 40 years ago, the federal deficit would disappear overnight—and that's without eliminating a single direct subsidy or handout." Nor would they have to document that "between 1983 and 1989, 99% of the increase in Americans' wealth went to the top 20% of the population, and 62% of it went to the top 1% of the population (currently made up of families whose net worth is $2.35 million or more)." They would not have to document that, "$13 billion the Pentagon handed out to weapons contractors between 1985 and 1995 was simply 'lost.' Another $15 billion remains unaccounted for because of 'financial management troubles.'" I don't know about you, folks, but this is fantastic news. It means that all of our financial woes will be gone overnight once these people who are in control recognize that their thriftlessness is poor judgment. Talk about a reason to celebrate!

The next dozen pages are a bevy of chunks from other books addressing the economy, starting with Donald L. Barlett and James B. Steele's *America: Who Stole the Dream?* (also authors of *America: What Went Wrong?*). In one segment they bring to light that corporate Washington's "deception" has outdone itself so fantastically that it's literally beyond deception: they're so confident that they're not accountable that they don't think it necessary to conceal legislation that undeniably illustrates that business and politicians are ("secretly") in cahoots. The following is undeniable evidence of politicians directly being preferential; (this is only one glaring example among many): "If you pick up a copy of the Internal Revenue Code, you can read the custom-tailored tax law written for American International Group, Inc. It states, in part, that this section of the new tax law will apply to everyone except 'any controlled foreign corporation which on August 16, 1986, was a member of an affiliated group (as defined in section 1504(a) of the Internal Revenue Code of 1986 without regard to subsection (b)(3) thereof) which had as its common parent a corporation incorporated in Delaware on July 9, 1967, with executive offices in NY, NY...' A.I.G. was incorporated in Delaware on July 9, 1967 and had its executive offices in New York."

Welcome to the surreal world.

Here's what author, lawyer and civil rights activist, Scott Turrow, had to say on the matter of poverty within poor black communities during his visit with Charlie Rose on October 21, 1996:

"…to me, the watershed event was when Dr. King was killed and white people were essentially evicted from the Civil Rights movement. There were good reasons for that in 1968, and I'm not—I'm not quarreling with all of that. But I did what a lot of white people of conscience did, which is to say, 'Okay, it's black power and black concern and let's let the black community figure this out.' I don't pay attention. And in 1989, [I was hired to handle some law work in Chicago]. I began to do it and I was incredibly moved and horrified to see what had happened to the poorest black Americans because--. We—they—we have created in this country what I refer to a as a 'fourth world." It's the—not the third world, it's a life of poverty, anxiety, neglect, irresponsibility that exists within the midst of great plenty and it can't be called 'third world' because the—one of the most significant factors, when you talk about my observations of life in housing projects, is these people know that they are the measure by which more fortunate people say, you know, 'There but for the grace of God go I.' And so they live with a terrible sense that—of being downtrodden and disregarded in this society. And it's—it's shocking, the—what, you know, I experienced as a lawyer, what I've seen walking through Robert Taylor Homes and, certainly, what I've experienced more through reading. We have got to do something about that in this country and the 'we' is everybody.

"The first thing we have to do, in my view, is put aside the blame game. There is blame enough to go around for both sides. The black community's made mistakes; the white community's made mistakes. What we have to do is have a sense of common resolve. We have to focus hard on education. We have to get rid of, you know, the various politically correct taboos. You now, we've got to talk about the fact that a lot of discrimination in this country is based on the way people speak and we've got to give people— poor black kids a real option to learn to speak the way I do, a real option. If there are various political or personal reasons that they don't want to do that, then God bless them, but they've got to have the option to learn to speak the way I do because nobody else has been able to join the mainstream culture without doing that.

"…But the problem, of course, is that a minority jury, which is constantly victimized by [police misconduct], cannot dismiss that kind of conduct.

"[My book], *The Laws of Our Fathers*, is about the way race and the criminal justice system work together. Near the end of the book, one of the lawyers says, and it's not without point, you know, 'Well, I don't know what happened, but all I know is that the black guy is still in jail.' And, you know, there's sort of a continuing truth to that."

Notice that Mr. Turrow is alerting us to a fact that we needed to address a 1989 situation in 1996 and, even still, this discussion did nothing to mobilize us.

Reality Check

The same weekend that STAR WARS was re-released I discovered George Seldes' monumental work, *The Great Thoughts*. This awesome collection of quotes contains much wisdom. The introduction has the answer to beat all answers. The following excerpt is from Henry George's 1879 landmark work, *Progress and Poverty*:

"This association of poverty with progress is the great enigma of our time. It is the central fact from which spring industrial, social and political difficulties that perplex the world, and with which statesmanship and philanthropy and education grapple in vain…it is the riddle which the Sphinx of Fate puts to our civilization, and which not to answer is to be destroyed.

"So long as all the increased wealth which modern progress brings goes but to build up great fortunes, to increase luxury and make sharp the contrast between the House of Have and the House of Want, progress is not real and cannot be permanent…

"This then is the remedy for the unjust and unequal distribution of wealth in modern civilization, and for all the evils which rise from it:

"<u>We must make land common property</u>."

Also in the introduction was this gem by St. Ambrose:

"Nature has poured forth all things for the common use of all men. And God has ordained that all things should be produced that there might be food in common for all, and that the Earth should be the common possession of all. Nature created common rights, but usurpation has transformed them into private rights."

"In the Colonies, we issue our own paper money. It is called 'Colonial Scrip.' We issue it in proper proportion to make the goods pass easily from the producers to the consumers. In this manner, creating ourselves our own paper money, we control its purchasing power and have no interest to pay to no one. You see, a legitimate government can both spend and lend money into circulation, while banks can only lend significant amounts of their promissory bank notes, for they can neither give away nor spend but a tiny fraction of the money that the people need. Thus, when your bankers here in England place money in circulation, there is always a debt principal to be returned and usury to be paid. The result is that you have always too little credit in circulation to give the workers full employment. You do not have too many workers, you have too little money in circulation, and that which circulates, all bears the endless burden of unpayable debt and usury."

~ Benjamin Franklin

"The Government Accountability Office said 72 percent of all foreign corporations and about 57 percent of U.S. companies doing business in the United States paid no federal income taxes for at least one year between 1998 and 2005."

If the corporate-controlled media wasn't, then perhaps you would already know about the following travesty that Charles Kernaghan of the National Labor Committee documented regarding the deplorable conditions that unnecessarily persist for Haitians due to an imbalanced scale of distribution:

"<u>Crying Out in Disbelief</u>:

Prior to leaving for Haiti, I went to a Wal-Mart store on Long Island and purchased several Disney garments which had been made in Haiti. I showed these to the crowd of workers, who immediately recognized the clothing they made. Everyone pointed to the parts of the shirt that they had sewed while explaining what the quota was for those operations. I asked the L.V. Myles workers if they had any idea what these shirts—the ones they had made—sell for in the U.S. I held up a size 4 Pocahontas T-shirt. I showed them the Wal-Mart price tag indicating $10.97. But it was only when I translated the $10.97 into the local currency—178.26 gourdes—that, all at once, in unison, the workers screamed with shock, disbelief, anger and mixture of pain and sadness, as their eyes remained fixed on the Pocahontas shirt. People kept yelling, excited. They simply could not believe what they had heard. In a single day, they worked on hundreds of Disney shirts. Yet the sales price of just *one* shirt in the U.S. amounted to nearly 5 days of their wages! In fact, one production line of 20 workers assembles 1,000 Disney shirts in an eight hour period. In effect, each worker assembles 50 Disney shirts in a day, which at $10.97 each, would sell for a total of $548.50 in the U.S. For her eight hours work sewing these shirts, the L.V. Myles employee earns just $2.22! You can only imagine their shock."

"This, then, is held to be the duty of the man of wealth: First, to set an example of modest, un-ostentatious living; …to provide moderately for the immediate wants of those dependent upon him; and after doing so to consider all surplus revenues which come to him simply as trust funds, which he is called upon to administer…in the manner which, in his judgment, is best calculated to produce the most beneficial results for the community—the man of wealth thus becoming the mere agent and trustee for the poorer brethren."

~ Andrew Carnegie

"Owners of capital will stimulate the working class to buy more and more of expensive goods, houses and technology, pushing them to take more and more expensive credits, until their debt becomes unbearable. The unpaid debt will lead to bankruptcy of banks, which will have to be nationalized, and the State will have to take the road which will eventually lead to communism

~ Karl Marx

"'I did everything I was supposed to! I worked hard, studied hard, got into college. Now I'm unemployed, with no prospects, and $50 to $80,000.00 in debt.' These were kids who played by the rules, and were rewarded by a future of constant harassment, of being told they were worthless deadbeats by agents of those very financial institutions who—after having spectacularly failed to play by the rules, and crashing the world economy as a result, were saved and coddled by the government in all the ways that ordinary Americans such as themselves, equally spectacularly, were not."

~ David Graeber

Reality Check

Hank Paulson's Inside Jobs, by Felix Salmon

What on earth did Hank Paulson think his job was in the summer of 2008? As far as most of us were concerned, he was secretary of the US Treasury, answerable to the US people and to the president. But at the same time, in secret meetings, Paulson was hanging out with his old Goldman Sachs buddies, giving them invaluable information about what he was thinking in his new job.

The first news of this behavior came in October 2009, when Andrew Ross Sorkin revealed that Paulson had met with the entire board of Goldman Sachs in a Moscow hotel suite for an hour at the end of June 2008. He told them his views of the US and global economies, he previewed a market-moving speech he was about to give, and he even talked about the possibility that Lehman Brothers might blow up. Maybe it's not so surprising that Goldman Sachs turned out to be so well positioned when Lehman did indeed do just that a few months later.

Today we learn that the Goldman meeting in Moscow was not some kind of aberration. A few weeks later, on July 28, 2008, Paulson met with a who's who of the hedge-fund world in the headquarters of Eton Park Capital Management—a fund founded by former Goldman superstar Eric Mindich.

> The secretary, then 62, went on to describe a possible scenario for placing Fannie and Freddie into "conservatorship" — a government seizure designed to allow the firms to continue operations despite heavy losses in the mortgage markets…
>
> Paulson explained that under this scenario, the common stock of the two government-sponsored enterprises, or GSEs, would be effectively wiped out…
>
> The fund manager who described the meeting left after coffee and called his lawyer. The attorney's quick conclusion: Paulson's talk was material nonpublic information, and his client should immediately stop trading the shares of Washington- based Fannie and McLean, Virginia-based Freddie.

When we found out about the Moscow meeting, I asked how on earth Paulson thought such behavior was OK. But now I think he was downright pathological in giving inside information to his old Wall Street buddies. And the crazy thing is that we have no idea how many of these meetings there were, or how long they went on for — the only way that we ever find out about them is when reporters like Sorkin or Bloomberg's Richard Teitelbaum manage to find a source who was in the meeting and is willing to talk about what happened.

Given that it's taken two years since the release of Sorkin's book for the Eton Park meeting to be made public, it's fair to assume that there were other meetings, too — possibly many others. Paulson was giving inside tips to Wall Street in general, and to Goldman types in particular: exactly the kind of behavior that "Government Sachs" conspiracy theorists have been speculating about for years. Turns out, they were right.

Paulson, says Teitelbaum, "is now a distinguished senior fellow at the University of Chicago, where he's starting the Paulson Institute, a think tank focused on U.S.-Chinese relations". I'd take issue with the "distinguished" bit. Unless it means "distinguished by an astonishing black hole where his ethics ought to be".

Pivot

From Thom Hartmann's *Threshold*:

After George W. Bush rolled back the modest income tax increase of the Clinton years, and cut more than half the maximum income tax paid by people who "earn" their income by sitting around the pool waiting for the dividend of capital gains check to arrive in the mail (that tax rate, set in 2002, is still at the Bush maximum of 15 percent as of 2008), the September 20, 2005, issue of *Forbes* magazine noted that the combined worth of the Forbes 400 richest Americans went from $221 billion (combined) to more than $1.13 fucking trillion. Just from 2002 to 2005—the first three years of the Bush tax cuts—the number of millionaires in America went up 62 fucking percent.

The result is that in the first three years of the Bush tax cuts, the number of Americans who had to get food stamps just to feed their families jumped 49 percent, to more than 25.7 million people. (p.137)

Would it kill Leslie Stahl et al. to ask John Boener et al. the simple question: "What the fuck is wrong with you people?"

Millionaire Congressman Rep. John Fleming (R-LA) says he can't afford tax hike because he only has $400K left after "feeding my family."

Yes, these people are for real.

A sad letter from a realtor about banks and foreclosures by "doctor o" on Daily Kos

I was given the following letter by a friend who received it in the mail from a local real estate agent. I have redacted the names and places at the agent's request, but it is a powerful statement of why we were, at the time, Occupying Wall Street.

Oct. 20, 2011 Dear XXXXX:

The home at XXXXX was foreclosed upon on Oct. 4, 2011. I want to explain what happened in the 271 days that I had this property on the market as a short sale. A short sale is when there is more money owed on the home that it is worth.

I brought XXXX bank 17 offers over a 9 month period in which they turned them all down. I even had an all cash offer where a buyer said he would close in 7 days with no inspections. The bank's goal was to foreclose and wipe out the lender in second position. With the second gone, their profit margin is greater. The negotiator at XXXX bank made it quite clear that they do not concern themselves with what happens to property values in a neighborhood when they foreclose. It is strictly a numbers game to the guy sitting behind the desk.

The bank gave the listing to an agent in a city who has never sold a property in your county.

Sincerely,

XXXXXX   XXXXX Realtors

The home in question, which is now abandoned and for sale, was owned by a fully-employed surgeon who got into financial trouble when his wife died after a long and expensive illness and with probate, he missed some payments. He could have done a short sale and paid off the mortgage, but the bank - one of the nation's largest - saw an opportunity to profit from his loss. Now he is houseless as well as a widower.

To paraphrase John Malcovich's character from "In the Line of Fire":

START SHOWING ME SOME GOD-DAMN EMPATHY!!!

America's corporate tax obscenity, by Andrew Leonard

In 2010, Verizon reported an annual profit of nearly $12 billion. The statutory federal corporate income tax rate is 35 percent, so, theoretically, Verizon should have owed the IRS around $4.2 billion. Instead, according to figures compiled by the Center for Tax Justice, the company actually boasted a *negative tax liability* of $703 million. Verizon ended up making even more money *after* it calculated its taxes.

Verizon is hardly alone and isn't even close to being the worst offender. Perhaps most famously, General Electric raked in $10.5 billion in profit in 2010, yet ended up reporting $4.7 *billion* worth of negative taxes. The worst offender in 2010, as measured by its overall negative tax rate, was Pepco, the electricity utility that serves Washington, D.C. Pepco reported profits of $882 million in 2010, and negative taxes of $508 million — a negative tax rate of 57.6 percent.

Altogether, according to "Corporate Taxpayers & Corporate Tax Dodgers 2008-10," a blockbuster new report put together by the Citizens for Tax Justice and the Institute on Taxation and Economic Policy that will have you reaching for your hypertension medicine before you finish reading the third page: 37 of the United States' biggest corporations paid *zero* taxes in 2010. The list is a blue-chip roll call.

The "high taxation" lie

Reading through this report, you will find yourself seized by an irresistible desire to hurl yourself headlong into the nearest OccupyYourLocalCity protest. In an era of crushing government deficits and mass unemployment, corporate America is not only skating blissfully free of its civic responsibilities, but continues to complain that it is paying *too much* in taxes. Even worse: Congressional Republicans and many Democrats agree! Listening to our politicians talk, you would imagine that corporate America's neck is permanently under the tax man's steel-tipped boot. When, in fact, the exact opposite is the truth.

The list of companies that paid zero taxes is only the beginning of the travesties documented by the report. The authors looked at the tax filings from 2008-2010 of 280 of the nation's biggest, most successful corporations. These companies reported $1.4 trillion worth of profit during a period when most Americans were struggling to stay afloat. The authors discovered that the average *effective* tax rate — what the companies really paid after government subsidies, tax breaks and various tax dodges were taken into account — was only 18.5 percent, less than half the statutory rate. Fully a quarter of the 280 companies paid under 10 percent.

The most distressing part of the tale is the big picture: The overall trend line is pointed in exactly the wrong direction. If you break out just the years 2009-2010, the effective tax rate was 17.3 percent. "In 2008, 22 companies paid no federal income tax, and got $3.3 billion in tax rebates. In 2010, 37 companies paid no income tax, and got $7.8 billion in rebates." When measured as a percentage of total GDP, over the last three fiscal years, "Total corporate income tax payments fell to only 1.16 percent of the GDP … a new sustained record low since World War II."

> "Corporate taxes paid for more than a quarter of federal outlays in the 1950s and a fifth in the 1960s. They began to decline during the Nixon administration, yet even by the second half of the 1990s, corporate taxes still covered 11 percent of the cost of federal programs. But in fiscal 2010, corporate taxes paid for a mere 6 percent of the federal government's expenses."

How have these companies managed to cut their tax liabilities so far? The answer includes a mixture of targeted tax breaks that impact specific industries or companies, accounting games that corporations play with stock options, and sweeping adjustments to tax law such as changes in the rules in how companies can write off the value of depreciating equipment. The accounting rules for so-called accelerated depreciation are now so accommodating that companies can write off 75 percent of the cost of new equipment *immediately.*

A look at the list of the 10 corporations receiving the biggest tax-subsidy breaks from the U.S. government will defeat the ameliorating effects of *any* medication: Wells Fargo, AT&T, Verizon Communications, General Electric, International Business Machines, Exxon Mobil, Boeing, PNC Financial Services Group, Goldman Sachs Group, and Procter & Gamble. "56 percent of tax subsidies," write the authors, "went to four industries: financial, utilities, telecom, oil/gas/pipeline."

The companies that pay

However, not all companies are tax dodgers. Of the 280 companies analyzed by the authors of "Corporate Taxpayers & Corporate Tax Dodgers 2008-10," about 25 percent of the total paid close to the statutory rate, a little over 30 percent. But there's no rhyme or reason to who pays or who doesn't.

> "DuPont and Monsanto both produce chemicals. But over the 2008-10 period, Monsanto paid 22 percent of its profits in U.S. corporate income taxes, while DuPont actually paid a negative tax rate of –3.4 percent. Department store chain Macy's paid a three-year rate of 12.1 percent, while competing chain Nordstrom's paid 37.1 percent. In computer technology, Hewlett-Packard paid 3.7 of its three-year U.S. profits in federal income taxes, while Texas Instruments paid 33.5 percent. FedEx paid 0.9 percent over three years, while its competitor United Parcel Service paid 24.1 percent."

And that, ultimately, is the most enraging fact about the new report from the Citizens for Tax Justice and the Institute on Taxation and Economic Policy. It won't make a darn bit of difference.

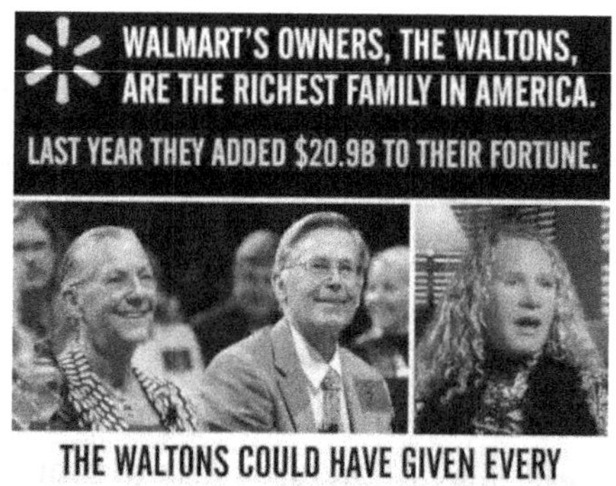

More Bank Chicanery: Double Charging on Escrow Fees, by Yves Smith

As we have reported repeatedly, based on independent reports from numerous consumer attorneys and investors, servicers engage in numerous forms of petty larceny which they pass off as "mistakes" when caught. The problem with this excuse is that servicers are set up to be highly routinized environments, so any reasonably widespread error is not a mistake, but policy. However, it is remarkably difficult for borrowers to get servicer internal records, even in litigation, and even then, borrowers need to incur considerable costs (as in hire an expert witness) to dispute the accuracy of the bank's charges.

Despite the general "missing in action" posture of bank regulators, one office has taken a tough stance of abuses, namely, the US Bankruptcy Trustee. A *New York Post* story by Catherine Curan reports that the Trustee is investigating double dipping in the New York City area by Wells Fargo and GMAC (now Ally). Borrower attorneys contend this practice is common at all servicers:

> Many homeowners opt to pay part of their property taxes and homeowners insurance with their mortgage every month. The funds are then put into an escrow account and used to periodically pay the taxes and insurance.
>
> But after falling behind on a few payments, troubled borrowers in Chapter 13 often find that their bank or mortgage servicer tries to collect twice on the escrow funds — once as part of the overall mortgage payment, and again as a separate "escrow shortage" charge. The average double charge is about $2,000, said forensic accountant Jay Patterson of Full Disclosure in Arkansas, who sees escrow issues in half the cases he examines.

The New York Post does a quick and dirty calculation and guesstimates that the level of overcharges could easily have been $180 million in 2011.

Now understand the asymmetry. $2000 is not chump change to most people, particularly people going through bankruptcy. Yet in aggregate, this scam over the last few years adds up to the billionish level over the last few years. The public has gotten so used to discussions of banks getting subsidies ranging in the trillions that a consumer scam in the upper hundred millions to something over a billion doesn't register as being significant, even though, by any other standard, that would be a very large consumer fraud.

And that is what the banks rely on, that their malfeasance is a bit too hairy to find and prove, and that it is way too costly for the parties damaged (borrowers and investors) to prove the abuse exists and beat it back. In many ways, this is close to a perfect crime.

As Senator Everett Dirksen allegedly said (apropos defense budgets), "A billion here, a billion there, and pretty soon you are talking real money."

Reality Check

"No to Oligarchy," by Senator Bernie Sanders

"While the middle class disappears, and poverty increases, the wealthiest people in our country are not only doing extremely well, they are using their wealth and political power to protect and expand their very privileged status at the expense of everyone else. This upper-crust of extremely wealthy families are hell-bent on destroying the democratic vision of a strong middle-class which has made the United States the envy of the world. In its place they are determined to create an oligarchy in which a small number of families control the economic and political life of our country.

"The 400 richest families in America, who saw their wealth increase by some $400 billion during the Bush years, have now accumulated $1.27 trillion in wealth. Four hundred families! During the last 15 years, while these enormously rich people became much richer their effective tax rates were slashed almost in half. While the highest paid 400 Americans had an average income of $345 million in 2007, as a result of Bush tax policy they now pay an effective tax rate of 16.6 percent, the lowest on record.

"Last year, the top 25 hedge fund managers made a combined $25 billion but because of tax policy their lobbyists helped write, they pay a lower effective tax rate than many teachers, nurses, and police officers. As a result of tax havens in the Cayman Islands, Bermuda and elsewhere, the wealthy and large corporations are evading some $100 billion a year in U.S. taxes. Warren Buffett, one of the richest people on earth, has often commented that he pays a lower effective tax rate than his secretary.

"But it's not just wealthy individuals who grotesquely manipulate the system for their benefit. It's the multi-national corporations they own and control. In 2009, Exxon Mobil, the most profitable corporation in history made $19 billion in profits and not only paid no federal income tax -- they actually received a $156 million refund from the government. In 2005, one out of every four large corporations in the United States paid no federal income taxes while earning $1.1 trillion in revenue.

"But, perhaps the most outrageous tax break given to multi-millionaires and billionaires happened this January when the estate tax, established in 1916, was repealed for one year as a result of President Bush's 2001 tax legislation. This tax applies only to the wealthiest three-tenths of 1 percent of our population. This is what Teddy Roosevelt, a leading proponent of the estate tax, said in 1910: 'The absence of effective state, and, especially, national restraint upon unfair money-getting has tended to create a small class of enormously wealthy and economically powerful men, whose chief object is to hold and increase their power. The prime need is to change the conditions which enable these men to accumulate power which is not for the general welfare that they should hold or exercise.... Therefore, I believe in a ... graduated inheritance tax on big fortunes, properly safeguarded against evasion and increasing rapidly in amount with the size of the estate.' And that's what we've had for the last 95 years -- until 2010.

"Today, not content with huge tax breaks on their income, not content with massive corporate tax loopholes, not content with trade laws enabling them to outsource the jobs of millions of American workers to low-wage countries and not content with tax havens around the world, the ruling elite and their lobbyists are working feverishly to either eliminate the estate tax or substantially lower it. If they are successful at wiping out the estate tax, as they came close to doing in 2006 with every Republican but two voting to do, it would increase the national debt by over $1 trillion during a 10-year period. At a time when we already have a $13 trillion debt, enormous unmet needs and the highest level of wealth inequality in the industrialized world, it is simply obscene to provide more tax breaks to multi-millionaires and billionaires."

If only Bernie would ask the disingenuous, destructive, depraved, dastardly, delusional, despicable, disgusting, dumb, dissembling, disastrous, demented, deleterious, demonic, deceitful, divisive, dangerous, deliciously-ridiculous, despair-inducing, devoid-of-shame, downright-evil, demonstrably-anti-democratic, detached-from-reality, definitively-inaccurate, dirtbag-esque, unfuckingbelievable Republican fucking dickheads why they claim that the United States is a Christian nation, yet all of their policies are antithetical to Jesus' teachings. One would think that it would be that easy to completely undermine any remaining credibility the Republicans have among their ill-informed supporters.

For example: Did you know that 157 countries offer paid maternity leave? …None of which is the United States. I wonder how the Corporatist Republicans would reconcile that with their version of Family Values.

But even more telling… "As promised, Senate Minority Leader Mitch McConnell (R-KY) this week introduced legislation proposing to make the budget-busting 2001 and 2003 Bush tax cuts permanent. The so-called Tax Hike Prevention Act wouldn't merely drain $3.9 trillion from the U.S. Treasury over the next decade. At a time of record income inequality, the Republicans' $700 billion windfall for the wealthy would virtually ensure a **perpetual income gap**.

Last month, the non-partisan Joint Committee on Taxation examined the impact of the Democratic proposal to let the Bush tax cuts of 2001 and 2003 lapse for just the top bracket households making over $250,000 year. "Taxpayers with income of more than $1 million for 2011 would still receive on average a tax cut of about $6,300 compared with what they would have paid under rates in effect until 2001," the *New York Times* reported, adding, "that compares, however, with the roughly $100,000 average tax cut that households with more than $1 million in income would receive under current rates." In words and pictures, *The Washington Post* explained the payday for the rich if the GOP gets its way:

New data from the nonpartisan Joint Committee on Taxation show that households earning more than $1 million a year would reap nearly $31 billion in tax breaks under the GOP plan in 2011, for an average tax cut per household of about $100,000.

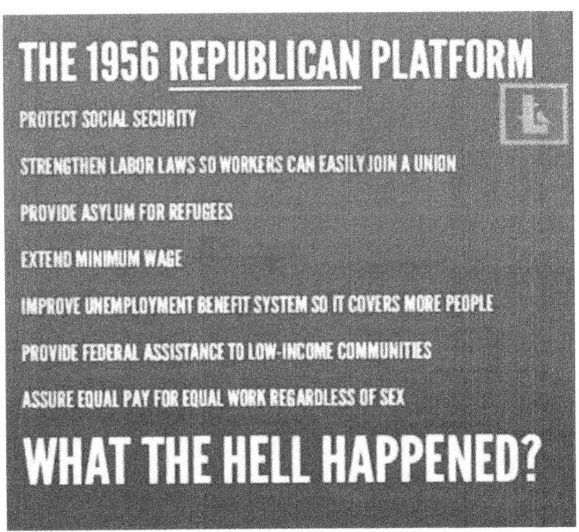

Reality Check

I'll spare you any details from David C. Korten's "devastating" book, *When Corporations Rule the World*. Suffice it to say, such a book exists. However, I can't afford to leave out a portion of John Ralston Saul's international bestseller The Unconscious Civilization, copyright 1995, "whose publication is widely regarded as a pivotal event." (I'll see your pivotal publication, and raise you, John.) …The title speaks for itself:

"The acceptance of corporatism causes us to deny and undermine the legitimacy of the individual as citizen in a democracy. The result of such a denial is a growing imbalance which leads to our adoration of self-interest and our denial of the public good. Corporatism is an ideology which claims rationality as its central quality. The overall effects on the individual are passivity and conformity in those areas which matter and non-conformism in those which don't.

"Economics as a prescriptive science is actually a minor area of speculative investigation. Econometrics, the statistical, narrow, unthinking, lower form of economics, is passive tinkering, less reliable and less useful than car mechanics. The only part of this domain which has some reliable utility is economic history, and it is being downgraded in most universities, even eliminated because, tied as it is to events, it is an unfortunate reminder of reality.

"Over the last quarter-century economics has raised itself to the level of a scientific profession and more or less foisted a Nobel Prize in its own honor onto the Nobel committee thanks to annual financing from a bank. Yet, over the same 25 years, economics has been spectacularly unsuccessful in its attempt to apply its models and theories to the reality of our civilization. It's not that the economists' advice hasn't been taken. It has, in great detail, with great reverence. And, in general, it has failed. [("I made a mistake in presuming that the self-interests of organisations, specifically banks and others, were such that they were best capable of protecting their own shareholders and their equity in the firms." -- Alan Greenspan.)]

"A 'profession' implies both real parameters and professionals who bear some responsibility for the effects of their advice. If economists were doctors, they would, today, be mired in malpractice suits.

"Many are surprised that this management elite continues to expand and prosper at a time when society as a whole is clearly blocked by a long-term economic crisis. There is no reason to be surprised. The reaction of sophisticated elites, when confronted by their own failure to lead society, is almost invariably the same.

"To be precise: we live in a corporatist society with soft pretensions to democracy.

"A simple test of our situation would involve examining the health of the public good. For example, there has never been so much money—actual money—disposable cash—in circulation as there is today. I am measuring this quantity both in absolute terms and on a per capita basis. Look at the growth of the banking industry and the even more explosive growth of the money markets.

"There has never been so much disposable money, yet there is no money for the public good. In a democracy this would not be the case, because the society would be centered, by general agreement, on disinterest. In a corporatist system there is never any money for the public good because the society is reduced to the sum of the interests. It is therefore limited to measurable self-interest.

"I would argue that confronting reality—no matter how negative and depressing the process—is the first step towards coming to terms with it.

"[It is] my right as a citizen—my Socratic right—to criticize, to reject conformity, passivity and inevitability.

"It is worth trying to do better."

To simplify: we've designed a system which allows inordinate amounts of wealth to be held in the private sector while the government is left with its hands tied to actually effect noticeable change because they've got hardly any money to pay for anything.

The point: THE HOARDING OF WEALTH DIRECTLY CONTRIBUTES TO THE DECAY OF SOCIETY. Anyone with the slightest understanding of economics knows that the foremost rule to a healthy economy, and society, is CIRCULATION. We all "know" this, yet those of you at the top two percent with all of the money and control seem to think that the rules of cause and effect don't apply to you.

But instant karma IS going to get you, eventually.

"Property is theft. Nobody owns anything. When you die, it stays here. I read about these billionaires: Sam Walton, 20 billion; Daniel Ludwig, 15 billion. They're both dead. They're gone, and the money is still here. It wasn't their money to begin with. Property is theft."

~ George Carlin

"He who dies with the most toys still dies."

"During the fifty years preceding 1914 a host of brilliant, eloquent, and desperate artists sought to wake the ruling European bourgeoisie out of its deadly lethargy. The bourgeoisie did not at first believe it was lethargic, because it was so busy making money. 'Making money is not heroic action!' cried the artists. 'Making money is boring you to death!'"

~ Charles Van Doren

"It was the end of the fifties, and most young people were disillusioned with what was called the Establishment. There seemed nothing to look forward to but affluence and more affluence. The Conservatives had just won their third election victory with the slogan, 'You've never had it so good.' I and most of my contemporaries were bored with life."

~ Stephen Hawking

"They debated the NAFTA trade bill for a long time; should we sign it or not? Either way, the people get fucked. Trade always exists for the traders. Anytime you hear businessmen debating 'which policy is better for America,' don't bend over."

~ George Carlin

Reality Check

Okay, here's my last section of borrowed material on the economy. It's from the February 1997 issue of *The Atlantic Monthly*. It's by George Soros, "one of the world's most prominent financiers," warning that "leaving social decisions to 'the market' poses a danger to society itself":

"Although I have made a fortune in the financial markets, I now fear that the untrammeled intensification of laissez-faire capitalism and the spread of market values into all areas of life is endangering our open and democratic society. The main enemy of the open society, I believe, is no longer the communist but the capitalist threat.

"I contend that an open society may also be threatened from the opposite direction—from excessive individualism. Too much competition and too little co-operation can cause intolerable inequities and instability.

"Insofar as there is a dominant belief in our society today, it is a belief in the magic of the marketplace. The doctrine of laissez-faire capitalism holds that the common good is best served by the uninhibited pursuit of self-interest. Unless it is tempered by the recognition of a common interest that ought to take precedence over particular interests, our present system—which, however, imperfect, qualifies as an open society—is liable to break down.

"[…] Yet laissez-faire ideology, I contend, is just as much a perversion of supposedly scientific verities as Marxism-Leninism is.

"The main scientific underpinning of the laissez-faire ideology is the theory that free and competitive markets bring supply and demand into equilibrium and thereby ensure the best allocation of resources. This is widely accepted as an eternal verity, and in a sense it is one. Economic theory is an axiomatic system: as long as the basic assumptions hold, the conclusions follow. But when we examine the assumptions closely, we find that they do not apply to the real world. As originally formulated, the theory of perfect competition—of the natural equilibrium of supply and demand—assumed perfect knowledge, homogeneous and easily divisible products, and a large enough number of market participants that no single participant could influence the market price.

"As I have shown elsewhere, the condition that supply and demand are independently given cannot be reconciled with reality, at least as far as the financial markets are concerned—and financial markets play a crucial role in the allocation of resources. Buyers and sellers in financial markets seek to discount a future that depends on their own decisions.

"In the absence of equilibrium, the contention that free markets lead to the optimum allocation of resources loses its justification. The supposedly scientific theory that has been used to validate it turns out to be an axiomatic structure whose conclusions are contained in its assumptions and are not necessarily supported by the empirical evidence. The resemblance to Marxism, which also claimed scientific status for its tenets, is too close for comfort.

"[…] Unsure of what they stand for, people increasingly rely on money as the criterion of value. What is more expensive is considered better. The value of a work of art can be judged by the price it fetches. People deserve respect and admiration because they are rich. What used to be a medium of exchange has usurped the place of fundamental values, reversing the relationship postulated by economic theory. What used to be professions have turned into businesses. The cult of success has replaced a belief in principles. Society has lost its anchor.

"By taking the conditions of supply and demand as given and declaring government intervention the ultimate evil, laissez-faire ideology has effectively banished income or wealth re-distribution. I can agree that all attempts at re-distribution interfere with the efficiency of the market, but it does not follow that no attempt should be made.

"[….]Wealth does not accumulate in the hands of its owners, and if there is no mechanism for re-distribution, the inequities can become intolerable.

"The laissez-faire argument against income re-distribution invokes the doctrine of the survival of the fittest. The argument is undercut by the fact that wealth is passed on by inheritance, and the second generation is rarely as fit as the first.

"In any case, there is something wrong with making the survival of the fittest a guiding principle of civilized society. This social Darwinism is based on an outmoded theory of evolution, just as the equilibrium theory in economics is taking its cue from Newtonian physics.

"[…] The main point I want to make clear is that co-operation is as much a part of the system as competition, and the slogan 'survival of the fittest' distorts this fact.

"As I have hinted earlier, the cult of success can become a source of instability in an open society, because it can undermine our sense of right and wrong. That is what is happening in our society today. Our sense of right and wrong is endangered by our pre-occupation with success, as measured by money. Anything goes, as long as you can get away with it."

TESTIFY!

Okay, I lied: the following are the last quotes regarding the economy to completely put into perspective how, literally, retarded our so-called priorities are:

"'The 358 billionaires on the planet listed by Forbes in 1994 had a combined net worth equal to the combined income of the bottom 45 percent of the world's population.'

"In other words, 358 people's net worth = 2,350,000,000 people's income."

And on the other hand…

"In 1985, the wealthiest five percent had net worth of $8 trillion. Today, the top five percent have net worth of $40 trillion. **The top five percent have gained more wealth than the whole human race had created prior to 1980."** (David Stockman, October, 2010)

Can we say:

Reality Check

What

the

fuck

Pivot

Once Upon

Once upon a rhyme,
In the land of filth and crime,
I saw a girl upon a bus,
And thought, *might be meant for us.*

Once upon a dime,
In the land of wasting time,
They used to leave it on the floor,
Then say, "We're too good for that—ignore."

Once upon a bridge,
In the land of sacrilege,
She left her heart upon the "Gate,"
And wished, "Hope he's not too late."

Once upon my mind,
Before a land of every kind,
I saw a couple holding hands,
And knew: that's where lovers land.

(Once upon the chance,
In our land of marching ants,
Can we afford to not be strong?
For if not...it won't be long.)

Once upon an end,
There comes the time to mend.
Let's grow up for once with all,
And shout, "There's enough for all!!"

Reality Check

Clockwise

1. Don't read this poem, yet,

2. Wait until I say "when."

3. I didn't say "when" yet.

4. Now, go on to line ten,

5. (Which has not been written, yet.)

6. Who would be the last one on time?

7. I wind up as the first

8. To work backwards a rhyme

9. That goes in reverse

10. With this final line

COUNTRY	RATIO OF PAY CEO VS. AVG WORKER
JAPAN	11:1
GERMANY	12:1
FRANCE	15:1
ITALY	20:1
CANADA	20:1
SOUTH AFRICA	21:1
BRITAIN	22:1
MEXICO	47:1
VENEZUELA	50:1
UNITED STATES	475:1

The truth will set you free.

Pivot

<u>The Ash Study on the Power of Individual and Group Opinion</u>:

"A study done in the 1950's by Solomon E. Ash, then a Professor of Psychology at Swarthmore College, investigated the power of individual and group opinion. His experiments were conducted at Swarthmore, Harvard's Laboratory of Social Relations, and at other universities.

"In 124 different experiments, groups of seven to nine male college students were shown sets of two large white cards, about 18" tall and a little wider, on which lines had been drawn. On one card a single vertical line appeared; on the second, three vertical lines of varying lengths, one line matching the length of the line on the other card, were presented to the group. The groups were asked to identify the line on the second card that matched the line on the first. Each group was shown 18 pairs of cards. The test was rigged; all group members but one (the subject) had been coached. In Part I of the experiment, the coached group members correctly identified the matching line about six times; in the other twelve cases they identified a line that did not match. In an average of 37% of the rigged instances, the subject, who went last or near last, also named the wrong line. Only 25% of the subjects held their opinion against the rest of the group. In Part II of the experiment, one of the coached members in each group broke by instruction from the majority and identified the matching line. Wrong choices by the uncoached subjects were then reduced by 75%. The study demonstrates that the opinion of the group, unless challenged, can suppress individual opinion; but that an individual who speaks the truth can change another's opinion, even if both remain in the minority. Speaking your mind does make a difference!"

Incidentally….

"The human faculties of perception, judgment, discriminative feeling, mental activity, and even moral preference are exercised only in making a choice. He who does anything because it is the custom makes no choice. He gains no practice either in discerning or in deserving what's best. The mental and moral, like the muscular, powers are improved only in being used. The faculties are called into no exercise by doing a thing merely because others do it, no more than by believing a thing only because others believe it. If the grounds of an opinion are not conclusive to the person's own reason, his reason cannot be strengthened, but is likely to be weakened, by his adopting it: and if the inducements to an act are not such as are contentious to his own feelings and character (where affection, or the rights of others are concerned), it is so much done toward rendering his feelings and character inert and torpid instead of active and energetic. How he lets the word, or his own portion of it, choose his plan of life for him is in no need of any other faculty than the ape-like one of imitation. He who chooses his plan for himself employs all his faculties. He must use observation to see, reasoning and judgment to foresee, activity to gather materials for decision, discrimination to decide, and when he has decided, firmness and self-control to hold to his deliberate decision."

~John Stuart Mill

Reality Check

One night, Pauline asked me a very good question.

She was a setting a dry leaf on fire, got burned and said "Ow!" Her question: "What do you think the world would be like if every time you did something bad, something bad happened to you?"

My reply, in effect: "That is exactly how the world works. The only difference, though, between doing bad things and then having bad things happen to you immediately like with fire, is that the fire we create by doing bad things often doesn't burn us until much, much later, so we are not aware that we are actually burning ourselves/each other. And even those of us who are aware of a thing called "long-term consequences" can't really stop perpetuating those consequences since we have only one system to survive in. And it is a system that was created a long time ago, inadvertently, to perpetuate long-term problems. And now that a long time has passed since the creation of this system, those long-term problems are finally catching up with us and becoming more and more evident.

"Now, if we want to survive, that system forces us to do one of two things, play by the rules and perpetuate our demise, or we can walk into another system. The latter choice is only theoretical, though, as there is no other system to walk into. Besides, even if there were, it would serve no purpose to join it since that system would still be within the larger system. So, when the larger system self destructs, it will take all of the others systems within it, as well.

"Oh, yeah, there is one other theory, actually, and that is to change the main system. For now it is only a theory that it can be done, because it hasn't yet been proven possible. I believe it is possible to create this hypothetical system."

Pauline then said, "I don't believe it's possible. You're wrong."

"Perhaps. But wouldn't you like me to prove you wrong?"

(Actually, to be honest, I didn't give such a long-winded answer. I merely said, "You know the phrase 'What goes around, comes around'?"

"Yeah."

"Well, look around.")

July 21, 1996

Pivot

January 2, 1997

A few weeks ago the television program "Politically Incorrect" moved to ABC, so now I can vicariously participate in its battle-royale discussions. I also happen to currently be involved in an ongoing correspondence with my Mormon friend Tim while he's on his mission. Between him, "Politically Incorrect" and a conversation I recently had with an A.C.L.U. lawyer while we were attending a rally on behalf of someone who was on death row, it's become evident that everyone's answers are absolute—yet everyone is in disagreement.

It was after last night's P.I. that this point became clear to me thanks to Dennis Miller's astute comment while they were discussing the death penalty. He really put a finger on why nothing ever gets resolved, and real progress is just a pipe dream. Dennis pointed out that everyone has their opinion on the matter, so it's kind of naïve of us to think that by batting back and forth our stances on the issue that the other guy is suddenly going to have some sort of epiphany and go, "'Hey! You convinced me! I'm wrong and you're right! You've made me see it the same way that you do!' In 10,000 years we'll all still be sitting here without having reached any sort of accord." (Dennis, the implication made in your recent *Playboy* interview was that it's doubtful we'll be here in ten years if we don't all agree to live or get off of the pot.)

In the first letter that Tim sent me after partially previewing *Reality Check* he acknowledged that he liked my ideas! And that what I've got written, "is a wonderful social commentary on society as a whole. Your plan calls for action. It deals with us taking charge of this world and solving problems. Your ideas can change people. Once properly organized, your work will become a permanent valuable work in the history of humanity."

Gosh, he sure sounds impressed; as if I've presented ideas which had not yet occurred to him.

He concludes the letter with, "I know all things pertaining to the point of life. I know why we are here, where we came from, and where we are going." He goes on to say that he knows these things because he relied on God for the answers. And he knows, "that these things are true because I <u>prayed to God sincerely, and he responded with a warm and peaceful feeling in my heart. HE WILL DO THE SAME FOR YOU!</u>" Several months later he writes that he "felt a burning in his bosom" when he prayed to God to confirm that his feelings were true. He also stated that "there is no such thing as reincarnation in any Jewish or Christian doctrine." …That last statement is easily disproved.

After witnessing Tim's absolute assurance and conviction about all these philosophical issues I requested he reconcile how some of my solid ideas conflicted with his notions, to explain why he's never written a book if he has all the answers, and to concede that, at the very least, he's never presented a solution to littering. But he's ignored my requests—yet he still continues to present himself as a pillar of credibility and correctness.

I asked the A.C.L.U. lawyer his opinion of censorship of pornography. He professed that censorship of pornography should absolutely not be permitted. Period. "If someone wants to display lewd, sexually explicit pictures on their suburban lawns [as you hypothesize], then, so be it—the neighborhood should simply ostracize them in order to get them to stop." (As if people who would do that would give a darn about scorn.) I asked him how one should explain the XXX signs and racy billboards to a child, if asked—or should we just hope that they don't ask? He didn't know. He suggested that maybe we should avoid those areas. (If it was left completely unrestricted, then I doubt that there would be any place in America left without it, except for maybe Utah.)

Reality Check

I'm not saying that I have a problem with his opinion because I disagree with him per se, but if he's not absolutely prepared to handle all sides of the coin then it doesn't seem as though he's justified in presenting any sort of absolute argument on any side without losing credibility.

With Tim I tried to force an open debate by asking him to admit that since there was disagreement, one of us, by the laws of logic, must be wrong—and that it could possibly be him. But he couldn't possibly admit to that, because it would be tantamount to "laughing in the face of God." Conceding that you are capable of making mistakes is blasphemy? Then how in God's name does He expect us to learn, let alone exhibit humility?

The point: by the very definition of the word "definitive," a claim of correctness and accuracy is malarkey as long as debate is necessary. Therefore, debating with a tone which implies the superior position is presumptuous.

Until everyone gets this then we're never going to have closure on anything. We're never going to apply the best answer in a consistent manner. So, if debate seems to be at an impasse, don't settle for agreeing to disagree. Roll up your sleeves and recognize that your current clarified argument is not clarified enough—and also acknowledge that you need to listen better. (Or, perhaps, pay anti-lefties to abide by certain rules to prevent them from debating unfairly, since they're otherwise incapable of not being disingenuous.)

Until a point reaches closure then it only remains a theory.

"Faced with a choice of changing one's mind or proving there is no need to, almost everyone gets busy with the proof."

~ John Kenneth Galbraith

P.S. #1: On April 26, 1998 I was looking through old letters and found one from Tim from July 25, 1995—five days into his mission: "Today I realize that nobody here knows who I am and what I am about, and I dare not reveal that I have an open mind, for fear that I would be sent home immediately. I don't confess to anything I've done or felt in the past. I suck it up and become mindless for the good of the whole." (L O L)

I Couldn't Have Said It Better

It behooves me to go overboard and take a moment to extensively quote from George Carlin's book, *Brain Droppings.* (Wait'll Uncle George gets a load of me.)

"The reason they call it the American Dream is because you have to be asleep to believe it."

"The news media are not independent; they are a sort of bulletin board and public relations firm for the ruling class—the people who run things. Those who decide what news you will or will not hear are paid by, and tolerated purely at the whim of, those who hold economic power. If the parent corporation doesn't want you to know something, it will be slanted to suit them, and then barely followed up."

"I have as much authority as the Pope. I just don't have as many people who believe it."

Regarding the alteration of language, George attempts to set the record straight on how certain items aren't being properly used, but then acknowledges that some people's attitudes are, "Well, many people are using it that way, so the meaning is changing." And he says, "Well, many people don't know what the hell they're talking about, too, so should we just adopt all of their standards?"

"Conservatives say if you don't give the rich more money, they will lose their incentive to invest. As for the poor, they tell us they've lost all incentive because we've given them too much money."

"What's all this stuff about retirement I keep hearing on TV commercials? People planning, saving; they can't wait to retire. One woman on TV says to her husband, 'At this rate, Jeff, we'll never be able to retire!' What is this all about? Why would someone spend his whole life doing something he can't wait to get away from?"

"What exactly is 'viewer discretion'? If viewers had discretion, most television shows would not be on the air."

"OUR ONLY HOPE IS INSANE LEADERSHIP"

"The extended hand of Adam Smith's seems to offer an extended middle finger to an awful lot of people."

"People should not get credit for having qualities they're supposed to have. Like honesty. What's the big deal, anyway? You're *supposed* to be honest."

"I think people have a lot of nerve locking up a tiger and charging four dollars to let a few thousand humans shuffle past him every day. What a shitty thing to do. Probably the only reason there are any tigers left is because they don't taste good."

"Each year, Americans eat 38 billion hamburgers. It takes 2,500 gallons of water to produce one pound of red meat. Cattle consume one half of all the fresh water consumed on earth. The sixty million people who will starve this year could be adequately fed if Americans reduced their meat intake by just 10 percent."

Reality Check

"Why don't we teach courses in how to be responsible, or how to be married, or how to be a good parent, or, at the very least, how to be a reasonably honorable human being? Unfortunately, such courses will never be taught, because the information gleaned would have no application in real life."

"What bothers me is all this crap about children being 'our future.' So, what's new? Children have always, technically, represented our future. But what does that mean? What is so important about knowing that children are our future? Life as it is right now—today's reality in this country—the people lying on the streets and park benches, living in the dysfunctional homes, the prisons, and the mental institutions, the addicts and drunks and neurotic shoppers, these people were all once children described as 'our future.' So, this is it, folks. This is what the system produces. The adults you see today are what kids become. Is anything really going to make it any different? To me, they're just another crop of kids waiting to become wage slaves and good little consumers. You know what I see when I look at today's kids? Tomorrow's fucked-up adults."

With that being said, now would probably be the right place to bring to everyone's attention the condition humanity is currently experiencing:

Learned Helplessness: a condition that occurs when someone becomes accustomed to things that they try to change, but see no affect, and stoicism develops.

(**stoicism**: lack of emotional responsiveness)

P.S. For lack of a better place to place something important…

"The same acre of land that would produce 250 pounds of beef would produce 40,000 pounds of potatoes—roughly the difference between feeding one person, and 160 persons!"

SLOWPOKE
©2011 Jen Sorensen
THE GOP REFUSES TO COMPROMISE ON THE DEBT CEILING
GIVE ME TAX BREAKS ON PRIVATE JETS OR GIVE ME DEATH!
WHAT OTHER THREATS MIGHT BE NEXT?

HEALTH CARE FOR POOR CHILDREN AXED UNTIL PASSAGE OF A PLASTIC SURGERY TAX CREDIT
I MUST KEEP MY FACE WRINKLE-FREE, DAHLING, OR AMERICA WILL LOSE JOBS!

NO MORE MONEY FOR AIR TRAFFIC CONTROL UNTIL BILLIONAIRE PLAYBOYS CAN WRITE OFF THEIR JOYRIDES INTO SPACE
WHEEE!
KA-BOOM!
LOOK AT ALL THE CHAOS THE DEMOCRATS HAVE CAUSED!

FUNDING FOR THE CORONER'S OFFICE STOPS UNTIL THE LOCAL COUNTRY CLUB CAN EMPLOY SLAVE LABOR
I HOPE THIS STANDOFF ENDS SOON!
I HAVE TO PAY FOR A CADDY AND THERE ARE CORPSES ALL OVER THE COURSE!

THE F-35 PROJECT WILL COST $1.35 TRILLION
NAVY
F-35
BUT TUITION FREE COLLEGE "COSTS TOO MUCH MONEY"
Bernie

Reality Check

A couple of days ago, Nov. 15, 1996, I received a letter from Marah. She recently finished reading *Reality Check* in its entirety and seems to think that it's not powerful enough despite how powerful it is—it's "mostly logic and words:

"[...]You seriously underestimate—at the same time that you are emphasizing it—the power of selfishness in determining human behavior. Most people are willing to philosophize on a larger scale for an hour or two about the sad state of the world, and most would probably agree with you that they would be happier if they started implementing some of your suggestions. But *Reality Check* proposes grand-scale disruption to the Average Selfish Joe's comfort and security without offering the sort of incentive for change that would appeal to him.

"Example: You say to Average Selfish Joe:

> "'You are living in a life of hypocrisy and perpetuating the legacy of falseness and lack of concern for others that has been handed down to you. Ironically, your insecurity and fears are directly attributable to this behavior. If you changed your behavior, you would be happier and the world would be a better place.'

"You then go on to back up your claims with incontrovertible proof that such is indeed the case. I think you do this quite well. Average Selfish Joe probably agrees that your claims are quite just, feels a bit guilty, maybe even tries to put some of these things into effect, tries—for a few days—to change. But very quickly—bored, after seeing little immediate result—Joe starts thinking, 'Well, my life and attitude may not be the best, but it's not as though I were a serial killer or something…I do the best I can,' and lapses back into the old ways. Now, [Pivot], I *know* that you specifically address this attitude of 'I'm only human,' but just reading your words is not going to be enough to change the Average Selfish Joe over the long-term. People only change when they have really hit rock bottom. No one is going to force themselves to completely alter their comfortable, familiar attitudes and behavior as long as some alternative exists, even if the alternative means living a less-than-fulfilling and, perhaps, unhappy life. *That's* how lazy and selfish most people are and you can't change that with logically-sound arguments, no matter how persuasive they may be. The only thing I can think of that might inspire a person to change is *true* fear: fear of being killed if they don't render their behavior in conformity with what is required, or fear of eternal damnation. (This is why Christianity is so effective.) Your work doesn't present a *personally* terrifying scenario of what will happen if the reader ignores your arguments; instead it relies on a broader, more general, fear that is only mildly disturbing to your Average Selfish Joe. It's like the destruction of the ozone layer: if true, this means the ultimate death of the planet. But the average person would be more likely to modify their behavior in order to get a boyfriend/girlfriend than to do so in order to preserve the ozone. No one can see beyond their own tiny little realm, and you need to take that into account."

(Oh, ye of little faith…) (And this is coming from the person who said back in March, before Part III even existed, "I find the second half very moving, and really quite inspirational. I really have tried to change my behavior for the better as a result of reading your work.")

Gee, if I knew that I was this naïve before I started this, then I wouldn't have.

First of all, she's not taking into account that Average Selfish Joe is outnumbered by Average Altruistic Joe. Also, I'm sure that when I and the rest of the visionaries on the planet put our heads together we'll be able to offer plenty of incentive. The transition doesn't necessarily have to entail great sacrifice if we adopt ideas from the likes of Paul Hawken's, author of *Natural Capitalism*. Also, Average Selfish Joe is outnumbered tremendously by many who *have* hit rock bottom, either through their own mistakes or the bullshit that the government/corporations have put upon them.

At any rate, grand-scale disruption is going to happen whether we implement it or not. If we choose not to do so voluntarily…

As for her other advice, well, since she insists, below are two choice quotes from two very different sources to accommodate Marah's suggestion:

From a Kabbalah class I took:

"Basically, you have two choices when you play the game of life. You can play it kicking, screaming and complaining, or you can play it for all it's worth. Here's the secret. God has His hand out to you all the time. All you've got to do is reach out, hold on, and your next move to the next space on the board will be painless, pleasurable and filled with certainty and joy. If you choose not, God will push you from behind. That can prove to be very painful and distressing. It's your choice, be held or be pushed; but be assured of one thing, move forward you shall.

"Enjoy the game."

Convinced? Okay, that was a tad compelling, perhaps, but not particularly scary. Maybe this will do the trick: "The path of the righteous man is beset on all sides by the inequities of the *selfish* and the tyranny of evil men!! Blessed is he who in the name of *charity* and ***good will*** shepherds the weak through the valley of darkness, for **he** is *TRULY* his brother's keeper and the finder of lost children!!

"And I will strike down upon thee with GREAT VENGEANCE and ***FURIOUS*** **ANGER** those who attempt to *poison* and ***DESTROY* MY BROTHERS!** And you will **know** my name is **THE *LORD*** when **I LAY MY VENGEANCE UPON THEE!!!**"

It's a lot scarier live; (with a large gun being waved in your face).

"Besides concealing the misdeeds of rulers, the doctrine that you can't change human nature has a larger purpose: defense of the existing social arrangements. Since these arrangements are, throughout most of the world, capitalist in character, the doctrine undertakes to show that, human nature being what it is, capitalism is the inevitable form of society."

~ Barrows Duncan

A group of elderly, retired men gathers each morning at a café in Tel Aviv. They drink their coffee and sit for hours discussing the world situation. Given the state of the world, their talks usually are depressing. One day, one of the men startles the others by announcing, "You know what? I'm an optimist."

The others are shocked, but then one of them notices something fishy. "Wait a minute! If you're an optimist, why do you look so worried?"

Reality Check

"You think it's easy to be an optimist?"

The Age of Anxiety

We would rather be ruined than changed

We would rather die in our dread

Than climb the cross of the moment

And let our illusions die.

~ W.H. Auden

"Living in A Bubble Is No Way To Live."
Posted by MineralMan Sun Jan 31st, 2010, 02:54 PM

My Sunday trip to the supermarket brought up something I've noticed for a long time, so I'm going to write about it just a little.

Looking around at the people near me as I shopped convinced me, once again, that most people live their lives in little bubbles. Inside their bubble, they are the most important people on the planet, and they seem unaware of all the other people around them. I can find no other explanation for the behavior I see again and again. For every person I encounter who makes eye contact and smiles, there are 20 who see nothing at all and act accordingly.

Today, the woman who parked her cart in the middle of the aisle and then wandered off to go to another aisle to find something, was an example. Another was the family of five who were shopping together and walking abreast through the entire store. I had to avoid them three times on this trip alone. Then, there's the guy who was entering the store just ahead of me who stopped just inside the automatic door to pull out his shopping list and study it, completely blocking the entrance. My "Excuse me, please..." got a glaring look from this one.

And it's not just the supermarket. The person driving their car down the middle of a residential street who does not move over to the right when encountering another car approaching is also in the bubble. The person who pulls into the gas station's empty lane and doesn't pull forward to the last pump is another. The driver who stares straight ahead and never consults the mirror and ignores the traffic merging from the on ramp is still another. The guy who carelessly parks halfway into the next space in a busy parking lot, or who pull into a space someone is clearly waiting for, is yet another example.

You see it at the movie theater, when people insist on two seats for themselves, piling their worldly goods on the seat next to them in a crowded theater, then being offended if you and your partner want to sit together in that and the adjacent seat. "Excuse me, but would you mind moving your things so we can sit here?" brings a harsh look or a "Fuck you." I understand when people want an aisle seat at the theater, but must they just sit there, unmoving, when others want to enter the row?

We appear, as a culture, to have forsaken our responsibility to be aware of our surroundings and assess the impact of our actions on others who share our space in public. Not everyone, of course, does this, but enough do that things slow down to an unacceptable level as we must go around, take another route, or beg permission to occupy space and move through life.

I could give examples of this bubble life for hours, and I'm sure most of us here could do the same. How do we make contact with the bubble people? How do we let them know that awareness is part of politeness? How do we move toward a more polite society if we cannot even contact those who live in their bubble world? I try very hard to always be aware of everyone and everything around me, and usually resist an angry response to those who do not. But politely asking people to behave as though they were not the only person on the planet often brings an imprecation rather than an "Excuse me." What can we do?

NEVER FORGET
SEPTEMBER 10, 2001
DONALD RUMSFIELD HOLDS A PRESS CONFERENCE
TO STATE THAT THE PENTAGON WAS MISSING
$2.3 TRILLION
BUT THE NEXT DAY SOMETHING HAPPENED AND
EVERYBODY FORGOT ABOUT THIS

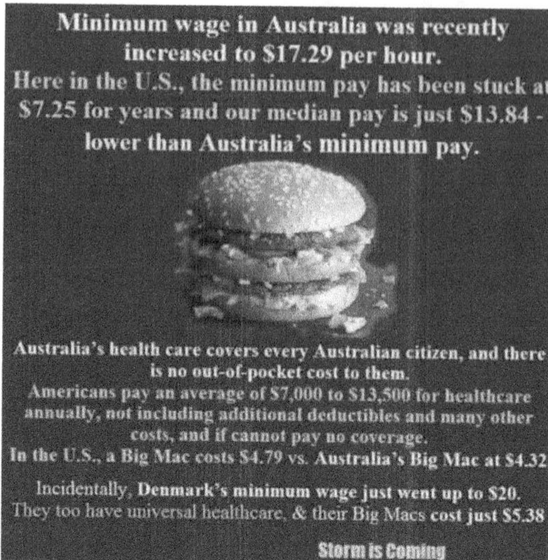
Minimum wage in Australia was recently increased to $17.29 per hour.
Here in the U.S., the minimum pay has been stuck at $7.25 for years and our median pay is just $13.84 - lower than Australia's minimum pay.
Australia's health care covers every Australian citizen, and there is no out-of-pocket cost to them.
Americans pay an average of $7,000 to $13,500 for healthcare annually, not including additional deductibles and many other costs, and if cannot pay no coverage.
In the U.S., a Big Mac costs $4.79 vs. Australia's Big Mac at $4.32
Incidentally, Denmark's minimum wage just went up to $20. They too have universal healthcare, & their Big Macs cost just $5.38
Storm is Coming

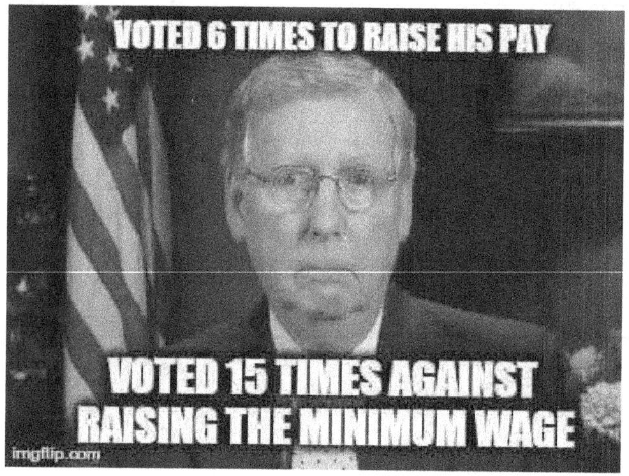
VOTED 6 TIMES TO RAISE HIS PAY
VOTED 15 TIMES AGAINST RAISING THE MINIMUM WAGE
imgflip.com

IF YOU THINK THIS COUNTRY IS GOING BROKE TAKING CARE OF THE POOR, YOU SHOULD SEE HOW MUCH IT SPENDS TAKING CARE OF THE RICH
$59 BILLION*
$92 BILLION*
SOCIAL WELFARE PROGRAMS
CORPORATE SUBSIDIES
*per year - http://thinkbynumbers.org/
Other98

Pivot

It occurred to me that even if aliens *had* granted me Superman's powers, it really wouldn't have made much of a difference. I mean, having the power to humiliate and forever imprison Bush, Cheney and Rumsfeld, et al.—and the five monstrous Supreme Court Justices responsible for turning America into a banana republic—would rock like nothing has ever rocked before, but Superman isn't immortal, so he doesn't live forever. So, once he's gone the problems will just resume at their normal pace. Plus, as I said earlier, once someone fires a gun, then the damage is already done, even if Superman were to snag the bullet.

Most of you probably didn't see the movie *Superman IV: The Quest for Peace*—because it stunk, big time. It was so lame that it made me embarrassed to be alive. I mention it, though, because I suspect that the person behind the premise of the movie also realized that even an army of Supermen couldn't solve all of the world's problems since it would be beyond even their means to hug all of the neglected children in the world. And all of the hugging in the world wouldn't make up for all of the affection that many adults didn't get as children. Right? (Especially with all of the "Mexican Jokers" to come.)

In *Superman IV* Superman goes on a crusade to personally rid the world of all the nuclear weapons by collecting them all and sending them into space. The whole movie was infantile and sappy. And, anyway, Superman failed. For better or for worse, though, I guess it is only fair that we acknowledge the person who wrote the important part of the movie. So, please, stand and take a bow for your heartfelt attempt to create world peace just by making a movie. (It seems, ladies and gentlemen, that our friend isn't going to be able to get up from his seat at the moment of this writing, but that's okay, because I'm sure that we can all wait as long as it takes for

Reality Check

Christopher Reeve.)

     "Golly, Mr. Kent, Superman's speech to the world sure was touching. He almost made me believe that just by saying a few words he could actually make it happen. Maybe if everyone really listened to him, then it *would* happen. If only he could find a way to get everybody to *listen*!"

     "Well, ya know, Jimmy, that's the beauty of the human language. Even if people don't hear your words the first time, they can always be repeated. Our bodies may have a time span, but our speeches are immortal. And I'm sure that someday there'll be another chance for the world to hear what Superman had to say."

To summarize:

     At the beginning of the movie, Superman was uncertain if he should attempt to get rid of the world's nuclear weapons, so he sought the advice of the ghostly elders from Krypton....

     "I know I'm forbidden to interfere in human affairs, and yet, the Earth is threatened by the same fate as Krypton's."

     "The Earth is too primitive," said one elder. "You can flee to other worlds where war is long forgotten."

     Said another elder, "If you teach the Earth to put its fate in any one man—even yourself—you are teaching them to be betrayed."

Despite their council Superman went before the United Nations:

I don't represent any country, but I'd like to address the delegates...

For many years now, I've lived among you as a visitor. I've seen the beauty of your many cultures. I've felt great joy in your accomplishments.

I've also seen the folly of your wars.

As of today, I'm not a visitor, anymore, because the Earth is my home, too.

We can't live in fear—and I can't stand idly by and watch us stumble into the madness of possible nuclear destruction.

And so, I've come to a decision: I'm going to do what our governments have been unwilling or unable to do. Effective immediately, I'm going to rid our planet of all nuclear weapons.

     At the end of the movie, after defeating a super villain and failing to accomplish his goal, Superman made an announcement to the press:

"Once more we've survived the threat of war, and found a fragile peace.

I thought I could give you all the gift of the freedom from war...but I was wrong: it's not mine to give.

We're still a young planet. There are galaxies…out there; other civilizations for us to meet, to learn from.

What a brilliant future we could have.

And there will be peace. There will be a peace when the people of the world want it so badly…that their governments will have no choice but to give it to them.

I just wish that you could all see the Earth they way that I see it.

It's just one world."

Here are a few excerpts from Superman's interview with Barbara Walters:

"There's something else coming. I don't know what it is, but I've got to find it."

"You know, one of the things I couldn't understand is, like, why, I mean—end up a quadriplegic on a training level jump? It's virtually impossible. I was not able to place that together. Why didn't I put my hands down?"

"This was an absolute freak accident."

"You can say that either the universe is totally random and it's just molecules colliding all the time and, you know, it's totally chaos and that our job is to make sense of the chaos, or you can say that sometimes things happen for a reason and your job is to discover the reason."

"See, it's like a game of cards and if you think the game is worthwhile, then you play the hand you're dealt. Sometimes you get a lot of face cards, sometimes you don't. But I think the game is worthwhile, I really do."

BONUS QUESTION:

What did Lex Luthor's father say to him when he was six years old?

Hint:

"Deeds of violence in our society are performed largely by those trying to establish their self-esteem, to defend their self-image, and to demonstrate that they, too, are significant…Violence arises not out of superfluity of power, but out of powerlessness."

~ Rollo May

Reality Check

Speaking of war and money, let me clear up a common misconception regarding the Cold War:

NOBODY WON WORLD WAR II, per se: "The U.S. and the former U.S.S.R. spent over $10 trillion on the Cold War; enough money to replace the entire infrastructure of the world; every school, every hospital, every roadway, building, and farm."

So, ask yourself why the daily talk shows are a constant barrage of dysfunctional souls without any sense of self-worth, direction, love or community.

We've invested so heavily in protecting ourselves from the enemy that we've become our own enemy, as they say. Every intelligent person I talk with confirms my assumption that things are without a doubt worse than they were thirty years ago. We can change our approach, but the core of society that will be implementing our future is already a precarious bunch inclined to pass on the same wretched apathy that their parents passed on to them. I mean, even my friends admit that they could use a lot of improvement; that their parents definitely could have given them more of a fighting chance to make the most out of life, and I keep pretty good company. What must it be like for all those who didn't get close to even half of the attention and direction that we did?

The good news, though, is that if we could afford to spend so abundantly on defense, then it also means that we have that much in abundance to clean up our act.

I used to believe that dropping the bomb on Japan was justified because, a) they were warned, b) they started it, and, c) it was a way to avert losing millions of more American lives.

But, looking back, I'd say that it was the worst mistake ever because it set a precedent. It set a precedent that said nuclear warfare is acceptable; in fact, it was to be expected. Growing up with that fear and expectation was a major hindrance that we could have done without.

Because warfare is unacceptable.

And nuclear warfare is impossible.

♪ "I hope the Russians love their children, too." [24]

I know it's irrational to try and talk sense into the kind of leaders who would set oil fields on fire as a military strategy, or someone asinine enough to burn Korans to make a point about how crazy Muslim fundamentalists are, but it's also irrational to not at least try.

So, here's an idea. Let's insist that our leaders all answer the following questions:

What do you personally want from life? What brings you happiness? Under what circumstances would you be able to die content knowing that you had lived life in a way that should be emulated?

What do you think the government is responsible for providing the citizens and how should it collect or create those funds to do so?

Do you find it immoral or unjust or sad or stupid that some citizens don't have access to ideal educations, diets and healthcare, while some citizens have *EXTREMELY* superfluous amounts of credit?

Do the above answers depend at all on how you would like to see the future in 150 years?

Are you still not convinced that it would be safe to just drop our defensive postures?

Let's talk about the bullshit in the Middle East.

Basically we've got feuding between Moslems and Jews and Christians. Is the conflict over land, or is it over principles?

What does the almighty encyclopedia say?

"The Koran, like the Bible, forbids lying, stealing, adultery, and murder. It teaches the virtues of faith in God, patience, kindness, honesty, industry, honor, courage, and generosity. It condemns mistrust, impatience, and **cruelty**.

"Muslims believe that **Muhammad** completed the sacred teachings of such earlier prophets as **Abraham, Moses,** and **Jesus**.

"Muhammad banned war and violence except for self-defense and the cause of Islam."

What does that mean, "the cause of Islam"?

Correct me if I'm wrong, but it seems to me that the logical assumption is that Muhammad and Abraham and Moses and Jesus all had essentially the same message. So, if all four of them got together to formulate rules for how we could all harmoniously live together, they could do so just fine. They would have no problem finding ways to overcome any minor details that they might find disagreeable since any "conflicts" which might arise would not be a hindrance upon anyone else's notions of how to live. Between the four of them justice and reason and amity would no doubt be the final outcome.

Again, from the encyclopedia:

"The most important teaching of Judaism is that there is one God, who wants people to do what is just and merciful. Judaism teaches that a person serves God by studying the scriptures and practicing what they preach. The most fundamental of these teachings concern behavior toward other people. Judaism teaches that all people are created in the image of God and deserve to be treated with **dignity and respect**. Thus, moral and ethical teachings play a more important role in Judaism than do the teachings about God."

ALL PEOPLE MEANS ALL PEOPLE

.

Excerpts from the Jewish High Holiday Prayer book:

"No concept of Judaism has been more persistently misunderstood than that of the Chosen People. It has been confused with false pride and national chauvinism. It has been mistakably identified with the pernicious doctrine of racial superiority. For the Jew, the concept of the 'chosen' people meant that more was expected of him than of others and that his actions would be judged by higher standards."

"There is not a single noble cause, movement, or achievement that does not call for great sacrifice and martyrdom."

First of all, ask yourself: Why am I fighting? What is the end result that I am trying to achieve? What makes my reason for fighting more right than the other guy's? WHY IS IT NECESSARY FOR ME TO FIGHT THE OTHER GUY?

Never Forget

Mike Pence's war on women led to an HIV outbreak in Indiana that required *federal intervention*.

In 2013 Governor Pence cut funding for Planned Parenthood by **nearly half** from 2005 levels. They were forced to **close five clinics**, none of which had ever provided abortions, but they **did** provide STD testing.

Scott County, Indiana, home to one of the closed clinics, became the hub of an **enormous** HIV outbreak.

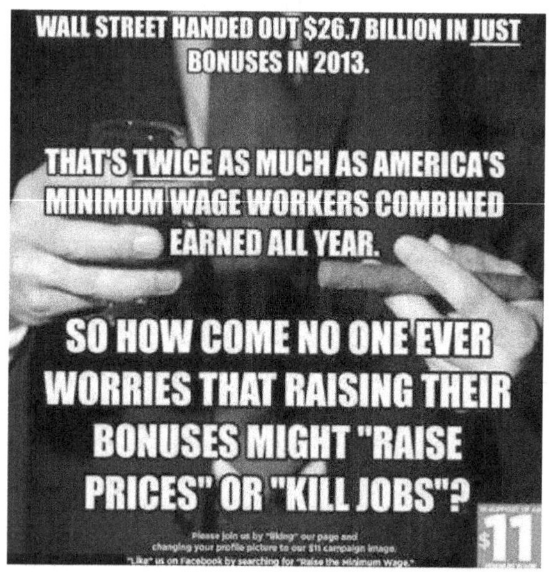

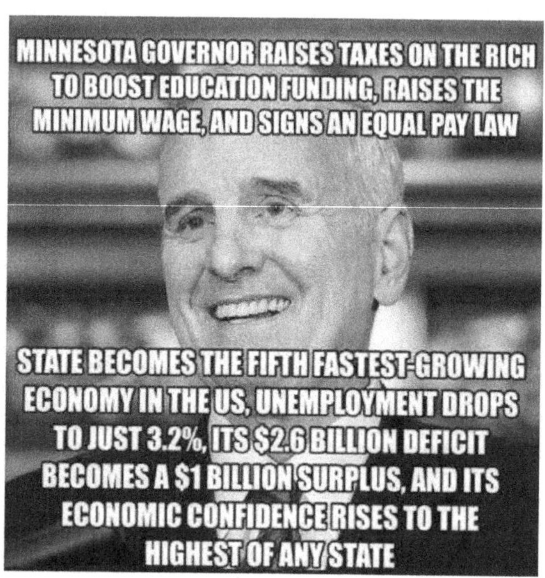

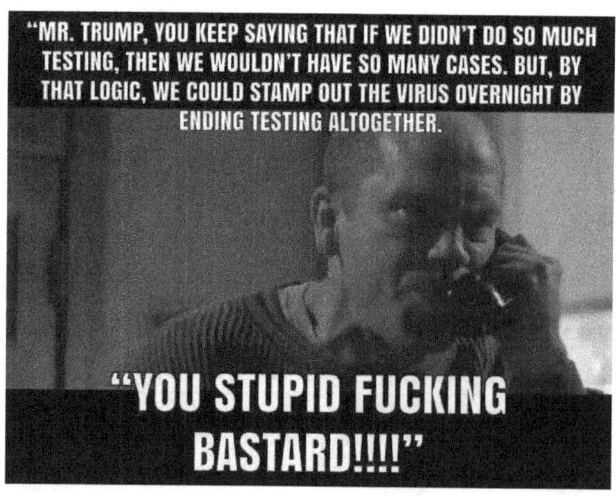

AFTERWORD

June 24, 1997

Over the last year I've been at my wit's end trying to find a connection to get this published; but, to no avail. The two concurrent trains of anxiety that I'm dealing with are: how do I find the right publishing avenue for this overwhelming work? And, once I do find a publishing outlet that has the chutzpah to take the ball on this, I wonder what the best strategy will be for distributing it. It may be a very, very necessary work, but, paradoxically, releasing it to the general public at large in one fell swoop could definitely be too much to swallow at once.

The reason I am prompted to write this Afterword is because of the difficulty I've had procuring a publisher or agent despite the fact that everyone in the business who has read it concurs that it is a necessary work. Apparently, I've left too much up in the air.

After receiving the first edition of the final draft Jarrod wrote that although it was the best draft yet, it was "in no-man's land." I knew what he meant, but did not know how to address the problem since I'm a novice writer who had to learn how to do this as I went along. I also told him that if a work is supposed to reflect how the author feels, well, then I definitely created the proper effect.

In March I thought that I had finally found an agency which was sure to pan out since I was paying them $300 to review it, so they were obliged to not only read it in its entirety, but also required to give me professional criticism. I didn't see how it was possible that they could acknowledge that they had read something this important, this potentially influential, and then proceed to deny me their assistance. I assumed that they would see it as their duty to take it to the next stage. Here's some of what I received:

> While intelligently conceived and often provocatively written, there are unfortunately too many substantive problems. There is no build-up to any sort of climax or resolution. The text isn't presented in any logical sequence, but rather jumps back and forth from subject to subject. ….Nor is your material really original—although the premise of self-fulfilling prophecy is interesting—you offer warnings about a doomed future, but not how to accomplish the goal of avoiding it. In only one instance do you suggest specific actions with The Initiative Movement.

Man, was I flustered over that. I was basically thinking: *Not really original?! What's he talking about?! How could he have read all of that, yet still not get that the first step isn't so much about the specific details of how to actually implement change as it is about simply disseminating certain information to the public in order to raise awareness. And why is he so gosh darn concerned about the unconventional format? What? Are critics and readers at large going to say, "Although he's presented a 'very unique and creative philosophical awakening' (as one literary agent's rejection letter put it), that is 'extraordinary in its barrage of references and diversity of ideas' (another rejection), not to mention that it's an emotional roller-coaster, his style is just too choppy—and therefore this gives us the luxury of being able to go on avoiding reality. It's a good thing that the man with the plan didn't have prior writing experience, otherwise we might actually have to take him seriously."*

However, I did see that they had a point about its lack of resolution and climax. My thoughts on that were: *What did they expect? That by the end of reading it the world would be fixed because the introduction said that that's what the intention was?* I thought it was clear that this was meant as a springboard for those with the clout and authority to sit down and go from here. I figured that this would precede *Reality Check*'s publication, but in the meantime all of those folks whom I've quoted would start stepping up to the plate and podiums to galvanize the masses to not just wallow in the status quo, any longer. Because, for now, I'm just Mr. Anonymous without any power to do anything other than distribute this to one person at a time until it finds its way to someone who will see it to fruition.

At any rate, I took this literary agent's rejection with a grain of salt. After all, as Jarrod reminded me, their job is to sell books, not save the(ir) future; (and this book "wouldn't be salable to a publisher in the currently highly selective market." (Right, why would a book that incorporates practically every cultural icon on the planet, and goes this deep to the heart and funny bone, have a mass appeal? Especially in light of the runaway success of *The Celestine Prophecy*.))

But, you know me, I'm incapable of being daunted—and I knew that sooner or later some publisher out there would be willing to go the mat with me. Then, lo and behold: a couple of months later I found the listing of a non-profit publisher whose "goal is to provide books that encourage critical thinking and constructive action, thereby helping to create fundamental social change."

Bingo. After telling me on the phone to send it in I knew that it was a foregone conclusion that they'd have to take it. Even Jarrod concurred that, "by the letter of the doctrine, they *have* to take it."

Alas, they receive up to a thousand submissions a year, yet only publish ten to fifteen, so they have to be very selective and reject works that are otherwise well written and contain interesting proposals. Needless to say, I was bewildered. But I sure as hell would love to see what they *do* put out if they've got works more effective than this one. You would think that we'd all be familiar with their material if it's brought about fundamental social change.

When I sum this up for prospective publishers I tell them that I've got quotes from all over saying that we need a huge coming together or else we're going to have a huge falling apart. A main point of this work is that there can't be such a coming together unless it is communicated to everyone IN CONCERT that this needs to happen. Now. Secondly, since it's primarily our attitudes and ignorance that are killing us, I've attempted to change people's attitudes. After all, conventional wisdom says that the first step towards bringing about change is to raise people's awareness.

In the introduction I neglected to mention two of the stronger impetuses that inspired me to write this. One was the Chomsky quote in the introduction; the other was the Billy Bragg song from Part I, "Waiting for the Great Leap Forwards." It dawned on me that we were all waiting for someone *else* to step up to the plate. But, "substantial change," as Chomsky put it, isn't going to just happen. WE HAVE TO *MAKE* IT HAPPEN. *But*, I thought, *if someone as respected as Noam Chomsky, "the world's foremost intellectual," is ostensibly unwilling and/or unable to implement a "profound democratization of the society and the economic system," then there's no hope. Because, apparently, there is no individual or group able to use their clout in order to raise the red flag on our entrenched stampede towards resource depletion.*

Frankly, it's embarrassing to be in a position of self-appointed coach of the world; even if I did it with an arsenal of so many spirited persons "to whom Nature hath given the **Power** of **Feeling**," as Thomas Paine put it. And now that I've spilled my guts I feel partially apologetic to the relatively small minority who aren't currently directly affected by the gross societal imbalance of resources, so they would rather not have to be bothered to participate in a democratization of the economy. I also apologize to the majority of folks who were by no means getting a free ride, therefore you would have no qualms with seeing the tables turned on opportunity, as it were, yet you've been content settling for the humdrum status quo because rejecting the comfort and security of its stability and predictability was not something you were ready for. However, despite any apprehension, we will indeed be taking a course of action to divert us from the dead-end path we're on. It's understandable to be apprehensive about this. As Philip Howard put it in *The Death of Common Sense: How Law is suffocating America*:

> Like prisoners in a dungeon too long, we want to get out, but the prospect frightens us. We have grown accustomed to a static system in which no one, including us, has to take responsibility. Our memory of anyone making decisions is so distant that we equate giving responsibility with anarchy. We have been lead to believe that government should operate like an error-free machine. Like the bureaucrats we despise, all we think about is what might   go wrong, not what might get done. (p. 177)

So, I'm sorry if I'm ruining the party, but the party is going bust without *Reality Check*, which means the only alternative is to pre-empt it. But, not to worry, the handbook to transforming us into a self-sustaining society has already been written: Paul Hawken's *Natural Capitalism*. My hope is that it will be the vehicle for a new, more direct form of vicarious living whereby those nearer the top of the self-actualization pyramid will lift up those nearer the bottom. The business of healing and re-building will become quite lucrative, I imagine.

In regards to the general despair and depravity of the population at large, James Redfield wrote, "nobody cares." And when George Carlin was on "Politically Incorrect" in June of 1997, he, rhetorically, asked, "Is society really worth saving?" And he was right to suggest that it isn't worth saving; up to a point: If nobody cares, then it isn't worth saving.

Of course, though, there are already droves of people out there who are up to the page of accepting that the status quo has got to go; and when they all get on to this page they're going to be saying, "Yes! FINALLY; an intellectual and emotional and spiritual articulation of exactly why we've been telling the government/business/teachers/parents/society to go jump in a lake!" And all of those people are clearly itching for the opportunity to focus and channel their collective ire and hope into collectivism, if you will.

So, while Donald Trump may be waiting to die, I'm dying to live. But in the months before writing this I had given up. I was resigned to accepting that there was no reason to try, anymore, because the near-term future was hopeless. I had given up a life-long pursuit of prosperity and success. I was willing to accept whatever paltry rewards would come from life without hope or goals (and, hence, much cash), while waiting time out as we "spiraled down the drain," as Carlin so eloquently put it. And I knew that it wasn't just me (and Chomsky) when I saw the excellent movie "Seven" in the fall of 1995. It played a key role in helping me to crystallize that it was a necessary matter of *articulating* everyone's collective (un)conscious, along with the irony that so many are quitting for the same reason that everyone else is—because everyone else is quitting. As Brad Pitt's character said to Morgan Freeman's, "You say, 'The problem with people is that they don't care—so I don't care about people,' so, therefore, you're quitting the police force. But I don't think you're quitting because you believe these things you say. I think you want to believe them because you're quitting." (Who quit first, the chicken or the egg?)

Fortunately, I found a way to galvanize us. I'm not providing new solutions, per se, but I have achieved the means to enable the choir to GET THE ATTENTION of the policy makers and their corporate masters, thereby getting them to concede that they've got to abandon the status quo and seriously examine the scrutiny and alternatives being provided by the likes of David Korten and Lester Brown. In Rousseau's words, I've created the "appropriate necessary agent for the public force to unify and put it to work according to the directions of the general will." Creating "public enlightenment" will result in "the union of the understanding and the will in the social body, hence the precise concourse of the parts, and finally the maximum force of the whole."

Perhaps what is implied by our general concession is a grim truth that a monumental amount of sacrifice is necessary to achieve such a turn around. But what is actually required is that we stop thinking inefficiently.

When I was first reading Carlin's book on September 18, 1997, something struck me. Well, a lot of things struck me and I got pretty black and blue. But one thing in particular really gave me a bump on the head: "If lobsters looked like puppies, people could never drop them in boiling water while they're still alive. But, instead, they look like science fiction monsters, so it's o.k." That's so funny, because they really do look like science fiction monsters.

In 1992 the teacher of my speech class brought it to our attention that the production of veal entails very cruel treatment of baby calves. I thought: *Well, shoot, I guess I'll have to stop eating veal. I sure will miss that tasty dish.* But, I was also thinking, *All it would take to end the unnecessary suffering of these animals is for everyone to stop eating veal; it would be that simple. If only there were a way to let the entire public know about it, then they could make an informed decision the next time that they get a chance to order it. (But if everyone stopped eating it, then the people who produce veal would lose money and jobs.)*

Then, about two years later, in Dustin Penn's biology class, we learned about "the hamburger connection"—how our inordinate consumption of beef is a primary cause of our destruction. (For instance, as is reported in Anthony Robbins' *Awaken the Giant Within*: "Every time you buy a quarter-pound hamburger using rainforest beef, it represents the destruction of fifty-five square feet of tropical rainforests." "The fossil fuel required to produce one pound of beef is roughly thirty-nine times that required to produce the equivalent protein value in soybeans." "It takes 500 years to create one inch of topsoil, and we're currently losing one inch every 16 years!") Now, this time when I learned that there were bad consequences from partaking in a juicy, mouth-watering, flame-broiled Whopper I wasn't so quick to take a stand. I made a mock attempt to curtail my meat intake, but then went back to my old ways. *After all*, I thought, *it doesn't matter what I do, I'm only one person. The vast majority is going to do it, anyway, so I might as well indulge; (and, therefore, it's only a matter of time before something snaps in a big way).*

Again, it was this conscious thought that was a huge impetus for trying to get this off of the ground: HOW TO GET EVERYONE WHO IS THINKING WITH A CONSCIENCE TO ACTUALLY ACT WITH IT? TO GET ALL OF THOSE PEOPLE WHO ARE ALREADY AWARE THAT THE SYSTEM IS SELF-DESTRUCTING TO PUT THEIR FOOT *DOWN*; or to hit the pause button, as it were.

In all of my conversations with people who won't try to deny how precarious the fabric of society has become, I keep pointing out that, if nothing else, whoever happens to be president has the Power of the Podium, the most powerful weapon of all. So why doesn't he use it?! For instance, a president could get everyone to start implementing the voluntary picking up of litter. Or, perhaps like my grandfather, you scoff at such idealism as "ludicrous."

Here's how a president could *make the attempt*: First of all, for this purpose, you hand the microphone over to a neutral third party such as Regis Philbin to call for the stand against littering. That way people won't be able to resist a good idea merely out of spite for being told what to do by the government or some stereotypical politician. "But littering is the least of our worries," you say? Yeah, but since this problem is so simple to solve, LET'S SOLVE IT. Right now $12 billion of our taxes go towards dealing with litter. If we pick it up ourselves while simultaneously stigmatizing it, then we'll be able to start using that money and manpower to build wind turbines and plant flowers and trees

A president could also announce key books for all of us to read. For example, a president could say, "I IMPLORE YOU ALL TO READ David C. Korten's *When Corporations Rule the World*!" Because once this devastating testimony is brought into the public forum so that businesses and governments have to confront the fact that the public is hip to their chicanery (to put it mildly) and shortsightedness, then there's no way that we could allow the hoi polloi to continue marching blindly into the dead end.

Or how about this: You know how so many businesses display cash on their walls? Imagine how much money we could compile if we set up the "money on the wall fund." That's only one example of how we can consolidate our resources without really giving anything up. (Many more examples are in Hawkens' *Natural Capitalism*.)

So now the question becomes: "Okay, so we found a way to get most everyone to reduce meat intake, to stop targeting minors for cigarettes, to stop using fur, and to generally stop participating in money-making activities that they wouldn't otherwise avoid if they had permanent and excessive financial freedom. But what about the fact that millions of people's survival depends on these industries? If everyone started acting with a conscience overnight, then we'd all be fucked." Well, directly above the part about boiling puppies Carlin has this isolated statement in bold: "**We're all fucked. It helps to remember that.**" I say, fuck you, George! (But don't you dare hassle your horse.)

We don't necessarily have to be [fucked]. If we organize and consolidate operations by categorizing them as either discretionary or non-discretionary industries, then we'll be able to eliminate probably 75% of our inefficiency; then there will be ample time and supplies. As I've said before, there are already those with plans to implement a system that assures everyone gets the basic necessities, and then some (starting with The American Monetary Act). We *can* all be "modestly prosperous" as long as we act Collectively.

With that being said I leave you to proceed to finish this tour de force attempt to create the best possible possibility. There are just a few more poems of mine and appropriated bits of wisdom and inspiration to tie it all together. And, although I believe that it is the most stupendous climax ever, I recognize that, ultimately, it is actually anti-climatic. At least, it will seem that way at first…unless of course you are **will**ing **to believe** that we do in fact have the power and responsibility to utilize the opportunity to make it so.

Reality Check

So, Future, ready or not, here we come.

Pivot

"It's the lost causes that you fight the hardest for. You even die for them."

~ Mr. Smith, from *Mr. Smith Goes to Washington*

"Peace is not only the absence of conflict. It is the presence of justice."

~ from the movie *Air Force One*

"You fight the fights you can win!"
"And you fight the fights that need fighting!!"

~ from the movie *An American President*

"Hey, kids. It's mostly bullshit and garbage, and none of the stuff they tell you is true. And when your father says he wants you to amount to something, he means make a lot of money. How do you think the word *amount* got in there?"

~ George Carlin

"Yet the fact remains that war is a school of strenuous life and heroism; and, being in the line of aboriginal instinct, is the only school that as yet is universally available…What we now need to discover in the social realm is the moral equivalent of war; something heroic that will speak to men as universally as war does, and yet **will be as compatible with their spiritual selves as war has proved itself to be** *incompatible*."

~ William James

"We have a purpose now; we have things to do now. Whereas formerly only boredom and mania were available to us."

~ from the movie *Crazy People*

"With power comes responsibility."

~ Peter Parker's Uncle Ben

(Incidentally, Peter Parker is where the Republicans got their motto; i.e., "How is that my problem?" (But, then again, they could also use Daffy Duck as their fictional mascot; i.e., "MINE! MINE! ALL MINE!"))

By all means effective.

"It is the strangely irrational notion that there is something in the very flow of time that will inevitably cure all ills. Actually, time is neutral. We must come to see that human progress never rolls in on the wheels of inevitability. We must use time creatively, and forever realize that the time is always ripe to do right."

~ Dr. Martin Luther King, Jr.

Reality Check

Together

Superman can't even fight.

And Pivot's best strength? Insight.

But, together our hope is Our might.

And, together, we all shall put right.

Life!

Approach life with Alacrity,

In all that comes your way.

Yes, it can get quite unbecoming,

But it's coming, either way.

The Next Level of Love

When I'm feeling love,

I *know* that I'm feeling love.

So I don't just feel it, I know it:

I know the feeling of knowing love.

(And I know that I wrote the above.)

Pivot

Keeping Things Whole

In a field
I am the absence
Of field.
This is
Always the case.
Wherever I am
I am what is missing.

When I walk
I part the air
And always
The air moves in
To fill the spaces
Where my body's been.

We all have reasons
For moving.
I move
To keep things whole.

~ Mark Strand

"And I believe that poetry is an action, ephemeral or solemn, in which there join as equal partners solitude and solidarity, emotion and action, the nearness to oneself, the nearness to mankind and to the secret manifestations of nature. And no less strongly I think that all this is sustained—man and his shadow, man and his conduct, man and his poetry—by an ever wider sense of community, by an effort which will forever bring together the reality and the dreams in us because it is precisely in this way that poetry unites and commingles them.

"From all this, my friends, there arises an insight which the poet must learn through other people. There is no insurmountable solitude. All paths lead to the same goal: to convey to others what we are. And we must pass through solitude and difficulty, isolation and silence, in order to reach forth to the enchanted place where we can dance our clumsy dance and sing our sorrowful song—but in this dance or in this song there are fulfilled the most ancient rites of our conscience in the awareness of being human and of believing in a common destiny."

~ Pablo Neruda

"Poetry is a way of taking life by the throat."

~ Robert Frost

"Nothing great was ever achieved without enthusiasm."

~ Ralph Waldo Emerson

Reality Check

If Jesus were alive today,
He'd surely feel despair,
Amidst a world of plenty,
And a bounty that's not shared.

If Jesus were alive today,
He wouldn't understand,
The system of oppression,
And how so few give a damn.

If Jesus were alive today,
He'd certainly be distraught,
Because the animals of Earth,
Are not treated as they ought.

If Jesus were alive today,
His eyes would have some tears,
And based on all the evidence,
I'd say he was sincere.

If Jesus were alive today,
He'd have to jump and shout,
To wake us from our slumber:
"THE FUTURE IS IN DOUBT!!"

If Jesus were alive today,
You know he'd try in vain,
To save us from each other...
(No doubt he'd go insane.)

If Jesus were alive today,
I expect we'd be rebuked.
It is likely he'd remark:
"Knock it off before I puke."

If Jesus were alive today,
No way he'd vote for Bush;
To those who say he should,
He'd say, "Kiss my donkey!"

If Jesus were alive today,
With Bushies he'd be pissed:
"Ignorance is no defence!
"Otherwise, get yourself a psychiatrist."

If Jesus were alive today,
He'd put John Kerry in his place,
As the world's lamest candidate:
"Why'd they even let that Jackass race?!"

If Jesus were alive today,
Boy, would Congress get a smack,
For practically everything they've done,
Especially for trusting Jr. with Iraq.

If Jesus were alive today,
He'd say the media is to blame:
"Don't think I haven't noticed
That you ass-clowns have no shame."

If Jesus were alive today,
The Democrats he would scorn,
For keeping out Wes Clark:
"Was it fucking yesterday these fools were born?!"

If Jesus were alive today,
Obama he would ream,
For leaving B P in control:
"I'm so angry I could scream!!!!!"

If Jesus were alive today,
He'd cheer for Marianne;
Cuz she's the one with the chutzpah,
To make love cool, again.

If Jesus were alive today,
He'd say that Biden has to go:
"Just 'cause Trump is of the devil,
Ain't a reason to settle for Joe."

If Jesus were alive today,
With the dotard he'd be aghast:
"To those of you who support this fucker,
You've really shown your ass."

If Jesus were alive today,
His sense of humor would be great.
Too wry, perhaps, for some,
But that's how he'd get laid.

If Jesus were alive today,
He'd be branded as a cynic,
Because no one wants to hear,
If it's raining at their picnic.

If Jesus were alive today,
He'd force us all to see,
That hope and love are the answer,
To who we're supposed to be.

Humanity

Limousines and magic tricks,
Fax machines and politics
Shopping malls and roller-blades,
Basketballs and the Jack-of-Spades.
And, allegedly...
Bullet wounds and jellybeans,
Silver spoons and Halloween.
Lemonade and heroine,
Hand grenades and Letterman.
And, probably…
Wedding gowns and coffee shops,
Killer clowns and Peppermint Schnapps.
Slavery and goodnight hugs,
Bravery and litter bugs.
And, supposedly…
Prostitutes and trending 'tags,
Sunday suits and screaming fags.
Democracy and monkey bars,
Hypocrisy and movie stars.
And, presumably....
The Price is Right and Peter Pan,
The Bill of Rights and Aimee Mann.
Instagram and Kurt Kobain,
Uncle Sam and "Purple Rain".
And, figuratively speaking...
The Daily Show and animal testing,
C3PO and driving while texting.
"In Your Eyes" and the Yeah Yeah Yeahs,
Jesus H. Christ and all that jazz.
And, actually...
A Hootenanny

Reality Check

Originality

And what it means to be,

Another random star

In competition with an infinity,

Is how I found out that we truly are

All equal parts diversity.

Infinity

And what it means to me,

Are circles and souls,

In a round about way,

Beginnings and Ends without any close.

Okay, with that I've said my peace and have just 1 thing left to add:

Pivot

0. (Holy Shit.)

1.   A toast: To Humanity! God's greatest paradox!

1. ♪ "Happy birthday! Whoever's birthday it is today!" [7]

1. To all of the parents of the world: Good luck. We're all counting on you.

1. To everyone else: Good luck. They're all counting on us.

1. "Earnest Hemingway wrote that the world is a beautiful place, and worth fighting   for." [18]
   I agree.

♪ "The opposite of war isn't peace. It's creation!!" ♪

Rest in creation, Jonathon Larson.

1.   "There's still a lot of good in the world. Stay gold, Ponyboy." [50]

1. "Let us have faith that right makes might, and in that faith dare to do our duty as we understand it."

~ Abraham Lincoln

1.   To paraphrase Homer Simpson: Don't thank *me*, thank my brain.

1.   To paraphrase George Costanza: We are living in a democracy! We're supposed to be acting in a
   democratic way!

11. "'Roads'?"

(over)

Reality Check

"Where we're going, we don't need...roads."

Pivot

♫   *"History Will Teach Us Nothing"*

If we seek solace in the prisons of the distant past,
Security in human systems we're told will always, always last;
Emotions are the sail and blind faith is the mast;
Without the breath of real freedom, we're getting nowhere fast.

If God is dead, and the actor plays His part,
His words of fear will find their way to a place in your heart.
Without the voice of reason, every faith is its own curse;
Without freedom from the past, things can only get worse.

Sooner or later just like the world first day. Sooner or later we learn to throw the past away
History will teach us nothing

Our written history is a catalogue of crime,
The sordid and the powerful, the architects of time.
The mother of invention, the oppression of the mild;
The constant fear of scarcity, aggression as its child.

Convince an enemy, convince him that he's wrong,
Is to win a bloodless battle where victory is long.
A simple act of faith,
In reason over might: To blow up his children will only prove him right.

History will teach us nothing

Sooner or later just like the world first day. Sooner or later we learn to throw the past away

History will teach us nothing

Know your human rights
Be what you come here for
Know your human rights
Be what you come here for

Sooner or later just like the world first day

Know your human rights

Sooner or later we learn to throw the past away

Be what you come here for

Sooner or later

Reality Check

From the movie *Oh, God!*:

That's why I came; to tell everybody that I set the world up so that it can work.

You can't look to Me to do it for you.

I gave you a world and everything in it. It's all up to you.

"But we need help!!"

That's why I gave you each other.

"If You're so involved with us, how can You permit all the *suffering* that goes on?!"

How can *I* permit the suffering?

"Yeah!!"

I don't permit the suffering; you do: Free will. All the choices are yours.

You can love each other; cherish and nurture each other.

Or you can kill each other.

♪ "And as you feel it, you'll know how it was meant to be." ♪

Sooner or later

Pivot

They can be a great people, Kal-el; they wish to be. They only lack the light to show the way.

For this reason above all—their **capacity for good**—I have sent them you.

~ Superman's father, Jor-el

The sun is gone, but I have a light.

~ Kurt Cobain

Reality Check

The End

This poem is over,

But don't let it end.

No, don't think it is over,

Even after "The End"

Pivot

This page was supposed to have an image from the cartoon strip, "The Far Side," by Gary Larson, but permission was denied. Otherwise you'd be seeing a scene of the sun coming up upon four squirrels atop a branch chanting, "Nuts! Nuts! Get 'em!...Nuts! Nuts! Get 'em!..."

And the bottom caption reads: "Before starting their day, squirrels must first pump themselves up.'

♫

Cue theme song from "SUPERMAN: The Movie."